# RE-LIVING

# THE AMERICAN

# FRONTIER

**FANDOM & CULTURE**

*Paul Booth and Katherine Larsen, series editors*

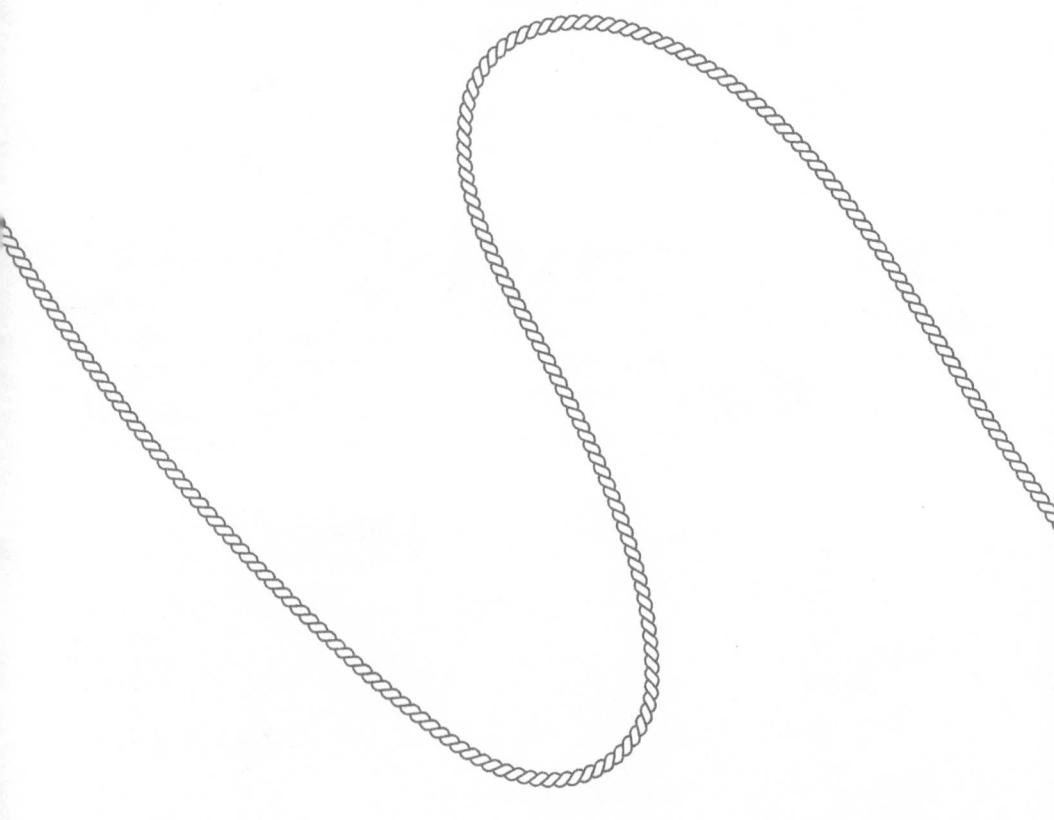

# RE-LIVING THE

# AMERICAN FRONTIER

Western Fandoms, Reenactment, and

Historical Hobbyists in Germany

and America Since 1900

## NANCY REAGIN

UNIVERSITY OF IOWA PRESS, IOWA CITY

University of Iowa Press, Iowa City 52242
Copyright © 2021 by the University of Iowa Press
uipress.uiowa.edu
Printed in the United States of America

Design by Ashley Muehlbauer

Printed on acid-free paper

*Library of Congress Cataloging-in-Publication Data*
Names: Reagin, Nancy Ruth, 1960—author.
Title: Re-living the American Frontier: Western Fandoms, Reenactment, and Historical Hobbyists in Germany and America Since 1900 / by Nancy Reagin.
Description: Iowa City: University of Iowa Press, [2021] | Series: Fandom & Culture | Includes bibliographical references and index.
Identifiers: LCCN 2021001154 (print) | LCCN 2021001155 (ebook) | ISBN 9781609387907 (paperback) | ISBN 9781609387914 (ebook)
Subjects: LCSH: Frontier and pioneer life—West (US) | Historical reenactments—Germany—history. | Indianists—Germany. | Indian hobbyists—Germany. | Cowboys in popular culture—Germany. | Fans (Persons)—cross-cultural studies. | Heritage tourism—Middle West. | Wilder, Laura Ingalls, 1867–1957—appreciation. | Frontier and pioneer life—West (US)—historiography.
Classification: LCC F596.R3593 2021 (print) | LCC F596 (ebook) | DDC 978—dc23
LC record available at https://lccn.loc.gov/2021001154
LC ebook record available at https://lccn.loc.gov/2021001155

*For Bill*

# CONTENTS

## ACKNOWLEDGMENTS

I have lived with this project for a long time, and I am grateful to many people and institutions for their support for my work. It is a great pleasure to be able to thank them.

Pace University provided research support for this book in the form of a sabbatical and research funding. Even more, Pace has given me a community of colleagues who support each other in teaching and research; I'm very fortunate to have such colleagues and friends there. Pace's interlibrary loan staff provided indispensable support for my research, as well.

I am also deeply indebted to the many people who shared their stories and insights about their communities and organizations with me. In Germany, Robin Leipold, Hans Grunert, and Michael Petzel went out of their way to help me access their archives, allowed me to work with a rich variety of sources, and answered my many questions. Mr. Leipold also allowed me to interview him, generously shared many of his private photos, and read through a draft of the manuscript; my work was enriched as a result. In the United States, the volunteers and staff of the Wilder homesites welcomed me, helped me find sources and information, and generously shared their enthusiasm for Laura's world along with their expertise. I want to thank Rev. Nicholas Inman, Vicki Johnston, and Tana Redman of the Mansfield Laura Ingalls Wilder Home and Museum; Tessa Flak and Amy Ranfelt at the DeSmet Laura Ingalls Wilder Memorial Society; Sue Fedie, at the Pepin Laura Ingalls Wilder Museum; LaDonna Albertson of the Walnut Grove Laura Ingalls Wilder Museum; and Maeve Maguire at the Malone Wilder Homestead. I also enjoyed and benefited from many conversations and interviews with people who were active in all of the fan communities discussed here. I particularly want to thank Bill Anderson, who allowed me to draw on his deep expertise and history in the Wilder community; Pamela Smith Hill, Sandra Hume, Catherine Latane, Laura McLemore, Brenda Miller, and Julie Frances Miller, who helped me to connect with a broad swath of Wilder fans; and Cathy Sorensen, Sarah Uthoff, and Barbara Walker. The love and enthusiasm of all of them for their respective communities and hobbies was palpable. I am also grateful to fans who spoke with me and shared their insights, but asked me not to mention them by name.

My friends helped me in many ways: hosting me when I did research near their homes, listening to me for hours as I thought through the issues discussed in this book, and giving me affection and encouragement when needed. I am blessed to count them as friends: Erica Appel (who drove with me to the Malone, New York homesite), Viki Bankey, Buka and Dietz Denecke, Diedl Denecke, Beth Haddrell, KC Kleinman, Siegfried Müller, and Anne Rieke-Müller. Anne Rubenstein was this book's fairy godmother. She read several drafts, showed me where I needed to improve it, and listened for hours to stories about what I'd found in the archives or during interviews. At every stage, this book benefitted from her insights.

While I was still developing this project, my first drafts also benefitted from the feedback and questions I got from the members of the German Women's History Study Group: Bonnie Anderson, Dolores Augustine, Renate Bridenthal, Belinda Davis, Atina Grossman, Marion Kaplan, Jan Lambertz, Mary Nolan, and Krista O'Donnell. This group of historians has helped to improve everything I've ever published, while providing me with friendship and professional support. Finally, Kristina Busse offered scores of smart suggestions and ideas for my manuscript, and supported and encouraged the project almost from its inception; she lives the truth that scholarship flows from communities.

I've been fortunate in my choice of publisher, as well. The University of Iowa Press is the home of skilled production professionals; the staff and their associates supported and accommodated my research and writing schedule repeatedly. I am grateful for the work that Ann DeVita, Alisha Jeddeloh, Susan Hill Newton, Jacob Roosa, and Meredith Stabel put into my project; their efforts improved the finished book.

I would not have begun this research if I had not belonged to fan communities that are *not* the subject of this book: the science fiction and fantasy fandoms that I have been active in for decades. In fan studies terms, I am an acafan: an academic who is also a fan, and who draws on both scholarly training and personal experience in fandoms for her research. I am not a Western fan, however, and have generally chosen to keep myself out of my narrative here because I have largely relied on historical methods and sources. This study is thus not an autoethnography, but I am nonetheless deeply indebted to the fan communities I've been active in. That experience and personal history made it easier for me to pick out and understand characteristics of the Western fandoms discussed here, which showed a family resemblance to other twentieth-century fandoms: the ways that fans fall in love with a particular imagined world or set of characters; the propensity of fans to engage in endless parsing (and in sometimes intense disputes) over their canon; the creativity and passion that fans bring to their engagement with the object of their fandom; and the diverse ways that fans can adapt to new technologies and platforms for community organization. For all of these lessons, I am indebted to the fan communities that I've been active in and to the friends I made there.

Finally, I owe more than I can express here to my husband, Bill Offutt. He traveled with me for months during the period I was doing archival research in Germany, and undertook a road trip across the United States with me to visit the Wilder homesites. His deep understanding of American history was a tremendous resource, and he was always willing to visit and debate the history of another site in the American West. He has supported my research and hobbies at every turn, with affection and intelligence. Thank you. Thank you again. This book is for him.

# RE-LIVING

# THE AMERICAN

# FRONTIER

# Living in Someone Else's Past

*Now is now. It can never be a long time ago.*

—LAURA INGALLS WILDER, *LITTLE*
*HOUSE IN THE BIG WOODS*

For historically based fan communities, the past is still present:[1]

*In May 1962, more than six hundred German "cowboys and Indians" set up tents or built teepees in soccer and sports fields near Mannheim, West Germany, to hold their twelfth annual Indian Council. This gathering was the annual meetup of the members of thirty-six West German cowboy and Indian clubs. The founders of these groups drew inspiration from the Westerns written by Karl May (1842–1912), said to be the bestselling author in modern German history, as well as from other Western novels, circuses, and Wild West shows. Club members created their own costumes, crafting replicas of Indigenous North American feather headdresses, moccasins, tomahawks, elaborate beadwork, and other Western-style clothing and artifacts with painstaking accuracy. Some wore imported cowboy clothes, including real Stetson hats. A local newspaper report noted that "wandering around the fields, one could see every Indian costume that had ever been worn, from Florida to Oregon." The gathering was presided over by Wambli-Wiccara ("White Eagle," whose legal name was Ernst Dietzuleit), considered to be "the father of the German Indians." The German Indians staged knife-throwing contests and performed dances around magnifi-*

cent campfires, while German cowboys twirled lassoes and serenaded passers-by with "hillbilly songs." Their leaders—called chiefs, if they were in Indian roles, or sheriffs, if in cowboy roles—rode on horses.[2]

More than sixty years later, German "cowboys and Indians" continue to gather each year for summer councils. Some members are the children or grandchildren of those who founded the first clubs and grew up as part of these communities.

*In small towns across the American prairie (and elsewhere), there are a string of rural communities whose claim to fame—and draw for visitors—is that they were once home to Laura Ingalls Wilder (1872–1957), author of the Little House on the Prairie series, or a member of her family. Wilder's wandering family lived in farms and homes in upstate New York, Wisconsin, Minnesota, Kansas, Missouri, Iowa, and South Dakota. Many of the original buildings are now long gone. But Wilder fans love to research, discuss, and re-create or refurbish the homesteads and dwellings where Wilder or her relatives have lived, establishing Wilder memorial "homesites" or museums in these locations. Wilder homesite exhibits contain a plethora of objects and details described in the books: her Pa's fiddle; a pantry lined with jars and baskets with preserved foodstuffs and antique tools for processing foods, such as churns and butter molds; quilts and embroidery made by Wilder or her relatives; or replica dugout prairie dwellings. After Wilder's death, the number of fans who retraced her family's journeys grew steadily, attempting to recapture the sense of place, domesticity, and lifestyle of nineteenth-century white settlers, and what it was like to be Laura.[3]*

More than sixty years after Wilder's death, fans continue to organize their summer vacations around the circuit of Wilder homesites. Some fans come in costume, wearing long dresses and sunbonnets (or bring their daughters in prairie girls' dresses and calico bonnets), and refer to themselves as "bonnet heads." Fan tourism keeps the Wilder homesite towns alive in regions that are steadily depopulating, as other small communities around them fade away. In one homesite community that I visited, there was only one mom and pop café (open for breakfast and lunch only), one bar and grill, and no hotels. Without Wilder fans, one resident observed to me, "we wouldn't have any restaurants at all, and probably no gas station." But thousands of Wilder fans keep coming from around the world, year after year.

The vignettes describe two examples of historically focused fan communities, which have proliferated transnationally during the last century. What are the pleasures and consequences of living in someone else's past, and how have these communities changed over the last century? Why do members of these communities travel so far, devoting their free time to historical research and handicrafts, and their vacations to fan pilgrimages and gatherings? This book explores how fans position themselves against the historical backdrops that engage them, inserting themselves into quasi-fictionalized historical narratives. It asks how historically focused fan communities navigate the sometimes tricky interface between their present-day cultures and politics, and the problematic, even unmasterable aspects of the past cultures and imagined worlds that they celebrate. I am particularly interested in how these fans' self-understandings, interpretations, and activities developed over time in response to political and social changes in their present, as those changes drastically reshaped contemporary understandings of the distant, ever-receding past that historically focused fan communities celebrated and re-created.

A history of fan communities must necessarily make use of the scholarly literature and methods of both historians and fan studies scholars. This book draws on my training as a historian, using archival research and historical scholarship to explore changes over the last century in the communities featured here. I supplemented my archival research with field work at fan pilgrimage sites as well, and interviewed people who are deeply engaged with an imagined American frontier. My research was also shaped by work published over the last generation in fan studies by scholars from many disciplines; I have tried here to explain key concepts or events that might be well known to some readers, but not to others who come from a different background.

In fan studies, "fans" are people who have an unusual degree of immersion in or affective commitment to a particular hobby or interest. The term can denote a strong interest in or affection for a particular sport team or celebrity, or for a film, television series, video games, novels, or other forms of entertainment.[4] When gathered into clubs, societies, or less formally organized communities, groups of fans are called "fandoms." The word "fandom" was first used in print in 1903, and could refer to fans of varied forms of entertainment who exhibit quite different degrees of commitment to their hobbies. Fan studies scholarship has generally distinguished between fans who pursue their hobby as individuals, not associated with any larger group (individualized fandom) and those who belong to a "participatory" fandom or social fandom, who exchange ideas and undertake activities with a group of fellow fans. Communities and organizations are, of course, generally easier to research, although they make up only part of the entire group of fans devoted to a particular object of fandom.

To date, the bulk of fan studies scholarship has focused overwhelmingly on mid- to late-twentieth- and twenty-first-century fandoms. These are often rooted in a transmedial (multi-platform) imaginary world like *Harry Potter*, an entertainment franchise that extends across the formats of film, television shows, books, video games, plays, and other forms of entertainment. There is a substantial body of scholarly work on fans of science fiction series (e.g., *Star Trek* and *Star Wars*); East Asian anime and manga; popular television shows like *Doctor Who*, BBC's *Sherlock*, soap operas, genre horror or vampire series; and other modern entertainments. Earlier twentieth-century fandoms that scholars have also published on include mid-twentieth-century Sherlock Holmes communities and early science fiction fans; both communities emerged during the 1930s.[5]

Members of participatory fandoms also frequently engage in productive fan activities, going beyond intense consumption and enjoyment of the object of fandom to produce their own fan fiction, research and writing, fan art, fan videos and films, cosplay or role-playing games, and a wide variety of fan handicrafts related to the object of fandom. Fan handicrafts can include knitting, costume creation, creating props and other objects, quilting, and needlework. Handicraft products are frequently highly mimetic, seeking to reproduce artifacts or clothing seen or described in the original canon, but they sometimes also express commentary on the original story and characters.[6] The historically focused fandoms discussed in this book have been productive in many of these areas for decades, and for over a century in some cases.

Fan studies scholars have also explored the differences between what is sometimes called "affirmational" (largely celebratory) fandoms and "transformative" fandoms. Productive, participatory fandoms can fall into either category, and the line between affirmational and transformative fan activities can be fluid. Transformative fan works are those that rework the original object of fandom to reimagine, critique, or expand the original story world or object of fandom to reflect the fan's own desires, needs, and opinions. The depth of engagement and group organization for fans and fandoms thus varies widely, as does the degree to which fan works affirm, celebrate, or seek to rework or remediate their objects of fandom. Over time, individuals and communities of fans can move from one approach to the other. Participatory, organized fandoms were much smaller before the emergence of the internet, when connecting with other fans often required travel to conventions or other events. Over the last thirty years, the internet has enormously broadened many fan communities, since online access to organized fandoms is much easier.

In contrast to fans who are focused on fantasy or science fiction world-building, historically based fandoms are those in which fans' activities and interests are focused on historical cultures and peoples, imaginary or otherwise. Relatively little scholarly work has been done on historically focused fan communities and (as we shall see in chapter 6), most of that research has been done by historians who are generally not sympathetic to historical hobbyists, sometimes describing hobbyists as "antiquarians." How accurate—in the sense of being true to historical reality, as historians might see it—fans' understanding or re-creation of historical settings and cultures are, can also vary considerably.

Historically based fandoms are often inspired by a literary series set in the past, but in other groups like the Society for Creative Anachronism, a medievalism fan community founded in 1966, the past itself might be the "canon" that fans play with and retell to suit their own tastes. Fan communities that focus on historical events directly, instead of using a literary series as a point of entrée, shade into historical reenactment communities; there is no clear hard-and-fast line between the two categories of organizations. In the German fan communities I examine here, some fans and groups who were originally attracted to a literary series later split off in order to focus on historical reenactment.

Historically based fandoms run the gamut in terms of their imaginary locations, both temporally and geographically. Fan communities across the European Union re-create aspects of medieval Europe that appeal to them. Examples include the Cologne Horde of Huns, founded in 1958 by fans of movies about Atilla the Hun, or the group of Thuringian fans I met in May 2019 at the ruins of a local castle, who gathered there annually to celebrate Walpurgis Night with costumes, cooking implements and foods, and tents modeled on those of medieval German orders of knights.[7] Other hobbyist groups prefer historical cultures that are geographically quite distant from their own cultures, since they perceive the reenactment of someone else's past as being less politically problematic and thus less controversial.[8] This might be one factor underlying the global popularity of the American Civil War among non-American reenactment communities.

Fandoms organized around literary canons written more than a century ago, for example the Sherlock Holmes stories, may focus primarily on the characters and storylines, while still giving considerable attention to the historical setting of the stories. The members of the earliest Sherlock Holmes groups, the Baker Street Irregulars and the Sherlock Holmes Society, researched and published extensively on life in Victorian London. On occasion, they even dressed in Victorian clothes to re-create famous scenes in the stories, such as Holmes's struggle with Professor Moriarty at Reichenbach Falls. Yet for fans of literary works like the Sherlock Holmes stories, the vanished historical culture that the story world is set in forms only a backdrop to some fan activities. Sherlock Holmes could be (and was) successfully transferred from the Victorian period to other time periods, however, and the character lost none of its fascination for most fans.[9] For the fandoms discussed in this book, however, the historical cultural context is central to what brings fans amusement, and it defines their organizations and activities.

In scholarly discussions, historically focused fandoms have received less attention than twenty-first-century media fandoms. Historically focused fan communities, like those discussed in this book, are often distant—in geographic, cultural, or political terms—from the interests and cultural locations of academic fan studies practitioners and most academic historians. But like some other early twentieth-century literary series, these fandoms and their canons have been participatory, productive, and transmedial from their earliest stages.[10] In recent decades, their fans have eagerly participated in convergence culture, extensively using new media platforms as they pursue the re-creation of the past. They have never been insulated from the political discourses and concerns that affect other fandoms and the societies that they are embedded in. They have been largely overlooked in fan studies publications so far, however, which have been more intrigued by some forms of audience engagement and media platforms than others.[11]

In choosing historically focused fandoms as my focus, I am not only examining communities and fan works that have received limited attention in fan studies to date. Rather, the most important contribution this study tries to offer is a demonstration of what we can learn by using historical methods and sources to study fan communities over a longer period of time. Most work on fandoms has been synchronic, examining fans and their communities in the present, or over the course of a few years. But a historical approach to fan studies is diachronic, analyzing change over time both in fan communities, and in the cultures that they are embedded in.

A historical approach looks at how fans perceived and responded to the original story canon against the backdrop of the time and culture within which they were organizing their fandoms, and how those responses shifted over time. This book argues that fans' responses to their canon, their object of fandom, were also responses to the world around them, and that fans' activities and views changed substantially over time precisely because the cultures that they belonged to altered greatly as well, undergoing sometimes wrenching political, social, technological, and economic shifts. Examining historically focused fandoms throws these processes into particular relief, because the conflicts or tensions between the historical cultures and norms that the fans celebrate, and the contemporary politics and social structures that they live within, can highlight changes within the fandom itself. Historically focused fandoms are also among the oldest organized fan communities, offering examples of communities where we can trace developments over decades.

This study also suggests that drawing on the frameworks and terminologies of fan studies can also be illuminating for historians and scholars of popular culture from other disciplines, who have generally not made use of this framework. Historians have sometimes had as much difficulty understanding deeply engaged hobbyists and fan communities as these fans' contemporaries did, for example the German journalist who attended the 1962 West German Indian Council. Fan studies offers concepts and approaches that can be usefully applied to the study of popular historical entertainments and their enthusiasts.

The scholarly literature on German Western fans is limited. Only one of the fan communities (itself one segment of German Western fandom) discussed in this study has previously received significant attention from historians and other scholars: hobbyists who created "Indian" costumes and artifacts in order to perform as Indigenous *personas*, and who often referred to themselves as "Indianist" hobbyists after World War II.[12] One striking feature of both scholars' and journalists' work on German Western fans is the tight focus on the motives of German Indianist hobbyists, to the exclusion of almost every other aspect of German Western fans' activities, even where the Indianist hobbyists and other Western fan communities overlapped and interacted with each other.

Like the journalist who reported on the 1962 gathering of German "cowboys and Indians" mentioned earlier, historians and anthropologists have often been bemused, perplexed, or sometimes critical of German Indianists. Petra Kalshoven's and Glenn Penny's more recent studies of German Indianist hobbyists have offered a useful and well-researched addition to earlier research. Penny's book traces the lengthy history of Germans' engagement with Indigenous North Americans and gently suggests that scholars should take hobbyists' own explanations about their motives more seriously. Kalshoven's study supports this conclusion and examines communities of Indianist hobbyists in France, the Netherlands, and the Czech Republic, as well. Penny's work considers Indianist hobbyists using historical sources and literature, but does not analyze them within the context of German Western fans as a whole. In this study, I will examine the ways in which German fans' *Indianer* role-play first emerged within the context of "cowboy and Indian" clubs, with club members frequently alternating between both types of role-play for decades, and how these groups overlapped with or were connected to Karl May fans and other German Western fans.[13]

The historically based fandoms discussed in this book have relatively old pedigrees. German fans of the American West founded their first clubs before World War I, predating organized science fiction fans, while *Little House* fans first organized during the 1950s. These fans generally did not emphasize the creation of transformative works as fan studies scholars have traditionally understood the term, e.g., fan fiction. They were not so much interested in reworking the past as they were in experiencing it, or even entering it, in some cases. Over time, however, many of the groups examined here did end up tweaking or extending the story world that fascinated them. Some also challenged conventional historiographical understandings with performances that reinterpreted the past and the story world canon in ways to suit their own needs, stressing affect and the experiences of a daily life in historical cultures that were worlds away from their own.

The historically focused fandoms discussed in this book were and are heavily oriented toward the experiential. Their activities are usually less concerned with particular important historical events or long-term historical change than they are with the individual's personal experience of the past as a compelling foreign culture. Through role-play or other types of intensive engagement with historical artifacts, cultures, and settings, these fans seek to "touch" historic cultures and people they feel affinity for, and experience the past firsthand. They are fascinated by the taste of foods no longer eaten, the feel and design of clothes no longer worn, crafts and skills that have fallen into disuse, archaic forms of entertainment, and the social "rules" and mindset of a long-vanished world.

These are often simultaneously the foods, clothes, and norms mentioned in much-loved story worlds, as well as those from a historical culture. In Canberra, for example, Jane Austen fans come together annually for the Jane Austen Festival Australia, described by the organizers as a venue "where Austen and Napoleonic fans from all over Australia come and indulge themselves in everything Regency [the word denotes both a time period and a literary genre]—including dancing, music, food, games, archery, fencing, theatre, promenades, grand balls, talks, workshops, costumes and books. . . . Small soirees, concerts, a costumed promenade, theatre, archery, period games, fashion, food, lectures, and of course LOTS of dancing [are featured] over three days and four nights."[14] As one scholar of Danish historical reenactors noted, this type of engagement offers fans "the experience of achieving knowledge about the past through their own bodies."[15]

In the process, members of historically based fandoms create interpretations of a historical world which can be partly imaginary. The experiential nature of their engagement fosters the conviction that they *have* touched the past, however, and now know what it was really like: *wie es eigentlich gewesen*, as a nineteenth-century founder of academic history summarized his profession's goal.[16] And indeed, many fans have taught themselves an often impressive amount of information about material culture and daily life in the past. But as with academic historians' work, their interpretations necessarily involve creativity and imagination; they also display a strong affective identification with past cultures and actors. Indeed, their research and performances allow them to "co-construct and appropriate the very past that [they are] imitating."[17] This sense of identification and the creative, performative aspects of historical reenactors' work has underwritten a sometimes critical view of reenactment and living history by academic historians. Historians who have studied reenactment have noted that while reenactment fans might master the past's ephemera, they do not attempt to explain historical processes, nor do they always confront those processes or structures critically.[18]

Beyond an opportunity to "touch" and experience the past, historically oriented fandoms can have an antimodern appeal: they offer an entrée into a world that is—in popular imagination—a "simpler" time. In the past, as imagined in these literary historical story worlds, good and bad were clear. Life and gender roles were also thought to be more "natural," which can mean more essentialized. As we shall see, however, the antimodernist appeal of historically focused fandoms can evolve over decades, as the cultures that fans seek temporary escape from alter themselves. Historically based fandoms thus combine the pleasures of "escape" into a less bureaucratic, regulated past with the lure of detective work, as fans do sometimes extensive and painstaking research to uncover historical details. They also draw fans into a world of fascinating historic crafts and for many, offer membership in a cherished community of kindred spirits.

But research into and re-creation of the nineteenth-century American frontier, even to the point of cross-racial identification in the case of some German fans, ran into increasing criticism and opposition during the late twentieth century. In the case of these historically focused fandoms, the most critical appraisals of their communities and canons were rooted in changing views of white settler colonialism and Indigenous North Americans. This was not a dynamic unique to the fandoms examined in this study. Other historically based fandoms have had to grapple with changing contemporary views of past cultures, which engendered critiques of the values and social structures with which fan communities and their imagined worlds were engaged. German Western fans first began to face political pressures in Nazi Germany, which substantially changed and intensified in East Germany after 1948. In both the United States and Germany, political and social changes in the late twentieth century led to increasingly critical evaluations of white settler colonialism and of the depictions of Indigenous cultures which were, in very different ways, as intrinsic to each fan community's activities as these issues were to the history of the American West itself. As a result, fans' historical performances or interpretations led to accusations of cultural appropriation or of the erasure of Indigenous people's historical experience. These conflicts were rooted in the fact that the perceptions of white fans and those of Indigenous peoples proceeded from quite different ontologies and epistemologies.

Changes over the last century in how white settlement and Indigenous cultures were viewed are mirrored in the shifting vocabulary and terminology used to describe Indigenous peoples over the last century. During the early and mid-twentieth century, in the stories and fandoms discussed in this book, the first inhabitants of North America were usually referred to simply as "Indians," although Karl May might also use nineteenth-century names or specific cultures that were current among ethnologists and anthropologists, such as, the Mescalero Apache. But by the late twentieth century, Indigenous peoples and Indigenous Studies scholars used a wide range of descriptions. Where a specific individual from one tribe or that person's community is discussed, the preference now is almost always to include that nation's name, such as Lakota or Cree. But at this writing, there is no clear consensus beyond that. Canadians usually use the terms "First Nations" or "Indigenous Peoples." In the United States, Indigenous people and the scholars who study these cultures (whether they themselves are Indigenous or not) might use "Native American," "Indigenous," "Native," or simply "Indian" as a catchall term, or refer to lands or cultural spaces controlled by Indigenous people as "Indian country."

Since the Indigenous cultures that this study refers to extend across Canada and the United States, I have generally chosen to refer to them as Indigenous here when referring to Indigenous cultures collectively, and have used the specific community's name where available. When discussing the imagined cultures and characters that were part of the story worlds and the activities or role-play of the fandoms that this book examines, I have used the word "Indian" or (if the reference is to German hobbyists) Indianist. My goal is to try to make clear for readers the difference between the imaginary cultures and fictional characters that fan communities referred to, and the actual cultures of Indigenous North America. Where an Indigenous organization or individual used the terms "Native American" or "Indian," however, I respect and use the terms chosen by this person or group when referring to themselves.

The political challenges and changes that fans had to navigate went deeper than taxonomy and terminology. Fandoms that pursue historical re-creation cannot escape the fact that their hobbies have inherent political implications, since the past is the basis for nations' shared understandings of ethnic and social groups' origins and identities. The political connotations of historical re-creation can be subtle, or so obvious that they are inescapable, as with the American Civil War reenactors studied by Tony Horwitz.[19] Choosing to identify with someone else's past (as German Western fans did) can be seen as disloyalty to current political regimes at home, accusations that were leveled against Western fans in both Nazi Germany and East Germany. The politics of an imagined past can also become controversial in decades after the fandom was founded, as commonly held values and historical interpretations are challenged. Thus, white *Little House* fans—engaged with a popular and widely honored story world—were later forced to grapple with criticism about the representation of Indigenous cultures in Laura Ingalls Wilder's works. Fans in both Germany and the United States were compelled to negotiate the tensions between the values of the imagined pasts that they celebrated, and the politics and expectations of the cultures that they currently live in.

All long-term fandoms are ultimately founded on shifting historical terrain, a fact that historically focused fandoms cannot avoid. The fandoms discussed here were particularly confronted with changes over time in their societies' understandings of racial hierarchies. Understandings of white colonial settlement, Indigeneity, and national identities were crucial to each fandom's activities and to the culture that each was a part of, and these understandings were redefined over the decades this book covers. One example: fans in both the United States and in Germany were making quilts, blankets, and clothing, or re-creating historical foods as part of their engagement with an imagined American frontier. But as we will see, the meaning of what they were doing for themselves as individuals, and in terms of the politics of the culture they lived in, were wildly divergent. And these meanings and the political contexts of these activities altered over decades, as this study demonstrates.

Chapter 1 begins by tracing the historiography of the American West, and the entertainments and mythologies rooted in these historical narratives in both the United States and Europe since the mid-nineteenth century. Popular understandings of the American West have changed considerably over the last century, alongside the evolution of the technological platforms used for Western entertainments. In the United States, the "opening" of the American West was the dominant national identity narrative among white Americans long before Frederick Jackson Turner—a founder of American Western historiography—argued in 1890 that the frontier settlements formed the bedrock of American democracy and had shaped American national identity. For white Americans, the doctrine of Manifest Destiny had guided and sanctioned white expansion across the North American continent and the expropriation of Indigenous lands over decades.

Germans were generally more critical of the impact of white settlement on Indigenous cultures than white Americans were. But both groups were unified in seeing the "red race," as Karl May called Indigenous peoples, as doomed: vanishing Indigenous cultures, they assumed, would give way before the assertion of white Americans' right to the lands into which they were expanding. Even sympathetic nineteenth-century white depictions of Indigenous cultures were invariably elegiac.[20] In both nations, popular entertainments based on this view of American history became extraordinarily popular by the mid-nineteenth century, giving rise to bestselling Western dime novels and pulp fiction, Buffalo Bill's *Wild West Show*, other traveling circuses and exotic entertainments, and in the twentieth century to Western films and television shows. During the early and mid-twentieth century, Western entertainments—and the national mythologies they were rooted in—were huge draws in both the United States and Europe.

Chapter 2 turns to the emergence of Western fans in Germany, whose communities were inspired by both Karl May and other Western novels, and by the *Wild West Show* and other touring Western performances. German fans began to found "cowboy and Indian" clubs in the decade before World War I, and the number of such clubs grew steadily during the interwar period. The Karl May Museum, founded near Dresden by May's widow in 1926, served as an important pilgrimage site for the fandom; its first curator, Patty Frank, helped to connect regional clubs and dispersed fans with one another. Cowboy and Indian clubs were predominantly male, and members practiced the handicrafts, skills, and role-play of both Indians and cowboys; many individuals performed both roles, creating costumes and adopting special club names for both types of role-play.

The fandom during this period was shaped in part by the pressures and influence of May's copyright holder, which generally discouraged the type of literary society and fan scholarship that developed among British and American *Sherlock Holmes* and science fiction fans by the 1930s. After the National Socialists came to power in 1933, Patty Frank and the clubs had to manage their relationship with Nazi leaders in order to continue their Western activities. Some Nazi activists criticized May's novels, on the grounds that many of the leading characters were not white, and because the white protagonist at one point proposed marrying an Apache woman, which for them amounted to the promotion of miscegenation. May was also vulnerable to Nazi attacks because his later works were pacifist. This chapter examines why and how Frank and German fans were ultimately able to continue their work under the Nazis, even receiving support from the regime.

Germany was occupied and divided after its loss to the Allies in 1945, and Chapter 3 explores the bifurcated development of a now divided Western fandom, tracing its history against the backdrop of the Cold War. In East Germany, the Communist authorities suppressed the publication or sale of May's novels, since his stories were located in the United States, now the enemy of Soviet-led Eastern Europe. Some of May's leading characters were white American cowboys, and East German authorities took a very dim view of fans dressing and role-playing as cowboys. In order to reestablish their clubs, East German fans ultimately ceased cowboy role-play and organized interest in May, instead focusing on often intensive study of Indigenous North American cultures, developing elaborate mimetic handicrafts and an emphasis on "accurate" Indianist role-play. In West Germany, fans activities were part of an expanding consumer culture, which offered an ever-growing variety of Western and May spin-off products and entertainments. West German fans continued and expanded their range of Western role-play, supported a variety of commercial Western and May-related entertainments, and created a scholarly and productive May literary society. By the time the Berlin Wall came down in 1989, the two German fandoms had developed in quite different directions.

Chapter 4 crosses the Atlantic, to pick up the story of the fans of Laura Ingalls Wilder and her *Little House* series. It examines the development of the fan community in the first few decades after Wilder's death in 1957, against the backdrop of Cold War–understandings of American national identity and history. Wilder's fans were deeply engaged with fan scholarship about her life and that of her family. They also supported the development of a substantial fan pilgrimage circuit, organized around the Wilder "homesites," which re-created the material culture and lifestyle of nineteenth-century white settlers for fans to see and experience. This chapter explores the ways in which the Wilder fandom celebrated the experience of white settler women like Wilder, and how the story of the Wilders was connected to fans' and contemporaries' understandings of their own national, regional, and family heritages.

On both sides of the Atlantic, these fandoms were affected by changes set in motion by the social and political activism of the 1960s and 1970s, and the subsequent changes that followed. Chapter 5 traces the impact of these developments on each fandom. In the United States, the resurgence of Indigenous protest organizations like the American Indian Movement (AIM) ultimately affected Western fans in both Europe and America. AIM developed connections with both East and West German fans, who sympathized with and supported Indigenous activists.

Across the Western world, the social reform movements of this period ultimately supported a critical reassessment of American history that gave rise during the mid-1980s in the United States to a still-ongoing "culture war." Earlier narratives of American history and national identity were called into question by academic historians' heightened awareness of the racial conflict and injustices inherent in the project of white settlement along a "frontier" that moved ever westward; this awareness was shared by many people, both inside and outside of the United States.[21] New frameworks were introduced into a more multicultural historiography of the American West, provoking a strong response from American cultural conservatives.

Both German Western fans and fans of the *Little House* series were affected by these changes in popular historical understandings, and by a resurgence in Indigenous North American activism during the second half of the twentieth century.[22] For the *Little House* fan community in particular, Indigenous activists' criticisms of Wilder's stories found more sympathetic and widespread support than they had in the past. At the same time, the reunification of Germany in 1990 meant that East Germans had greater access to the "real thing," as American Indigenous performers and visitors came to Germany, sometimes reacting critically or bemusedly to German fans' Indianist role-play. Some Indigenous activists questioned the Karl Museum's holdings, demanding the return of Indigenous scalps on display at the Museum. Gradually, German Indianists were replaced in public performances at festivals by North American Indigenous performers, and slowly retreated from public view. Some German hobbyists continued their gatherings in private, while others branched out into American Civil War reenactment instead. The earlier elegiac myth of the "vanishing Indian" was now replaced by Indigenous activism and resurgence, challenging Western fans' understanding of their fandoms.

*Little House* fans and German Western hobbyists therefore confronted the question of how to acknowledge and respond to a complicated and sometimes problematic history, a challenge that presents itself to other historical fandoms as well. As we shall see, fans in both groups became entangled in the conflicts generated by changes in how their cultures evaluated the American West and entangled in a complex racial history that had little to do with the reasons that their fandoms were initially attractive to their members.

Both fandoms continue to be affected by these developments in the twenty-first century, and fans have developed their own accommodations and responses to changes in how the history of the American West is understood. Chapter 6 concludes by discussing recent developments in both fandoms, and the ways in which these fans are influenced by the growth of living history institutions, historical reenactment hobbyist organizations, and other historical hobbies. A variety of new ways of "doing" history as a public hobby or educational activity is increasingly important in how the past was remembered in both Europe and the United States. This chapter examines the recent history of Western fans against the backdrop of these broader changes, seeking to explain why, for example, fans who were active Indianists in East Germany now gravitate toward Confederate roles in American Civil War reenactment, and how Karl May fans have expanded their playful reinterpretations and revisions of the story world canon.

Fans have always been aware that the past cultures that they sought to connect with through experiential engagement are at least partially imagined, but they became invested in these histories and characters nonetheless. Their immersion into imagined historical pasts began decades before the internet, during a time when fans of historical story worlds had to go to some effort and expense to meet, parse, and play with their source texts. Immersion in imaginary worlds was more than an escape from the sorrows or stress of daily life: it helped to re-enchant prosaic lives, in some respects bringing magic or imaginative engagement into modern lives.[23] Historical cultures and settings became a pleasant refuge from daily life, a location where individual fans could incorporate their own perspectives and values, and thus create a more interesting site for play, which nonetheless reflected the political and cultural context of their present.

Fans of historical worlds could and still do get away to an imagined Old West, medieval Europe, or anywhere else their imaginations (and source canons) take them. Of course, humans have used myth and fiction for this purpose for thousands of years. But starting in the early twentieth century, the availability of historically focused fan organizations meant that readers who were passionately interested in a particular story and its historical world could go there on "group tours," with other fans. Once there, they could do their own research and even create new pieces of this world, sharing their products with appreciative audiences —fellow fans. Their communities varied greatly, since every fan community was shaped by a particular social or historical context.

As this book will demonstrate, the paths that their journeys took changed substantially over time, as the cultures and political contexts that they were embedded in changed as well. Each visitor to the past explored and created in his or her fashion, learning new skills and taking on absorbing projects, while the group immersed itself in a past culture that its members found fascinating. In the process, many found that the rewards included membership in tight-knit communities. This book explores the places they went, together.

# CHAPTER ONE

# Who Owns the West?

*Up to our own day American history has been in a large degree
the history of the colonization of the Great West.*

—FREDERICK JACKSON TURNER, 1893

The American West is a region whose boundaries and ownership are still disputed. In both an imaginary and material sense, it is an alluring and strongly contested intellectual, cultural, and political property. The West's historic and mythic elements—covered wagon trains, stockade forts, herds of buffalo that stretch as far as the eye can see, teepee villages, Indian warriors on horseback, men who make their own justice with their guns, cowboys on open ranges, "vanishing" Indian cultures, and white settlers "taming" a wilderness with their plows and log cabins—have spread across global culture and have been used in every type of art and story form over the last two centuries. All of these images and ideas came to form a storytelling archive of images and concepts, which both academic historians and Western entertainment creators drew on in their work.

For American audiences, Western stories were rooted in a shared understanding of American history that explained and often justified white settlers' displacement of Indigenous peoples, and the seizure of their lands. The frontier was crucial to this understanding of the West, and to white Americans' national identity and historical narratives. As the first academic historians of the West depicted it, the frontier—constantly receding as white settlement progressed westward—formed the boundary of a United States that ultimately expanded to incorporate land from the Atlantic to the Pacific, a transcontinental nation. Historians and politicians also argued that the frontier was the site of a special American experiment in democracy and freedom. The Indigenous peoples who found themselves located on this frontier, and ultimately inside the United States, disagreed and resisted. Their cultures were engulfed and decimated by white settlement, which entailed successive waves of settler immigration and the imposition, often by violence, of white Americans' legal and economic systems.

The elements of the frontier mythology that developed in dialogue with the advance of white settlement and Indigenous resistance were not only the property of academic historians and politicians. They were free for people both inside and outside of the United States to draw on as well, in constructing their own stories about the American West. Western entertainments were enormously popular in Europe, although European audiences developed their own interpretations of Western stories. Artists, writers, stage performers, modern media producers, and ordinary people around the world have mined frontier images, tropes, and settings since the early nineteenth century, often with joyful absorption and fascinated attention to the artifacts and cultures of the West. In recent decades, the historiography of the West has changed, and Western films and television shows have declined in popularity; but for almost two centuries, Westerns dominated American entertainment markets and were extremely popular around the world.

The imagined West proved to be an unstable cultural territory. Today, American popular culture more often looks outward, creating and exporting stories of other worlds and galaxies rather than stories of the American frontier. Throughout the period when mass entertainments were emerging, however, Westerns were the most popular American entertainment genre, attracting large communities of fans. Each community developed its own interpretation of the history of the West, the history that it wanted or needed. And what audiences and fans needed, changed over decades.

## The Historic West and the Frontier in American National Biography

*Where* is the West? The American frontier was a moving target for most of the eighteenth and nineteenth centuries, an imaginary line that white Americans used to divide the established states of the United States from the unorganized and lightly governed territories where white settlement and the displacement of

Indigenous peoples was still underway. This line moved steadily westward over two centuries, as white settlers seeking land pushed past the boundaries of the original colonies during the eighteenth century to the Old Northwest (the future states of Ohio, Indiana, Illinois, Wisconsin, and Michigan), and still later to the trans-Mississippi territories.[1] The Homestead Act of 1862 facilitated this process by allowing any white adult citizen or immigrant to claim 160 acres of public (government-owned) land if he or she settled and cultivated it for five years.

The lands coveted by white settlers were not uninhabited, of course. Sometimes, would-be settlers squatted on land that had not yet even been taken by the federal government, hoping to file homestead claims in the future. Indigenous cultures consistently resisted white encroachment, leading to endemic conflicts or outright warfare between white settlers, the US Army, and Indigenous peoples, and (in the far west and southwest) with Hispanic communities that often predated the foundation of the United States. Before the Mexican-American War, the American government pursued a policy of removal of Indigenous cultures to a point past the frontier's imaginary line, pushing them to territories farther west, some of which were promised to Indigenous tribes in perpetuity. But the acquisition of territory from Mexico and the creation of a United States that spanned the continent doomed the earlier federal policy, which had envisioned the Plains as "Indian Territory." Like Laura Ingalls Wilder's family, white settlers squatted on land inside of territories promised to Indigenous peoples; the US federal government then shifted to a policy of forcing Indigenous tribes off their lands and into diminishing, often resource-poor reservations, surrounded by white communities. By 1890, the population was sufficiently dense across the continent that the US Census Bureau declared that the frontier was now "closed."[2]

The imaginary boundary between settled and unsettled territories might no longer exist, but the frontier's importance to American national identity and mythology continued to grow for decades, even as the United States became more urbanized. The frontier's role in shaping American identity and democracy was articulated in scholarly terms by the influential work of historian Frederick Jackson Turner, whose research founded the field of American Western history and presented one of the most influential master narratives in American history. Turner first offered his "frontier thesis" at the 1893 meeting of the American Historical Association. His arguments developed, in a more detailed and scholarly form, the ideas that had been circulating even before Turner gave his presentation, e.g., in Theodore Roosevelt's popular history, *The Winning of the West*.[3]

Turner argued that frontier conditions had shaped both American national character and the development of American democracy. Experiencing both the challenges and the personal liberty that characterized frontier life, he claimed, pioneers from European cultures were released from the hierarchies and constraints of the Old World: European aristocracies, state-supported churches, standing armies, and habits of deference to one's social betters. The frontier, Turner argued, "is the line of most rapid and effective Americanization," a sort of melting pot that accepted people from many cultures and transformed them into a new composite but English-speaking nationality. The frontier experience also promoted egalitarianism and democracy. The American mindset that resulted, Turner concluded, featured "coarseness and strength combined with acuteness and inquisitiveness; that practical, inventive turn of mind, quick to find expedients; that masterful grasp of material things, lacking in the artistic but powerful to effect great ends; that restless, nervous energy; that dominant individualism, working for good and for evil, and withal that buoyancy and exuberance which comes with freedom, these are the traits of the frontier."[4] Turner's description fit Laura Ingalls Wilder's depiction of her father, "Pa" Ingalls, almost to a T. Wilder came to adulthood in a culture that had absorbed Turner's understanding of the frontier, and her own depictions of frontier communities reflected Turner's paradigm.[5]

In Turner's conception of American history, "the frontier is truly American because at some time, all of America has been the West," due to the fact that the frontier was first located in the East Coast colonies, and moved westward, while "interaction with the conditions of the frontier made Americans American."[6] Frontier life thus produced men who were free of European traditions of deference and social hierarchy, while the conditions of frontier life required that frontiersmen participate in public life, and in participatory democracy. Turner's farmers had conquered a wilderness, and simultaneously expanded the realm of liberty and democracy. His arguments ultimately shaped the teaching of American history for more than a generation: by the 1930s, 60 percent of leading American universities taught Western history in ways that reflected Turner's thesis.[7]

In *The Puritan Origins of the American Self*, Sacvan Bercovitch discusses the development of the "national biography" of the United States, a folk history or story that Americans share about their origins and foundational heroes.[8] In present-day America, the musical *Hamilton* is a good example of national biography; in the 1950s, the television series *Davy Crockett* represented another version.

National biography is not rooted in a strictly factual account of a nation's history, but instead it reflects people's affection for and pride in their national heritage. It is a form of popular mythology which helps a people explain themselves, to themselves, and to foreigners. At the same time, national biographies often align very well with (and indeed, can function as popularized segments of) the master narratives that create a framework for a nation's academic historiography, codified and passed down in school textbooks.

Nations are rather abstract concepts; they can have disputed or fluctuating boundaries. Their territories are often (but not always) governed by nation-state entities. But nations are also identity categories that seek to unite quite diverse populations and geographies, even those that are not currently governed by the same state entity, e.g., the concept of Germany and Germanness, which long predated the creation of a united German state.[9] The nation provides a framework for assembling collective memories, creating national myths and national biographies, and for teaching history to the citizens of a nation.

In nineteenth- and twentieth-century historical scholarship and teaching, the nation—its origin, growth, national struggles for unification or liberation from other nations or empires—often formed the center and focus of historical narratives. Nation-focused historical master narratives became pervasive, developing in step with the professionalization of academic historians. As two scholars who studied this process in Latin American national histories observed, "national master narratives act as both official and general interpretations of the past, but also legitimize the present and set an agenda for the future [for each national state]."[10] Turner's frontier thesis offered a national master narrative that provided an explanation and justification for the expansion of the United States and for the origins of American identity that integrated Americans from diverse European ethnic backgrounds while celebrating the creation and growth of American democracy.

It was a description of American identity that was inherently white, although Turner did not acknowledge this. In his telling, the settlers who homesteaded and developed frontier communities came from diverse European communities. Once in the United States, they were all re-socialized by the frontier experience, emerging as white Americans. Indigenous peoples, Hispanics, and other non-white peoples in the West were implicitly excluded from Turner's narrative of American identity and participation in frontier governance not only because of the origin cultures he traced Americans to but also because of the laws and theories that regulated land development and ownership in the United States. Under the Homestead Act white adults, whether they had obtained American citizenship yet or not, were allowed to homestead land on the frontier. Indigenous Americans were generally excluded from citizenship throughout the nineteenth century, and thus could not file claims on lands that their ancestors had lived on.[11] Property rights, nineteenth-century American legal theorists and jurists argued, were linked to the cultivation and development of land according to European standards, and were thus tied to the white forms of agricultural production and community structures celebrated by Turner. These writers did not recognize Indigenous methods of collective land stewardship and use, instead seeing such land as "unused wilderness."[12] This view of land ownership and property rights would be echoed by some of the characters in Wilder's books and by the protagonists of other Western entertainments.

Turner's arguments about the frontier as a crucible of American national character were well aligned with the popular visions of the American West promoted by Theodore Roosevelt, and by leading writers and artists like Owen Wister and Frederic Remington, all contemporaries of Turner. This understanding was carried forward in the work of a host of lesser-known writers, artists, and historians.[13] Turner thus named and articulated a theory of American history and identity that remained hegemonic for decades.

As Boyd Cothran noted in *Remembering the Modoc War*, the collective contributions of these writers and artists transformed "memories of the violent conquest of American Indians into the 'red-blooded realism' [of Western settlement tales] . . . Americans celebrated the open spaces, autonomous individualism, personal sacrifice, and masculine heroism endemic to the narratives of the American West."[14] During the late nineteenth and early twentieth centuries, these overlapping understandings of the frontier experience contributed powerfully to a national biography that was ultimately reflected across American popular culture. As Robert Hine and John Faragher observed about the frontier myth: "myth, like history, tries to find meaning in past events. But when turned into myth, history is reduced to its ideological essence. The Western—the characteristic story form of the frontier myth—is essentially a tale of progress, a justification of violent conquest and untrammeled [economic] development."[15] But it was simultaneously a powerfully appealing national biography that became the springboard for a range of enduring, compelling popular entertainments.

Cothran's recent study examines popular memories and entertainments rooted in the Modoc War, the final chapter in waves of violence between Indigenous peoples and white settlers in California and Oregon during the mid-nineteenth century; this war led to the near annihilation of Indigenous communities in the region. In California alone, the Indigenous population dropped from around 150,000 to less than 30,000 during this period, the worst example of genocide against Indigenous cultures in American history. The governor of California, Peter Burnett, argued that genocide was inevitable, commenting that "a war of extermination will continue to be waged between the races until the Indian race becomes extinct."[16] Cothran is concerned with what he calls the "marketplaces of remembering" that arose afterward: the development of entertainments, museum displays, plays, artifacts, memoirs, souvenirs, and other remembrances of the Modoc War, which received nationwide attention at the time and for decades thereafter. These commercial marketplaces required remembrances of the Modoc War that told the conflict from white Americans' points of view, remembrances that are popular cultural examples of the cliché that history is written by the winners of a war.

Cothran notes that the popular narratives and products that focused on the war were shaped by (and in turn helped to influence) the expectations of particular commercial markets, and the expectations of consumers of these narratives. In the case of the Modoc War and other episodes of US-Indigenous violence, Cothran argues, nineteenth-century Americans saw their nation as fundamentally innocent, in terms of the government's goals and values:

> The United States, they insisted, had to expand to maintain its freedom through a culture of broad-based white, male landownership [which had led to the Homestead Act]. The inevitable violence resulting from this expansion was thereby justified as innocent . . . in this context, Indians were the irrational aggressors and violators of a civilized nation's just laws.[17]

The entertainments discussed in this chapter were primarily created for the same white American and European marketplaces of historical remembrance discussed by Cothran. These novels, paintings, memoirs, theatrical pieces, and later films and television shows celebrated the natural beauty of the frontier, and the opportunities that it offered to settlers. The entertainments created for white American audiences, including Laura Ingalls Wilder's novels, also reflected the popular national biography that Turner and others had promoted, depicting white settlers as fundamentally innocent. No other narratives could have met the expectations of the American markets and consumers that writers and artists were creating for.

European marketplaces of remembrance for entertainments and products based on the American West would allow their creators more flexibility: mass entertainment markets outside the United States offered room for narratives in which white Americans were sometimes the aggressors, and culpable in US-Indigenous violence. Karl May's story world thus presented the same overarching framework of advancing white settlement and Indigenous retreat (and decline) that Wilder's novels assumed. But writing for German audiences, he did not subscribe to the understanding that white settlers were always innocent, acting in good faith.

## Western Entertainments

Painters and authors created art and stories about the American West and its peoples that fascinated both Europeans and Americans living east of the Mississippi throughout the nineteenth century. After 1820, a series of artists traveled west to capture images of the exotic landscapes and Indigenous peoples of the regions that white settlers were moving into. Often, they traveled as part of federal surveying parties, or with wealthy European or American naturalist patrons who wanted a record of their journey. Some of the best known were German-speaking or German American painters, whose images circulated widely in both the United States and Germany; Karl May drew upon some of this work in creating his own imagined West.

Karl Bodmer, a Swiss artist, created detailed studies of the daily lives and homes of the Mandans during the 1830s, while Alfred Miller became known for his watercolors of mountain men, trappers, and the Indigenous cultures that they traded with. George Catlin, well known before the Civil War, saw the Indigenous subjects he sketched as members of vanishing cultures; he sympathized deeply with them, and was determined to capture their images for future generations.[18] These artists' images of Indigenous cultures were reproduced in widely distributed US government publications, and were copied in authorized and unauthorized prints, as well as in magazines, dime novels, and popular books in both Europe and the United States.[19]

Other Western artists, like George Caleb Bingham, focused on pioneers and white settlement; his *Daniel Boone Escorting Settlers through the Cumberland Gap*

(1851–1852), was quintessential frontier iconography. Emanuel Gottlieb Leutze's *Westward the Course of Empire Takes Its Way* (1861) was a twenty-by-thirty-foot mural depicting pioneers, mountain men, and wagon trains headed West, celebrating the realization of Manifest Destiny as a quasi-religious pilgrimage; it still hangs in the US Capitol Building today. In post–Civil War America, Albert Bierstadt and Thomas Moran created gigantic landscapes that offered romantic, almost transcendent panoramas that envisioned the West as a sort of spectacular natural cathedral. Their work gave urban East Coast Americans and Europeans a sense of emotional connection to the natural beauty of the West, and to an earlier, now supposedly vanishing frontier experience.[20]

As the region considered by Americans to be the frontier moved west over time, so did the fictitious West in popular novels. James Fenimore Cooper's *Leatherstocking Tales* (widely read in both the United States and Germany during the mid-nineteenth century) were set in central New York, in Iroquois territories.[21] But the Mohicans featured in Cooper's tales were replaced in late nineteenth-century pulp fiction and novels, including in Karl May's work, by the Plains Indigenous peoples and the Indigenous cultures of the Southwest.

Dime novels set on the frontier began to appear during the 1840s, featuring purely fictional exploits by Davy Crockett and Kit Carson. Later novels showcased Buffalo Bill, Billy the Kid, and Jesse James, and offered stories where white heroes squared off against savage Indian characters, inscrutable Chinese, or "greaser" Hispanic antagonists. Calamity Jane was one of the earliest embodiments of what became an established trope in Westerns, the independent white woman with a gun, or even a whip, of her own. She would be joined in the pantheon of Western heroines by Annie Oakley, offering models for later female Western fans.[22]

One of the best-known Western novels of the early twentieth century was Owen Wister's 1902 *The Virginian*, which presented the frontier as a proving ground for American masculinity and the national character that Roosevelt and Turner had promoted. *The Virginian* paved the way for the flood of genre fiction written by Zane Grey and Louis L'Amour in later decades. Western fiction thus came to its peak during the same decades that triumphalist historiography and the Turner "frontier thesis" became dominant in popular narratives of American history.

But the most bankable Western entertainment of the late nineteenth and early twentieth century, which powerfully influenced the vision of the American frontier for a generation of Americans and Europeans, was "Buffalo Bill" Cody's *Wild West Show*. The hero of more than 1,500 dime novels, William Cody

(1846–1917) was a tireless self-promoter and gifted showman who successfully capitalized on his personal biography: this included a childhood in a homesteading pioneer family, and work as prospector, a trapper, a professional buffalo hunter, Indian fighter, and cavalry scout on the Great Plains after the Civil War, where he fought alongside (or against) men from a variety of Indigenous cultures. Cody played himself on stage and reenacted historical events and key elements of the frontier myth in an enormous, technically cutting-edge show that toured the world between 1887 and 1906.[23]

The diverse troupe of the *Wild West Show* included Annie Oakley, Buck Taylor ("King of the Cowboys"), buffalo and other exotic animals, and of course a contingent of Indigenous performers (often Lakota), including Sitting Bull himself during one season. The show emphasized the authenticity of its performances to its audiences. It featured actual artifacts such as scalps, weapons, and uniforms, from historical events and allegedly accurate historical reenactments that included the same men, like Buffalo Bill and Sitting Bull, who had fought for dominance of the West. Set pieces of the *Wild West Show* included scenes of Indigenous attacks on settlers' cabins (in which settlers were always innocent parties); a reenactment of the Pony Express mail delivery service; buffalo hunts; a train robbery; demonstrations of sharp shooting, lasso tricks, lantern shows, rodeo events, and square dances; Indigenous dances and demonstrations of their lifestyles on the Plains; and where the venue's infrastructure permitted, a re-creation of a Plains tornado. The show usually included a re-creation of Custer's Last Stand, in which Buffalo Bill arrived just a bit too late to save George Armstrong Custer. Shows ran three to four hours, and attracted crowds of thousands each day. Louis Warren summarizes the impact of the *Wild West Show* on its audience:

> Buffalo Bill brought together the wild, primitive past of the American frontier—buffalo, elk, staged prairie fires, real Indians . . . in his show's modern gun play, its glowing electric lights, and brilliantly colored publicity. It is hard to overstate the impact he had on his audiences. . . . From California to Maine, and from Wales to Ukraine, crowds who came to see Buffalo Bill's *Wild West Show* spoke so widely and fervently about it for years afterward that it became a defining cultural memory—or dream—of America.[24]

Turner's national biography of America stressed the civilizing effects of the plow and axe, peaceful homesteading and small towns' foundation, and the growth of local democracies. By contrast, Buffalo Bill's narrative emphasized the importance of the rifle and racial conflict between Indigenous peoples and whites in the settlement of the West, and justified cross-racial violence as necessary to protect innocent white settler families.[25] But both of them promoted a nostalgic, backward-looking view of the frontier, and their visions complemented each other well.

The crosshatching portrayals of American frontier life offered by Turner and Bill Cody, supplemented by the West presented in literature and art, created an attractive and compelling vision of American national identity and history that centered on white settlers' point of view and experiences. This national biography laid the foundation for the success of twentieth century Western genre fiction, films, and other entertainments. Western entertainments thus presented two interrelated frontier narratives: the Wild West of lawless violence and individual justice seen in *The Virginian, Gunsmoke,* and still later in *Deadwood*; and the frontier where, as in Turner's thesis, civilization was spread via the plow by white homesteaders, reflected in the novels of Willa Cather and Laura Ingalls Wilder and in stories of the Overland Trail.

Even Europeans who, like Karl May, were more critical of this vision were still persuaded that life in the West was truly a life of personal liberty, a region of wide-open spaces where people could control their own destinies. For many Europeans and Americans who lived in the eastern half of the United States, after the late nineteenth century the American West became a place known and understood almost entirely through fiction and other entertainments, more of a mythic space than a real geographic location.[26]

Stories of the West provided some of the most enduringly popular and marketable entertainments for white American and European audiences for almost a century. This marketability meant that the Western was re-imagined and retold on every new media platform—film, radio, television, video games, and other media—that emerged during the twentieth century. As Bill Cody's life—depicted on stage, in novels, and in films—demonstrated, the American West was among the earliest transmedial story worlds.[27] When silent films proliferated during the 1920s, at least one third of those made in the US were Westerns.[28]

Mid-nineteenth-century frontier dime novels gave way to the "pulps," stories told in serial form in magazines. The most successful pulp western writer, Zane Grey, became a bestselling novelist with his breakout *Riders of the Purple Sage* (1913). Grey published fifty-six Western novels during the interwar period. After 1945, Western genre fiction was dominated by Louis L'Amour, who published more than a hundred novels. Many of Grey's and L'Amour's novels were later adapted for film or television shows.[29]

The West that was the setting for the stories of Zane Grey, the *Wild West Show*, and later cowboy films was thus the dominant vision of the frontier in American popular culture for most of the twentieth century. But alternative interpretations of the history of white settlement of the West had always been possible. German writers had seen those possibilities from the genre's beginnings. While white American audiences generally identified with the pioneers in Western stories, Germans were reading the American West through a different lens: their pronounced affinity for Indigenous North Americans.

## The American West Abroad

The American West and fictionalized Indians were popular draws for global audiences, as reflected in the success of the *Wild West Show*'s tours across Europe, each of which lasted for years (1887–92 and 1902–06). But while Europeans from London to Romania flocked to Buffalo Bill's shows, Germans had a particularly strong and long-standing interest in Indigenous peoples. William Cody's recreations of Great Plains battles were therefore evaluated against the backdrop of German audiences' shared understanding of nineteenth-century travelers' accounts, artistic images, and fiction about American Indigenous cultures. These narratives had already suggested to some Germans certain parallels between their own national character and history, and those of North American tribes, leading to an emotional investment in Indigenous cultures that twentieth-century Germans would later call "*Indianthusiasm.*"[30]

James Fenimore Cooper's *Leatherstocking Tales* sold well outside of America, but his influence was particularly strong in Germany. During the nineteenth century, he was the most-translated American author, and easily one of the ten most popular foreign authors in Germany. His "good" Indian characters were presented as brave and noble members of cultures that were well attuned to their natural habitats but doomed in their struggle against white colonists; Cooper's stories established early and influential images of "Indians" in Germans' imagination.[31]

German writers who traveled to North America published bestselling travelers' accounts and novels during the nineteenth century that continued these tropes for German readers back home.[32] Balduin Möllhausen traveled with military expeditions during the 1850s as far west as the Grand Canyon and produced some of the earliest accounts and images of the Indigenous cultures of the Southwest. Möllhausen's observations confirmed ideas that he brought with him from Germany, derived from his reading of Cooper's stories. He made a successful career publishing a traveler's account and hundreds of Western short stories, novellas, and novels, which became familiar to many German readers.[33] His equally successful contemporary, Friedrich Gerstäcker, traveled in the American West between 1837 and 1843 and published the first German-language Western novel, *The Regulators of Arkansas*, in 1846.[34] Gerstäcker authored a series of influential and beloved Western stories aimed largely at adolescents over the course of his career. Germany's first literary prize for authors of children's literature bears his name today; the analogous American Library Association medal for children's literature in the United States would be named for another writer of the American frontier, Laura Ingalls Wilder.

In addition to fiction and travel accounts, many Germans also received information about frontier life more informally, through letters and exchanges with the flood of their relatives and neighbors who migrated to the United States, especially to the upper midwest. Roughly one-sixth of the immigrants to America between 1830 and 1930 were German-speaking. German-American communities in Wisconsin, Minnesota, and the Plains territories were often featured in German newspaper accounts, which also made Germans more aware of conflicts between Indigenous cultures and white settlers.[35]

Möllhausen, Gerstäcker, and other popular nineteenth-century German novelists reinforced German travelers' accounts in their categorization of Indigenous North American cultures as being either "uncorrupted" or "corrupted" by contact with white Americans and their government. Many Germans writers were critical of the US federal government's policies and white settlers' actions, which they saw as having an unnecessarily destructive impact on Indigenous cultures, the landscape, and wild animals. White Americans had confiscated Indigenous lands with inadequate compensation, Germans authors argued, and frequently used alcohol or legal tricks to rob unsophisticated tribal cultures. German accounts highlighted the remaining "uncorrupted" and admirable Indigenous leaders but concluded that these were doomed in their struggles against white American encroachment, which Germans did not see simply—as white Americans generally did—as progress. Rather, German authors saw the transformation of the West and the loss of territory by Indigenous peoples "as a predictable form of change driven by impersonal material forces and debased human motivations that could, with better leadership and higher ideals, be managed [more] humanely" by white Americans.[36]

Travelers and writers who had visited the United States sometimes drew sympathetic conclusions about perceived parallels between German and Indigenous cultures, none of which would be immediately apparent to most white Americans. Germany was a late-comer in the ranks of European powers and only unified as a single nation in 1871; divided into a plethora of small and medium-sized German-speaking states for centuries, German-speaking Europe had been conquered by Napoleon's armies during the early nineteenth century, and German nationalism had been spurred but also shaped by this period of military defeat and occupation. By the second half of the nineteenth century, many German speakers felt surrounded by more powerful nations and in competition with rapidly industrializing and growing European imperial powers, particularly Britain.

Some German writers felt an affinity for Indigenous peoples, whom they saw as fellow "tribal" peoples, as the Germans had been before their occupation by the Romans centuries earlier. German national origin myths were strongly influenced by the writings of the Roman author Tacitus, who provided some of the earliest written descriptions of tribes encountered by Roman armies, when they ventured into northern Europe. Tacitus admired the Germanic tribes that the Romans encountered, describing them as simple, virile cultures of the European woodlands, producing fierce warriors who resisted Roman incursions. For German readers, therefore, the trope of the "noble savage" of the North American woodlands resonated differently than it did for Anglophones, since it was read as showing similarities to their own nations' forbearers, and those ancestors' resistance against Roman invasion.[37]

In German eyes, Indigenous tribes in the United States seemed to be warrior peoples, like the ancient Germanic tribes, struggling against a foe ("Yankee" Anglophone Americans) who were even more militarily and industrially advanced than the Roman armies faced by Germanic tribes. Like the Germans who had resisted French occupation and confiscation of territory, Indigenous cultures were colonized and surrounded. As a result, some Germans began to argue that Germans were the "Indians of Europe," and emphasized what they saw as parallels between their own history and that of Indigenous American cultures.[38]

These parallels were fleshed out in the work of Rudolf Cronau, a German artist and writer who traveled across the United States in 1881–82. Relying on introductions facilitated by a network of German-American journalists in Minnesota and the Dakotas, Cronau met with many Indigenous leaders, particularly those from Lakota cultures. He repeatedly interviewed and sketched Sitting Bull and other Lakota leaders, and produced portraits of them; his painting and photograph of Sitting Bull made that leader particularly well known in Germany. Cronau was impressed with what he saw as the strength, bravery, dignity, wisdom, and pure, essential masculinity of these men, whom he perceived as uncorrupted by civilization. In lecture tours across Germany between 1884 and 1886, Cronau described the horrifying treatment of some Indigenous cultures by the federal government and military and bitterly condemned US Indian policies. Crowds filled auditoriums in cities across Germany to see Cronau's portraits and Indigenous artifacts, and to hear his thoughts on the Lakota and on the US government's dishonest dealings with American Indigenous cultures. In his lectures, Cronau argued that "American Indian tribes, much like German tribes more than a millennium earlier, suffered a devastating invasion from a better-organized and more technically advanced civilization."[39]

But Cronau noted that Indigenous peoples faced much longer odds than the Teutonic tribes had, a millennium earlier. The Yankee (Anglophone) settlers were greedy and wasteful, and did not manage the land and natural resources as wisely as Germans would have, and the frontier and Indigenous peoples were vanishing rapidly. Cronau's presentations to Germans received glowing press accounts and attracted appreciative audiences; his articles circulated widely in middle-class German journals.[40] The themes that Cronau and other nineteenth-century German writers stressed in their accounts of the American West—white Americans' thoughtless and destructive treatment of both Indigenous cultures and natural resources—were carried forward in the novels of Karl May, and throughout twentieth-century German discussions of the West.

Cronau ultimately immigrated to the United States. If he had remained in Germany, he would have had the opportunity to meet many more visitors from Indigenous cultures, since the decades that followed saw a considerable upswing in the number of *Völkerschauen*, German traveling shows of "exotic peoples."[41] Popular exhibitions of "exotic" Indigenous non-European peoples dated back centuries before Buffalo Bill brought his troupe to Germany. Exhibitions of non-European peoples within Europe can be documented as far back as the sixteenth century; Indigenous performers from the New World, including Cherokee, Creek, and Mohawk people, had occasionally been exhibited in German-speaking Europe since the early eighteenth century.[42]

With the development of academic disciplines like ethnology and anthropology in nineteenth-century universities, exhibitions of "exotic" peoples in Germany and elsewhere in Europe became more frequent and more professionally organized, with a greater emphasis on pedagogical content. They began to appear during the late nineteenth century at public educational sites such as zoological and botanical gardens, and were a staple at world fairs, colonial exhibitions, and circuses. Presentations and exhibits on Indigenous cultures were also created for natural history and ethnographic museums during the same period. One scholar has estimated that while fewer than twenty-five exhibits of "wild people" took place in the first half of the nineteenth century across Europe, more than a hundred exhibits in Germany alone were organized between 1875 and 1900.[43] Many of these exhibits exploited African performers, who were badly treated and presented as barely human, like the "Black Venus" Hottentot, Saartje Baartman.[44] During their heyday, between 1873 and 1931, *Völkerschauen* provided widespread and extremely profitable entertainments for German audiences, with over four hundred touring Germany. They were cheap entertainments, offering exposure to the exotic to those who might not be able to afford to travel abroad.

The popularity of travel accounts and stories about the American West ensured that Indigenous North Americans were among the most highly coveted performers in both circuses and *Völkerschauen* during the late nineteenth and early twentieth centuries. Indigenous American performers whose appearance and skills matched European preconceptions of what authentic Indians looked like—generally, those from Plains cultures, particularly the Lakota—could take advantage of the opportunity to travel and see other cultures, with wages and working conditions that were better than most opportunities on the reservations. Compared to African performers, Indigenous performers from the US could assume a somewhat more benign set of stereotypes and generally seem to have had more contract leverage.[45] Indigenous cast members often had more freedom of movement while on tour in Europe than they had on the tightly controlled reservations, as well. Some even saw the shows as a way to teach Europeans about their cultures, and they toured Europe repeatedly. On reservations and in regions that regularly supplied Europeans with show performers, Glenn Penny has observed, Indigenous Americans "increasingly thought of Germany as a place where they could go and often liked to go."[46] One Lakota performer in German circuses, Edward Two-Two, chose to be buried in Dresden. His grave has been maintained for decades by German Indianist hobbyists from the Old Manitou Club (discussed in Chapter 2).[47]

German entertainment companies like Hagenbeck and the famous Sarrasani Circus of Dresden had standing arrangements with particular American ranches or reservations to supply their constant demand for Plains-based Indigenous performers through the 1920s.[48] After 1900, Indigenous performers had additional opportunities to represent primitivism in other forms of modern popular culture, such as Western films and advertisements. Some Indigenous performers became entrepreneurs, offering their own club shows or lessons in Indigenous dance or other art forms to enthusiastic Europeans.[49] A few other Americans (sometimes actually African American in origin) passed as Indigenous people in interwar Europe, thus accessing the higher social status accorded to Indigenous North Americans by Europeans and the professional opportunities that this entailed.[50]

When Buffalo Bill's *Wild West Show* arrived in Germany for the first time in 1890, William Cody was therefore entering a market characterized by a long-standing romantic and nostalgic fascination with the American frontier, and particularly with Indigenous cultures. Germans evaluated the *Wild West Show* against their own prior exposure to information about Indigenous peoples, and in the context of a sometimes critical distance from US policies toward Indigenous cultures.

Scripted by Cody and his associates, many of the *Wild West Show*'s scenes assumed that white settlement and expansion was inevitable, and they staged racial conflict in terms that assumed that white Americans were the heroes of the story, as in the Indian characters' attack on the settlers' cabin scene, or in re-creations of Custer's Last Stand. German audiences and journalists reviewing the *Wild West Show* proved less interested in the struggle for white supremacy on the frontier, however, than they were in the ethnographic and romantic aspects of the show. The troupe's living quarters were set up as open villages that members of the public could wander through and interact with show performers, and German journalists and visitors to the show were interested in meeting with Indigenous performers offstage, where they were seen as behaving more "authentically" (that is, matching German preconceptions) than in the staged scenes of the show. Germans were also intrigued by Annie Oakley, who received visitors in a tastefully furnished tent, impressing journalists with her grace and ladylike deportment, combined with formidable sharpshooting.[51]

German audiences also admired other skills demonstrations in the *Wild West Show*, such as lasso demonstrations, rodeo events, and trick shooting. These performances were evaluated by German reviewers as being more "realistic"; this preference might explain why these same activities became the focus of German Western clubs a few years later. Overall, the *Wild West Show* was as successful in Germany as it had been in other European nations, but German visitors "re-appropriated the ideological messages of the *Wild West Show*, which were tailored to an American context but did not correspond with German notions of the West and especially Native Americans."[52]

Unsurprisingly, German newspaper reviews of the *Wild West Show* sometimes included critical comments on US Indian policies. As a result, William Cody apparently felt the need to justify white settlement to German audiences in some conversations with the press. In Berlin, he defended the Indigenous performers in his troupe as brave and hardworking men, but, echoing white Americans' understanding of the linkage between property rights and white approaches to land management, he added that "it is sad that this noble race had to give way to civilization. But it was inevitable. They let millions of acres of fertile land lie fallow and that had to change. Where my ranch lies today 25 years ago was wilderness."[53] In spite of Germans' reservations about the US treatment of Indigenous cultures, audiences nonetheless flocked to see the show. In Dresden, a local newspaper estimated that one hundred thousand local people saw the *Wild West Show* during its two-week stay there in June 1890, and the troupe's tour was equally successful in other German cities. Overall, Germans' exposure to Buffalo Bill's show was "massive."[54]

The dominance of the Western in popular entertainment continued on both sides of the Atlantic through the late twentieth century, although it would be modified and adapted in both Nazi and East Germany. Westerns became somewhat "grittier" during the 1920s and suffered a dip in popularity during the Great Depression, but Hollywood revisited and expanded the genre with the films that followed John Ford's landmark *Stagecoach* (1939), which made John Wayne a star. The film was an example of how Westerns would be repeatedly re-invented over the twentieth century to explore the current issues that interested Americans or Europeans (for example, *Brokeback Mountain*, 2005), an evolution that produced bleaker and quite different late twentieth-century visions of the West like Clint Eastwood's meditation, *Unforgiven* (1992).[55]

In the post-1945 period, Westerns were the most popular genre in American fiction, selling thirty-five million copies each year in the United States during the 1950s. Between 1945 and 1965, Hollywood produced an average of seventy-five

FIGURE 1. Advertisement for the German tour of a competitor to Buffalo Bill's *Wild West Show*, the Barnum and Bailey Circus, 1900. Courtesy of the US Library of Congress.

Hollywood Westerns annually, making up 25 percent of all films released in the United States and distributed globally. The postwar media form *par excellence*, television, also turned to a proven winner during its first decades: by 1958, American viewers could choose between twenty-eight television Westerns including *Gunsmoke, Wagon Train, Bonanza, Maverick,* and *The Rifleman,* providing seventeen hours of prime-time entertainment per week.[56]

*Bonanza* literally went around the world; as late as 1978, it was still showing in ninety nations with combined audiences of roughly four hundred million viewers. The show was so popular in Germany that historians of German television referred to the 1960s as their "*Bonanza* decade."[57] *Gunsmoke* and *Bonanza* were shown on Sunday afternoons in the same time slots used for American Western film broadcasts in Germany, and although it was illegal for East Germans to watch West German television, US Westerns found audiences among Germans on both sides of the Berlin Wall.[58] Ben Cartwright and his sons became part of the common cultural currency of not only Americans but also of Germans and other Europeans.

The United States was not the only source of Western genre entertainments, however. Germans avidly consumed the so-called spaghetti Westerns made in Europe during this period. In both East and West Germany, film producers created immensely successful German-language Westerns of their own, while a torrent of new German-language Western genre fiction, authored in both East and West Germany, continued to be published after 1945 and throughout the Cold War.

In both Germanies, producers of Westerns lightly reworked the genre's tropes to reflect German readings of Indian characters and the American West. Like fans of *Bonanza* around the world, Germans were getting to see the Ponderosa Ranch and the Cartwright family, along with the whole vocabulary of American Western images and tropes deployed in the other Hollywood productions of this period. But as in other cultures where American popular culture was syndicated, Germans on both sides of the Wall reinterpreted the tropes of American Westerns and used these fictional building blocks differently in varying cultural and political contexts. Ultimately, both West and East Germans got the American West that they needed from these shows, even if this often entailed a sometimes different reading of the American West than Hollywood producers had intended, that is, emphasizing the importance of Indian characters.[59]

Some of the most popular series imported to West Germany were helped in finding enthusiastic viewers because they staged frequent encounters with Indigenous cultures that were of particular interest to Germans, for example *High Chaparral*, where the white protagonists had frequent contact with Apaches, well known to German audiences from Karl May's novels. Not all episodes of even a popular series like *Bonanza* were broadcast in West Germany, but those featuring Indian characters or plot arcs were invariably dubbed and shown.

*Bonanza* episodes were often retitled to emphasize the episode's Indian content for German audiences. An episode originally shown in the US as "Far, Far, Better Thing," for example, was retitled for German distribution as "Lucinda and the Indians." Episodes with titles that might seem insulting to German admirers of Indigenous cultures were also retitled; thus the American episode titled "The Savage" became "White Buffalo's Wife" when it was broadcast in West Germany.[60]

Although global audiences tweaked the stories to get more of what they wanted, throughout the 1970s what they still wanted was a Western—on both sides of the Atlantic. Westerns were cornerstones of Americans' national biography, and their cultural calling card to the rest of the world. For much of the twentieth century, therefore, Westerns (told across a variety of media platforms) filled the same profitable niche in the marketing of American popular culture to the world that American superhero movies and video games fill in the twenty-first century.

## Who Won the West? Shifting Historiographical and Cultural Terrains

The social reform movements of the 1960s and the debacle of the Vietnam War—in which the American military regularly used tropes and images from Westerns to describe and justify their intervention—divided and polarized American culture. As a result, the national biography that had enjoyed consensus support in the United States was increasingly challenged after 1970 by those who no longer saw the Western as a narrative of optimistic progress.[61] The historiography of the American West was changing as well, as historians buried Turner's frontier thesis in a flood of new social history that reimagined the American West.

Turner's argument had been critiqued and modified by earlier generations of American historians after the 1930s, but the frontier itself remained the dominant paradigm for research on the history of the West for decades. The underlying assumptions of histories that focused on the concept of the frontier were seriously challenged after 1980, however, by a group of historians led by Patricia Nelson Limerick, Richard White, and others. These historians recast the study of the American West by emphasizing the roles played by race, class, gender, and environment in the development of the trans-Mississippi West. Rather than focusing on the progress of the frontier's imaginary line and the gradual expansion of the nation-state, the new historiography saw Western history as the story of all the peoples and cultures in the region, a complex multicultural tale of encounters between varied social and ethnic groups, and their impact on the land itself.[62]

In an early explanation of this new approach, Limerick argued that historiography should reject the frontier as the organizing principle for US master historical narratives as a white ethnocentric concept, since the frontier was "in essence, the area where white people get scarce." Instead, the New Western history would deploy approaches that focused on "invasion, colonization, exploitation, [and] development of the world market" in the West; these processes involved "women as well as men, Indians, Europeans, Latin Americans, Asians, Afro-Americans" and "their encounters with each other, and with the natural environment."[63]

The West had always been a disputed property, but the new historiographical emphasis on the West as a site of cross-racial violence, conquest, and oppression challenged and undermined the more inspiring frontier narratives (both literary and scholarly) of previous decades.

Although the New Western history rapidly became dominant in scholarly research and teaching about the history of the American West, the popular response to this revisionist historiography was sometimes resentful. Turner and his descendants had celebrated white settlement and took the supremacy of whites in frontier communities as written; the Western mythology that this supported was compelling to many white Americans, who disliked the new histories.[64] The *Arizona Republic* editorial writers reflected on the reluctance of many white Americans to embrace what they saw as a historiography of disenchantment, asking "why can't the revisionists simply leave our myths alone?"[65] As discussed in Chapter 5, by the 1990s, the reaction against the new historiography and its impact would support a polarized culture war, as conservatives vehemently rejected the New Western historians' conclusions.

Many Indigenous people had a different perspective. The New Western history developed during a period of concerted Indigenous American activism and resurgence, in which Indigenous communities mounted effective resistance against federal attempts to erase Indigenous peoples' agency and identities. The US government moved to "terminate" its remaining treaty obligations to Indigenous tribes and to eliminate tribes' last remnants of sovereignty on their lands after the mid-1950s, which inspired Indigenous organization and resistance during the 1960s and 1970s. The activism of the American Indian Movement (AIM) and other Indigenous Americans' organizations, allied with some Americans' increasingly critical and disillusioned view of the American government following the Vietnam War and Watergate, meant that the longstanding frontier tropes of the American national biography had diminishing appeal for particular segments of the American public.

For many Americans, however, the frontier myth still helped them to make sense of American history and identity. Ronald Reagan's success was rooted in his ability to insert himself into the frontier narrative and exploit its appeal to American voters. Born in the Midwest, Reagan had some success as an actor in Hollywood Westerns and was a skilled horseman, riding and chopping wood on his Southern California ranch in his free time. As a politician, he recast himself as a "cowboy president," wearing Stetson hats, Levi's, and boots when riding, and frequently drawing on the frontier myth in appeals to voters. In the first debate of the 1980 presidential election, he claimed that

> I have always believed that this land . . . was placed here [by divine plan] to be found by a special kind of people—people who had special love of freedom and who had the courage to uproot themselves and leave hearth and homeland and come to what in the beginning was the most undeveloped wilderness possible. We came from 100 different corners of the earth. We spoke a multitude of tongues—landed on this eastern shore and then went out over the mountains and prairies and the deserts and the far Western mountains of the Pacific building cities and towns and farms and schools and churches.[66]

Frederick Jackson Turner could not have put it better. Perhaps unsurprisingly, the television series *Little House on the Prairie*, broadcast between 1974 and 1982, was one of Reagan's favorite shows; he watched it regularly in the White House.[67]

For most of the twentieth century, the frontier experience had been a touchstone of white Americans' national biography: the broad consensus support that it enjoyed ensured its appeal in popular entertainments for decades. But by the later decades of the twentieth century, Reagan's understanding of American history and the political lessons he drew from it were being challenged by a variety of American groups: academics, the New Left, and activists from different ethnic minority groups. The American West itself was understood in increasingly diverse ways by conservatives and progressives. Progressives accepted the new scholarship, while conservatives often found it objectionable and uncomfortable. The older folk history was therefore increasingly associated with one political party, and no longer enjoyed automatic assent from the overwhelming majority of white Americans. The American West was still a contested property but in a different sense than it had been during the nineteenth century. In Germany, as we shall see, regime changes had already forced additional and repeated reconsideration of the West's meaning for Germans, both in Nazi Germany and in East and West Germany, after 1945.

The foundation for what had been a hegemonic national identity and folk history was now eroding, and so was the popularity of the entertainment genre rooted in that national biography, Westerns. During the last half of the twentieth century, audiences for Westerns would shrink. The historically focused Western fandoms that this book explores would ultimately be forced to grapple with the fallout. Like the story worlds they loved, the *Little House* fan community, Karl May fans, and German Indianists and other Western fans were initially well-aligned with the dominant narratives of the West in their respective nations. But over time, both scholarly and popular understandings of the West were changing. Ultimately, this would require a reconsideration of the fictional West that members of all the fandoms discussed in this book found so compelling.

# CHAPTER TWO

# Buffalo Bill and Karl May

## The Origins of German Western Fandom

The past is always with us, even when it is not our own. One example: *Brigadoon*-like pockets of a re-created American Old West can be found across Germany. Some come alive only in the summer, while others can be visited year-round. Like imagined pasts everywhere, these sites offer the lure of the exotic, a visit to a foreign land.

In Munich and Berlin, cowboy clubs maintain private grounds containing meticulously reconstructed settings worthy of any Western film, complete with Western saloons and trading posts. Members gather on the weekends to practice twirling lassoes, throwing knives, and other rodeo skills; the Munich club members tan leather using historic Indigenous methods. They re-create the lives of cowboys and sometimes Indian *personas*. The Berlin club's grounds, called "Old Texas Town," is open to the public one day each month. Like the Western settings of some other German cowboy clubs, Old Texas Town is surrounded by a stockade-like wall, which protects against both outsiders' curiosity and (for those on the inside) from reminders of the twenty-first century.[1]

The Munich Cowboy Club, founded in 1913, occasionally hosts performances of the Wild West Girls and Boys Club, whose historically costumed members perform can-cans worthy of a nineteenth-century movie saloon, country western style dancing, and a "flag parade" tribute to American history. The flag parade performance features cowgirl-cheerleaders and cowboys twirling batons as well as a variety of US flags, including the Confederate flag.[2] Other German clubs consist solely of Indianist hobbyists, who often specialize in re-creating the historical clothing, artifacts, and customs of a particular North American Indigenous culture. Many German Indianist hobbyists and cowboys meet up annually at summer camps, where Western-style tents mingle with teepees, and participants revel in private, extended gatherings of fan communities that have existed and gathered annually for generations.[3]

Open-air theatrical performances based loosely on novelist Karl May's stories run in cities and small towns across Germany each summer. The largest is in Bad Segeberg, north of Hamburg. Based on Karl May's Westerns, its performances attract hundreds of thousands of spectators each summer; over thirteen million visitors have attended since the Karl May shows began in 1952. A Western town was constructed outside of the performance amphitheater in Bad Segeberg, called Indian Village. In spite of the name, the town combines teepees with the typical buildings seen in Western films and television shows, including a sheriff's office, a general store, and of course a saloon.[4] Dozens of other Karl May performances are offered each summer in other parts of Germany, as well. Large productions with professional actors, and small local groups of volunteer amateurs, even troupes that include only children and youths, re-create stagecoach robberies, battles with Indian warriors on horseback, and other tropes of Western fiction for appreciative German audiences.[5]

East of Munich near the Austrian border, a Western theme park, Pullman City, offers visitors the chance to visit a potpourri of fictionalized sites associated with North American history: a Mexican cantina; a store named for Hudson's Bay and "Scarlett's" restaurant; a hotel with a Victorian Western theme; a show arena where performers offer rodeo demonstrations; and a reconstructed Mandan earth lodge where a "half-blood Cherokee" instructs visitors in his presentation of Indigenous lore. The highlight of each day's performances is an "American History Show," a parade with vignettes from eighteenth- and nineteenth-century American history, complete with a small group of buffalo. In the summer, visitors to Pullman City can see theatrical performances based on Karl May's Westerns—*Winnetou and the Curse of Gold* ran during the summer of 2019—and the park hosts a "Civil War Weekend" for reenactors each September. One area of the park is used by historical reenactors, who have created a variety of nineteenth-century American *personas* and dwellings for themselves.[6]

The historic heart of the German Western fandom, however, is found in Radebeul, outside of Dresden. Radebeul was where Karl May built his home, which he called the "Villa Shatterhand," named after the Western protagonist that May claimed was modeled on his own life, the hero Old Shatterhand. The villa became the Karl May Museum after his widow's death; it preserves the author's library and workspace, along with many knick-knacks and pieces of art that he collected during his life, and offers small exhibits about his life. Behind the Villa Shatterhand stands a second building, the Villa Bärenfett ("Bear Fat"), a log cabin style building housing a collection of artifacts from many Indigenous North American cultures. A few of these belonged to May, but many of the displays originally came from the personal collection of the museum's first curator, Patty Frank. The museum's archive houses not only May's papers but more than a century's worth of correspondence, press clippings, and publications from a wide variety of German Indianist hobbyist and Western-focused organizations and fan groups.

One of the museum's directors, Robin Leipold, has observed that many of the fans who visit it make a beeline for either one villa or the other. Some visitors are most interested in Karl May himself. They climb the stairs to see the desk where he created a fictional world that still engages Germans more than a century after his death, and they gaze at the reference works and maps he used to craft descriptions of a region of the world that he never visited himself, and at the ephemera of his life. Other visitors spend all or most of their time at the Villa Bärenfett. For them, May and his novels are less interesting than the historic artifacts from the Indigenous cultures that the second building displays. The Indianist hobbyists, Leipold noted, can spend considerable time looking at the diorama "Returning [Home] From Battle" in Villa Bear Fat; it shows life-sized figures depicting a Lakota household welcoming returning warriors, and displays nineteenth-century Lakota clothing and handicrafts. Some visitors spend long periods of time examining the diorama's details, along with the exhibits of other Indigenous cultural artifacts, which for some hobbyists are almost sacred in their importance and significance.[7] The different experiences sought by fans who visit the museum reflect the broad diversity in the German Western fandom: some hobbyists seek to reenact, re-create, and personally experience historic life worlds and cultures, while others are enthralled by a story world and characters that they know were always imaginary. Some fans embrace both: enjoying the story world, while still seeking historic authenticity. The Karl May Museum welcomes them all; its curators have served as a contact point for the entire spectrum of German Western fans for almost a century.

German devotees of the American frontier have created some of the earliest, most varied, complex, and extensive examples of historical reenactment, while also pursuing a broad spectrum of other fan activities. For more than a century, and in four quite different political environments, the tropes and artifacts of the American West have been repurposed and recycled by German fans and hobbyists to express a range of political positions, personal values, and formulations of race and gender. In Weimar Germany, Nazi Germany, in the divided nations of East and West Germany after World War II, and in reunified Germany after 1990, German fans of May novels and of a broader imagined American West "broke up" and reworked their favorite texts. They pulled out bits and details that they could knit together in new combinations and use as a springboard for their own interpretations and performances about what the Old West had "really" been like, or perhaps should have been like. In so doing, they made the historical American West their own, by creating their own versions of the stories, characters, and real cultures that Western novels were based on, and circulating these interpretations among other fans.[8] Under each political regime, they altered and adapted their understandings and re-creations of the West and Karl May's world to reflect the economic and political circumstances they lived in.

As discussed in Chapter 1, German readers were enthralled by the American West decades before Karl May began to publish, and some Indianist hobbyists later disdained his stories as insufficiently realistic and accurate in their depictions of Indigenous cultures. But Karl May is still central to any account of German Western fans. As one East German Indianist hobbyist observed—a woman who spent years researching and seeking strictly historical authenticity in her re-creation of Indigenous North American cultures—"Karl May was more or less the godfather [of German Indian hobbyist clubs]."[9] Another East German Indianist, who researched Indigenous musical traditions as part of his hobby and who recognized that Karl May was "clearly of no importance" to any fan seeking accurate information on Indigenous cultures, nonetheless noted that "for the German reader, Karl May's Indian novels established a deeply effective romantic-emotional tie to the American Indian . . . [ultimately inspiring them to seek] authentic material on Indians."[10]

Although his work is almost unknown in America, the enormous German fan community that took the novels of Karl May as one of its starting points dwarfed any early twentieth century contemporary fandoms of fiction series in the English-speaking world. May, who died in 1912, is generally considered the bestselling author in modern German history. Over one hundred million copies of his works have sold, even though the National Socialists suppressed publication of some of his works, and although his books were not published at all in East Germany before the 1980s.[11] His stories were popular throughout Central Europe, and his books have been translated into forty-six languages. The producers of derivative works that have sold millions of copies or tickets—comic books, songs, spin-off novels, heavily-attended open-air shows based on his books, movies, toys, etc.—have capitalized on the fact that his characters have been household names in Central Europe for more than a century. May's most popular novels are set in the American West or in an idealized Middle East. His story world is thus a literal embodiment of "orientalism," but over decades it developed into something rather different.[12] May's Western novels attracted the bulk of fans' attention and enthusiasm, and the heroes of his Westerns, such as Old Shatterhand and Winnetou (the son of an Apache chief), became particularly beloved and mythologized. They were the heroes of a series of blockbuster films made in West Germany in the 1960s and 1970s, provoking the East German government to authorize the production of a second, competing set of popular Western films. A parody of the May films, *Shoe of the Manitou*, is said to be the single most popular German language film of all time.[13]

May published more than a dozen Western novels and many short stories, most of which featured his two most important characters, Old Shatterhand and Winnetou, and the core of his story world is depicted in a series of novels named for Winnetou (*Winnetou, the Red Gentleman*, published in 1893, and its sequels). The series is told from the point of view of Old Shatterhand, a German immigrant to the United States, who is given his new name in America after he demonstrates the ability to knock out an opponent with a single blow. Old Shatterhand is originally hired to do a land survey through Apache territory, as a preparation for laying a railroad line, but he soon realizes that most of the white Americans he is working with are corrupt, lazy, and greedy. He quickly learns the skills of the "Western man" from an old scout, Sam Hawkens, who teaches him to catch wild horses, track buffalo, etc. Old Shatterhand shows an amazing aptitude for acquiring these skills, and is also a crack shot and expert knife-thrower. In modern fandom terms, the character is what is known as a "Mary Sue," but one with whom the German reader is invited to identify strongly.[14]

Old Shatterhand meets Winnetou and Winnetou's father, the chief of the Mescalero Apaches, when they come to protest against the railroad's land grab.

After a series of trials and adventures, Old Shatterhand becomes the "blood brother" of Winnetou in a bonding ritual, and attracts the attentions of Winnetou's sister, Nscho-tschi. Both Winnetou and Nscho-tschi seem to be impressed by European culture, and Nscho-tschi professes a desire to be trained in house-keeping in a white household, so that she might thus become a suitable bride for Old Shatterhand. But during their journey to take Nscho-tschi to St. Louis for her re-socialization, both Nscho-tschi and her father are murdered by greedy whites who are seeking gold.

Winnetou then succeeds his father as chief of the Mescalero Apaches. Win-netou and Old Shatterhand have numerous adventures separately and together —although not all of May's Westerns feature these two characters—in May's many other novels, which include the *Old Surehand* trilogy, *Old Firehand, The Treasure of Silver Lake, The Son of the Bear Hunter,* and *The Black Mustang.* In these novels, both Winnetou and Old Shatterhand, and another German-Amer-ican "Western man," Old Surehand, are usually portrayed as heroic fighters for justice, often against venal white (Anglo) Americans. Before the end of the series, Winnetou professes his conversion to Christianity and ultimately dies heroically.

Literary critics have speculated that May's stories became so popular because they were built upon and reproduced the tropes and historical backdrops of earlier popular Western authors' works, with which Germans were already fa-miliar. His novels create a fictional world in which the stories all follow similar but familiar plots, recycling earlier tropes. As Karl Markus Kreis observed, it is a "dream world" with an American backdrop but in which the heroes are often German immigrants, who sing German folk songs and express German values: they "embody familiar traits in their origin and behavior: the stories are permeated with German figures, German associations of ideological or social nature—in short, the hero is always a conventional German in a conventional environment."[15] But it is also a story world in which the "good" Indian charac-ters and the white (often German American) "Westernmen" are presented as deeply authentic: they are connected to nature, able to determine the course of their own lives, adhering to a clear moral code. This formed a sharp con-trast to the lives of many German readers, who lived in a rapidly modernizing and industrializing society that imposed an increasing number of formal and bureaucratic demands on everyday life, which made the American West so appealing to German readers.[16]

Perhaps May's heroes were too German to become popular with American readers. Although his stories are known to many Indigenous North Americans (since they have encouraged generations of German tourists to visit Indigenous communities), May's books have never sold well in the United States. Characters who have been household names for more than a century across Central Europe are almost unknown in the United States, outside of US reservations. May shared his German predecessors' sympathy for Indigenous cultures and condemnation of rapacious Anglo-American whites and their government. The fact that Old Shatterhand was a "blood brother" of an Indian character and had hoped to marry Winnetou's sister would also have made it harder to sell his stories during the late nineteenth and early twentieth centuries in the United States, since white men who married Indigenous women were socially marginalized and distrusted by other white Americans as "squaw men."[17] Combined with the imaginary descriptions of May's American West, his inversion of the American Westerns' view of heroes and villains might have dampened sales in the United States: the gift "to see ourselves as other see us" is not always a welcome one.

The dearth of sales in the United States hardly hampered May's career, however. His stories were at the very heart of German popular culture for most of the twentieth century, even though May's life and work were profoundly problematic from a variety of standpoints, particularly for those who wanted to see him as an authentic witness to the history of the American West. May's public *persona* invited controversy and for later fans, discussion and analysis, since he had served jail terms after being accused of small thefts and impersonating an official. He concealed this history, and instead claimed to have spent those years traveling abroad, living through the Western and Middle Eastern adventures that allegedly formed the basis for his stories. He promoted himself and his works with a series of famous photos taken of himself in both Arab dress (as his Oriental character Kara Ben Nemsi) and as Old Shatterhand, in a buckskin shirt, with a lasso, hunting knife, and rifles, claiming that all his stories were autobiographical and that Winnetou had been a real person. His calling cards introduced him as "Dr. Karl Friedrich May, known as Old Shatterhand"; the doctoral title was also an invention. In fact, May only visited the United States once, late in life, and never traveled farther west than Buffalo, New York. In order to make his stories persuasive as autobiography, May relied on maps, travelers' accounts, anthropological studies, and guidebooks for the information given on Middle Eastern and Indigenous cultures in his stories.[18]

In short, May was a fabulist. His assertions about his personal history were investigated by critics after 1900, as May became the target of repeated German newspaper exposes and attacks. This led May (by this point, a celebrity author) to file a series of widely-publicized lawsuits and countersuits, in which his past and his lies were exposed. Another "problem" with May's stories during the Nazi period was that he had expressed pronounced mystical and antimilitarist sympathies in his later novels, which were distinctly pacifist. He was also a friend of Bertha von Suttner, a well-known early twentieth-century pacifist who was the first woman to win the Nobel Peace Prize.

During the first half of the twentieth century, there was something in this biography to offend almost everyone. May's lies, and his denials once these were exposed, entangled his early fans and supporters in a web of charges and counter-charges, since to celebrate May's work was tantamount to supporting someone who was correctly suspected of perpetrating a swindle on the German public. For his early readers, the appeal of May's stories was inextricably interwoven with the fact that they truly *were* "authentic" and portrayals of "the real thing," just like Buffalo Bill. The powerful nostalgic appeal of Winnetou and his world—a world into which fans could escape, if only in their imaginations—was rooted in the fact that it had all indeed been "real" at some point in the past, as well as in Germans' long-standing affinity for Indigenous cultures. If a fan was deeply invested in Winnetou and Old Shatterhand (and this is a given, for almost all May fans), then the thought that May had simply made it all up, and that Winnetou had not lived, must have been quite painful for the first generation of his fans.

By the late twentieth century, May fans had come to terms with this self-invention and were no longer troubled by it; as one noted, the "the fact that he lied was among the best things about him."[19] But the first generation of fans had accepted his self-representations at face value, and tended to deny any evidence to the contrary. The scandal among readers and the public, when the "truth" about May first came out, was therefore substantial. His most devoted readers sometimes struggled to come to terms with the facts.[20]

Authentic or not, after 1933 the fact that May had idealized nonwhite cultures and later became interested in pacifism made him unacceptable to some National Socialists. National Socialists vehemently opposed any "racial mixing," and in one of the *Winnetou* novels, Old Shatterhand became engaged to Winnetou's sister. By rights, and taken strictly on their merits and ideology, May's books should probably have been censored during the Nazi period. One Nazi social critic proposed banning May's works, asking "how can we raise our youths to support colonialism, when they read such books, which attack imperialism, a powerful state, and colonialism in the ugliest fashion?"[21]

As if these were not obstacles enough to the development of an organized fan community, his publisher and copyright holder, the Karl May Press, sought to control what was published about his work. Through the Weimar period, at least, the Press tolerated only a hagiographic depiction of him in the "official" yearbook for Karl May fans.[22] Given the often-hostile attitudes of both political authorities and the copyright holder, it was a testimony to his fans' engagement with the stories that any fan groups emerged at all in the time before the works entered the public domain in West Germany during the 1960s, a time and place where they were, at long last, seen as unproblematic by most Germans.

And yet, May had powerful admirers as well. He was popularly thought to be Hitler's favorite author, and Hitler was said to have attended May's last public lecture in Vienna in 1912. But his enthusiasts also included some of the best-known leaders of the Left and social reform movements: Marxist philosopher Ernst Bloch; Nobel Prize–winning poet and author Hermann Hesse; Albert Einstein; humanitarian physician (and Nobel Peace Prize winner) Albert Schweitzer; and the German socialist leader Karl Liebknecht, a founder and martyr of the German Communist Party. May's stories were simply universally popular and seen by most readers as apolitical; they appealed across the Central European political spectrum.

Most Germans came across May's stories as schoolchildren or teenagers, since they became part of the standard repertoire of youth literature before World War I and remained so for more than fifty years. True fans continued to cherish May's characters and world into adulthood. Many looked back to later recall their own first encounters with May's books, which often echoed the "falling in love" accounts offered by Sherlockians and other fans about their first reading of their canon stories. In "first time" or "falling in love" stories in many fandoms, fans relate how they were immediately taken by the first story they encountered and pulled into a deep engagement with the story world.[23]

Lisbeth Barchewitz, a schoolteacher in Weimar Germany and lifelong May devotee, looked back fondly at her first reaction to May's stories, which she discovered at the age of sixteen:

I was staying with my uncle and aunt, who took me to visit some friends of theirs [and the hostess lent her a book to read] ... The book was *Winnetou,* by Karl May. An Indian story, I thought, leafing through it. Then I began to read it from the start and was so enraptured and enchanted by it that I couldn't bear to put it down. When we left [the house] I begged to borrow it, which the lady gladly allowed. She was so kind as to offer me access to her entire May library. On this day I thus made the acquaintance of what became my favorite author.

[Other stories] lost all charm after I read *Winnetou.* The May books were what now excited me. Karl May understood not only how to entertain, but indeed he found the way to my soul. There was so much that was good and noble in his exciting tales that my heart was on fire for them. I read all thirty volumes; I read them again and again ... it became the greatest wish of my life to meet the writer of these wonderful books.[24]

Some May fans became readers as a sort of "follow-on" to their experience of Buffalo Bill's *Wild West Show* or after seeing Indigenous performers at a circus or other traveling "exotic people's show." For May readers and all German Western fans, Indian characters and the American West evoked adventure, freedom, and unrestricted spaces: above all, and throughout the twentieth century, they were thus associated with an escape from the strictures and constraints of "civilized" daily life in urban Germany. May's novels also capitalized heavily on the trope of the "lost world" of American Indian characters and cultures, always a source of nostalgia for German readers.[25] His hero Winnetou believed that the whites would soon triumph and displace his people, and Winnetou himself was an impossibly noble "last Indian" who died in a heart-breaking fashion.

May thus offered readers a now-vanished world in which a German, Old Shatterhand, was endowed by his creator with what were commonly seen—by Germans—as stereotypically German virtues, and who had been accepted as the "blood brother" (as Winnetou put it) of one of the last and most noble of Indians. The profound bond of loyalty and affection between Old Shatterhand and Winnetou became one of the most attractive aspects of the story world for many readers.[26] The *Winnetou* novels were indeed a compelling early example of a dynamic that often inspired the formation of later fan communities: a genre of fictional "buddy" or best friend stories, where the adventure revolves around two male leads united in close friendship. As one leading member of the Karl

May fan community noted in conversation with me, for him the central core of the stories was that they revolved around the hero having a real friend, a true friend, a lifelong friend. Other fans took the bond between Old Shatterhand and Winnetou as the model for their own friendships. One founding member of the Karl May Society, Erich Heinemann, recalled the origins of his friendship with another Karl May enthusiast, Kurt Morawietz: "Do you remember back then, in 1948? We became friends, because Karl May was our friend, and we both wanted to do something for him. . . . We pledged lasting friendship to each other in the spirit of Old Shatterhand and Winnetou, friendship unto death."[27] The historical nostalgia, idealized national character, exotic setting, and the true bonds of friendship proved a heady combination. These attractions continued to underwrite the appeal of Karl May's story world throughout the twentieth century, although later generations would also contribute their own readings of the characters and cultures on top of this base.

Although some fans eventually drifted away from a focus on May's works to focus on the historic American West, German Western fandom owed much of its inspiration to Winnetou's world. Cowboy and Indian clubs formed only one segment of a broader spectrum of German hobbyist organizations and activities which were sometimes focused broadly around painstakingly "authentic" Indianist and Western activities, while others were organized to celebrate May's stories. By the late twentieth century the "Karl May scene" (as it came to be called) grew to include: fan tourism to the Karl May Museum in the author's former home in Radebeul and to May's birth home in Hohenstein-Ernstthal; fans of the 1960s Karl May films and of the films' stars, who organized their own tours to view the filming location sites in Croatia; the often scholarly discussions and exchanges of the Karl May Society, which published voluminous commentaries on the author after the works entered the public domain; performances of May's stories in open-air festivals staged on large outdoor stages that drew hundreds of thousands of spectators each summer, along with small local amateur theatrical performances; and the "Karl May Days," an annual American Western folk festival held near Dresden.[28] Collectively, these groups grew to form substantial and variegated fan communities, sometimes rooted in both the appeal of May's dream world, and more broadly in Germans' long-standing engagement with and affinity for Indigenous cultures.

Fandoms that developed during the 1930s around the stories about Sherlock Holmes or early science fiction often began as literary groups, focusing on discussions of the author and the stories. But a Karl May literary society analogous to the Sherlockian Baker Street Irregulars only came into being in the 1960s, in West Germany. For the first half of the twentieth century, several factors tended to delay the formation of the type of book discussion groups and published fan commentary which predominated in other literary fandoms, and which could produce transformative fan works. Instead, these factors pushed May fans toward cowboy and Indianist re-creation, and varied forms of experiential and participatory fan communities. Before World War II, both the problematic biography of the author and the attitude of his publisher (who held the copyright on the stories) tended to undermine literary organizations devoted to May, which all proved short-lived.[29]

None of these early fan societies produced lasting infrastructure or organizations; internal disputes over the scandals then surrounding May's biography were certainly one reason for this. The problematic legacy of May's lies about himself, and the scandals and disputes surrounding his lawsuits entangled his fans and inevitably became the source of divisions among them, since most had not yet come to terms with the "truths" of May's biography and assertions about himself. May's estate and publisher also guarded his reputation (and copyrights) jealously, which handicapped any serious examination of the writer or his works by fan publications.

The sort of extensive, elaborate parsing of the author's life and story world and the production of fan fiction, or the torrent of nonfiction publications produced by Sherlockians starting in the 1930s, would have been a difficult minefield for May devotees to negotiate during this period, given that so much of what May had said about himself and his characters was simply untrue. Nor would the publisher have been willing to tolerate further exposure and criticism, or the sort of derivative fan fiction that came naturally to fans in other fandoms. Arthur Conan Doyle had a general *laissez faire* attitude toward Sherlockian derivative or fan publications, but most May enthusiasts remained wary of antagonizing his publisher.[30] During the Weimar period, when fan publications faced no state suppression, fans were still constrained by these challenges. After the Nazis came to power in 1933, and in East Germany after 1948, May literary groups and fan publications were banned outright by the state.

Other types of engagement with the American West were easier to pursue in Germany before World War I and during the Weimar period, including cowboy and Indianist clubs. Hobbyist Western clubs that pursued historical crafts and skills were also generally immune to the political and legal pressures that could undermine May literary groups before the 1960s: no one could claim copyright over the concept of an American Indian or cowboy, after all. Such clubs also reflected the other crucial inspiration of early German Western fandom—fans' exposure to cowboys and Indigenous performers in Buffalo Bill's *Wild West Show* and in circuses—and could explore the entire historical world of the American West.

Hobbyist clubs were also part of a larger interest in cultural primitivism across the Western world during the early twentieth century, as Philip Deloria reminds us. During a period of widespread interest in "primitive" (non-Western) cultures, North American Indigenous cultures attracted particular interest among white Americans and Europeans because "they reflected nostalgia for community, spirituality, and nature."[31] This was also the heyday for traveling circuses and exotic "people's shows," which featured Indigenous and other nonwhite performers.

When seen against this set of well-established turn-of-the-century cultural trends and enthusiasms, cross-racial identification with Indigenous North Americans, even to the point of role-play, is less surprising than it would appear to us today. Participation in cowboy and Indianist clubs also did not require the level of formal education typical of enthusiasts who published in literary societies, which made these clubs more accessible to a broader audience of Western fans. German clubs, with their focus on participatory, experiential fan activities that did not require much education or cultural capital compared to literary fan groups, attracted members from working-class and lower middle-class backgrounds as well as university-educated fans.

The career of Patty Frank (1876–1959), who became a key figure in the world of German cowboy and Indianist clubs and among Karl May fans, reflected all of these influences. Frank's name was an adopted American-style cowboy name (at least, to German ears) and he usually dressed the part of a cowboy; his legal name was Ernst Tobis. Like May, Patty Frank was a fabulist and raconteur, with a gift for promoting both himself and his cause, which was the German Western fandom. For him, as for enthusiasts in other fandoms, engagement with a fan community became a way to fashion a new and different identity, one which ultimately helped him to establish a successful career.[32]

Enthusiastic about May's novels and also enchanted by Buffalo Bill's *Wild West Show* as a teenager, Frank ran away from home to follow the show and later trained as a gymnast so that he could tour with circuses. During his travels, he assembled a collection of artifacts from many Indigenous cultures of the New World; his collection became a springboard for his career as the Karl May Museum's first curator. Later, in the politically repressive regimes of both Nazi Germany and East Germany, Frank's political flexibility and the fandom's emphasis on role-play and reenactment helped ensure the fan community's survival, since cowboy and Indianist clubs could more easily distance themselves from the quite different political problems that the novels would pose under the later two regimes.

The Munich Cowboy Club 1913 was among the first Western hobbyist groups founded in Germany, and Frank maintained close contact with the group. Other clubs were founded in Weimar Germany, including the "First Dresden Indian and Cowboy Club 'Manitou,'" the Cowboy Club Buffalo and a Wild-West Association (both in Freiburg), and a Karlsruhe group devoted to studying and reenacting the customs and lifestyles of the Dakota Indian cultures exclusively. Some German clubs chose one Indigenous culture to specialize in, while others did role-play as both cowboys and Indians. Both the Munich and the Dresden clubs had connections to local circuses, where they could purchase Indigenous North American artifacts and learn from Indigenous show performers. Both clubs also had close relationships with Patty Frank and the Karl May Museum, and members of the Dresden club visited Frank there regularly.[33]

By 1933, the Munich Cowboy Club had about sixty members; its leader, "Fremont Fred" Sommer, estimated in 1933 that forty of these were primarily Indianist hobbyists (including ten "squaws"), while twenty preferred to re-create roles as cowboys or cowgirls. The club collected Indigenous artifacts; by the 1930s, its collection was fairly extensive, and members met in local parks to offer demonstrations of skill with lassoes and knife-throwing. The Dresden club began to meet during the late 1920s but boasted only seven members in 1934, along with three "squaws," who were seen as auxiliary members; members' preferred club names were equally divided between cowboy and Indian roles. All of the Dresden club's members were from working-class or lower middle-class backgrounds. As seen in photos of other interwar cowboy and Indianist clubs, the overwhelming majority of the Dresden club, like its Munich counterpart, were men.[34]

Women might have been less likely to have the resources needed to participate in hobbyist groups during the interwar period: money for costumes, publications, or artifacts; resources for occasional travel; and especially time free from household obligations. While many of May's readers were women, audience surveys showed that his readership consisted disproportionately of young men, and thus the clubs' memberships might have reflected the social composition of Western fans as a whole. And finally, many women might have simply preferred to join hobbyist groups that included more women; sociologists of play and leisure time organizations have found that such "leisure subcultures" tend to be homosocial. One scholar who studied other postwar role-playing societies in the United States noted that they, too, were overwhelmingly masculine partly due to "the different interests of men and women, but ...[also because] of patterns of recruitment and acceptance."[35]

Although May's stories (and all Western entertainments) delivered many more role models for men than for women, it still would have been difficult to reenact American Western cultures without them. As in club members' daily lives, women were sometimes responsible for creating clothing for group members, although many men did make their own costumes, or traded for them. The cowboy and Indianist clubs encompassed a significant amount of "arts and crafts" work that easily included women, and the costumes they crafted were crucial both to maintaining club members' *personas* and also to establishing the visual boundary between club members and spectators from the outside, mundane world.

The Manitou Club built a club house in the mountains near Dresden, furnished with a buffalo skin, teepee, and Western saddle. In 1934 the club chief wrote that each weekend "we lead the lives of real Indians and cowboys," practicing with lassoes, bows and arrows, and knife-throwing. They also spent one evening each week reading aloud and studying ethnological materials about Indigenous cultures lent to them by Patty Frank.[36]

Members of German cowboy and Indian clubs typically began by adopting a "Western" name (occasionally taken from a Karl May novel), creating a costume to match the *persona*, and setting about to learn the skills and crafts that their adopted role(s) required. The correspondence between the Munich and Dresden clubs indicates that most members had preferences in terms of a cowboy vs. Indian role, but that hobbyists in this generation were also fluid, crossing back and forth between cowboy and Indian clothing and names, depending on the skills they were practicing. One Old Manitou member, Harry Morche, whose Indian name was Lone Bear but whose cowboy name was Tom Mix (named after the American Western movie star), managed the training of his "tribal brothers." Morche reminded them to attend lasso practice in their cowboy costumes, since

FIGURE 2. Members of the Old Manitou Club in 1939, with Patty Frank (*seated, on the left side of the table*), inside the Karl May Museum in Radebeul. The members are about equally divided between cowboy and Indian *personas*, and their club president (*back row, center*) is dressed as an Indigenous chief complete with a floor-length feather headdress, holding what appears to be a peace pipe, an important object in Karl May's stories. Courtesy of Karl May Museum Archive.

"a rope-twirling cowboy looks better than an Indian [doing the same]," but noted that they should come to "Indian celebrations" dressed as Indian *personas*. The Munich club members did the same, he added.[37] Photos taken of Munich and Dresden club members during the 1930s show them dressed in a mixture of Indian and cowboy/cowgirl costumes.

Real, imported Stetson hats and Colt revolvers for cowboy costumes were expensive for club members to acquire, but creating convincing Indianist outfits was an even greater challenge. Club members immersed themselves in Indigenous arts and crafts as far as they could obtain information about these. They sought contacts with American sources for moccasins and beads to use for decorating clothing, sometimes trading with Indigenous people who were interested in obtaining eagle feathers from Central European birds, or club members purchased materials for clothing from Indigenous show performers.[38] Costumes that were as authentic as possible helped them to re-create and interpret how members of particular tribes and characters mentioned in the novels had looked. They practiced using throwing knives, whips, and lassoes, all skills featured in Karl May novels and in the *Wild West Show* performances that many had seen, and taught themselves how to create teepees. They educated themselves about Indigenous songs and dances.

Hobbyists tried to learn Indigenous languages, but were often stymied in these efforts before World War II. As the leader of the Munich club acknowledged, even when they met Indigenous North Americans, show performers often spoke only in English to each other, and to German hobbyists. He noted that while one member of the Munich club was a Lakota from the Dakotas, George White Eagle, that even this member could not help them to learn Indigenous American tongues, since he had left his tribe at a young age.[39]

Interestingly, club members did not role-play cowboys *versus* Indians, as was common in children's play both in Germany and the United States. Instead, like Old Shatterhand and Winnetou, both sorts of roles coexisted in the same group and members might play both roles in turn. Because they strove for authenticity no matter what their *persona*, many hobbyists ultimately came to distance themselves from Karl May's stories after 1945, particularly in East Germany, where he fell out of favor with authorities. But before World War II, early club members acknowledged that May was a major source of inspiration.[40]

Since they strove for authenticity in order to increase the attractions of their performances, Germans tended to role-play cowboys and Indians quite seriously. Indeed, German fans were noticeably less ironic about their activities than Sherlockians were from the start: certainly, they did not envision what they did as a droll Great Game, as Sherlockians did.[41] Instead, until the late twentieth century, this fandom generally tried to recapture, in minute detail, a "lost" world that they saw as having existed in the past, even if it was now gone.

All of these influences, aspirations, and activities were on display at a 1938 celebration of the Munich Cowboy Club, described by a sympathetic local reporter:

> The club might strike some as a costumed masquerade and games, and others as an expression of a passion for ethnology and deep compassion for a people who are rapidly dying out. One thing is sure: all of us who read Cooper and Karl May as children still feel the pull of the romance of a

Wild West that is probably now vanished forever. Everything that they [the club members] do is authentic: the gestures and expressions, the clothing (some costumes were those worn by famous redskins), the war paint, and even how they smoke the peace pipe. And they can do everything that real cowboys and Indians can do . . . for the celebration, Karl May Museum Director Patty Frank was invited . . . [a film of a Karl May story was shown, probably made by the club members] and we saw Old Shatterhand and Winnetou greet each other in a primordial forest. That was Karl May's magical world . . . [followed by club members'] demonstrations of lasso throwing, knife throwing, archery, displays of whips and Winchester rifles. The celebration closed with an Indian war dance; participants and demonstrators included Bob Cloud, Sitting Otter, Charlie and Blondy Nelson, Pecos Kid . . . Daisy Gordon and Doris Cumberland [these were club names of the members] . . . . In the demonstrations that displayed the athletic prowess of the members, the "Squaws" showed themselves to particularly good advantage.[42]

This account included elements that could still be found in cowboy and Indianist clubs decades later: the emphasis on role-play or reenactment (a distinction that depended on the point of view of the fan who was performing) and on re-creating the arts, crafts, and skills of an allegedly lost world. The fan activities across the spectrum of German Western fans were striking in their desire to make palpable and real the historical world of the American West. Literary fan groups elsewhere focused on creating fan art or produced vast quantities of derivative fiction and nonfiction essays. The re-creation of the material aspects of the imagined world with the use of props or costumes, as well, was an occasional feature of almost all literary fandoms in the mid-twentieth century. But very few fan communities elsewhere in early and mid-twentieth century Europe or the United States could compare with the abundant, painstaking, and impressively detailed mimetic creations of German cowboys and Indianist hobbyists.

This last part of the newspaper report also hints at the ways in which cowboy and Indianist role-playing could simultaneously reflect established gender roles, since Indigenous women, cowboys, and Indigenous men were all often seen in essentialized terms, naturalizing qualities ascribed to both sexes, while also allowing women in the club to transgress social norms, if they chose.[43] A German (male) cowboy who gave rifle and lasso demonstrations might feel that

FIGURE 3. Members of the Old Manitou Club, at a ceremony held by club members at Karl May's mausoleum in Radebeul, near Dresden, ca. 1930. Courtesy of Karl May Museum Archive.

he represented the personal liberty of a real "Western man," while a woman who painstakingly crafted an Indigenous woman's costume for herself and prepared foods that resembled those of historic Indigenous cultures was also enacting a role in which femininity was naturalized in an Indianist role-play context. But a woman who dressed up like Annie Oakley's little sister and participated in knife-throwing or sharp-shooting exhibitions was offering a performance of quite a different sort. And yet all of these roles could be accommodated within the flexible framework of May's world and the Old West, as interpreted by club members. Club members interpreted the "freedom" of the American West as granting individuals the liberty to create their own interpretive *personas*.

Clubs corresponded among themselves, but they were also connected to one another through the efforts of Patty Frank, who sometimes referred Western fans

FIGURE 4. An Old Manitou Club associate (women could not be voting members), dressed as a cowgirl, poses in a public knife-throwing exhibition, late 1930s. Courtesy of Karl May Museum Archive.

he met to their local cowboy and Indian club, so that they could connect with kindred spirits. Frank was a networker of the first order; having assembled a large collection of Indigenous artifacts during his tours of North America as a circus performer, he was seen as an authority on Indigenous cultures and languages back in Germany, cultivating contacts with ethnologists who were friendly with May's publisher. The silver-tongued Frank had met and discussed his collection with May before the author's death, and negotiated the sale of his collection some years later with May's widow and publisher, concluding the sale in 1926. He also persuaded them to build a large building in 1926 (complete with living quarters) modeled on a log cabin to house the collection. Along with some Indigenous artifacts that Karl May had purchased, Frank's collection became the focal point of a new museum where Frank would live and work. The Villa Shatterhand had long been a focal point for May fan tourism and visits, and May's widow agreed to locate the museum behind her home in Radebeul, the new Villa Bear Fat.[44]

Frank lived upstairs in the Villa Bear Fat above its exhibition rooms and ran the museum until his death in 1959, offering tours and talks to visiting fans under three political regimes. He encouraged German Western fans to form new cowboy and Indian clubs and connected them with one another across Germany, acting as a clearing house for such information. He also invited small groups of local fans to meet at his museum: the high point of such visits, one hobbyist recalled later, was always when Frank brought out his collection of real scalps.[45] He was as good a storyteller as May himself and a fitting curator for the Karl May Museum, possessing a fine sense of showmanship and a great deal of charm. Frank used his political and public relations skills to support German Western fans and to keep May's legacy in the public eye under both National Socialism and after 1945 in East Germany, where the museum and May's birthplace were both located after Germany's division.

Frank saw to it that the Weimar press regularly reported in positive terms about the museum and May himself. Soon after the museum's opening, for example, Frank worked with the Dresden's Sarrasani Circus to stage a widely reported "ceremony" at May's grave, in which a group of the circus's Indigenous performers, led by Chief Big Snake from the Lakota Pine Ridge Reservation, came to honor May's memory. Wearing feather headdresses and face paint, the visitors played drums and sang in their own languages before laying a large wreath on the grave that read "The Chief of the Sioux Indians greets his great white brother." Hundreds of people attended the ceremony and watched the Indigenous visitors perform a "ceremonial dance" afterward. Newspaper accounts framed the event as a spontaneous tribute offered by the visitors to one of their own, as reflected in the account of the ceremony published in the Karl May Press's yearbook, which attempted to shore up the authenticity of May's story world by linking it to nostalgia-drenched admiration for Indigenous North Americans:

> The real costumes and weapons of American Indians are hardly to be found nowadays, and are collected by museums. Their languages are dying out with the people themselves, along with their prayers, hymns, and love songs, and those who seek their lore will no longer find them out in nature, but rather only in books in a library or in a museum. But Winnetou lives, lives in the hearts of youths . . . therefore I was deeply moved when

I saw the Sioux Indian stand before Karl May's grave and give a eulogy in his own language . . . the thanks of a dying race to a man who could not save their lives but who did save something much more important: the soul of their people.[46]

Frank worked to promote the May legend for decades, providing a focal point for fan tourism and gatherings throughout the Nazi period and after 1945 (more discreetly) in East Germany. His ability to navigate the politics of the Nazi period, and to attract Nazi youth groups to his museum, is indeed a testimony to both his political skills and those of May's publisher. But the museum's success in both Nazi and East Germany also reflects the fact that Indigenous peoples could be repurposed in symbolic terms by very different political regimes.[47]

The letters, newspaper reports, and photos discussed above date from the late 1920s through mid-1939. During these years the Depression began, the Weimar Republic entered a state of political gridlock, and the Nazis took control of the German government in 1933, developing a racial state over the next few years before launching World War II with the German invasion of Poland in September 1939. But cowboy and Indianist club life continued through the start of World War II, apparently unhindered. The National Socialist government outlawed other political parties and labor unions or any groups that might oppose the Nazis, and effectively compelled many German adults and youths to join Nazi affiliate organizations during the 1930s. But groups that were seen as unpolitical, like the hobbyists' clubs, were allowed to continue their activities. National Socialists did require all organizations to purge their ranks of Jewish members so that they were *Judenrein* (purified of Jews), and the Western clubs must have complied. But they continued their activities, attracting favorable press, while Karl May publications and spin-offs and other Western entertainments remained very popular throughout the Nazi period.

On their face, May's stories could have been problematic for the Nazi leadership. May's pacifism and opposition to both imperialism and militarism had become pronounced after 1905, and these values were explicitly articulated in some of his later novels. His Westerns clearly preferred nonwhite characters and cultures to those of the "Aryan" Yankee Americans, and even endorsed what the Nazis would have seen as miscegenation, as shown in the proposed marriage between Old Shatterhand and Winnetou's sister. The political subtext here was not lost on some readers, both inside and outside the Party.

A supporter of the Nazi Party, teacher Wilhelm Fronemann, filed repeated complaints against the books with Nazi educational authorities, asking that they be banned. Fronemann had published critical analyses of May earlier—May's publisher had filed lawsuits against him during the Weimar period—and he saw in the new Nazi regime the opportunity to push back on May's popularity. "May's world view," he argued in one petition, "is extremely pacifist. . . . he is an opponent of National Socialist racial thinking and promotes mixed marriages . . . Karl May fits with National Socialism no better than a fist in one's eye."[48] Some May enthusiasts certainly read May's stories as promoting the same values that Fronemann saw in them, but drew different conclusions. Klaus Roxin (a later founder of the Karl May Society) was taught anti-Semitic lyrics to a song at a meeting of a Nazi organization for schoolchildren, and wrote later that he immediately realized that "Karl May would not have approved of this song. So, I closed my lips and refused to sing along with the rest of them."[49]

But Fronemann's crusade against May failed completely. The National Socialist Teacher's League, which was responsible for evaluating and approving children's literature, rebuked Fronemann and urged him to stop publishing critiques of the author. The National Socialist Teacher's League added Karl May's novels to their catalog of "good" literature for youths in August 1933, thus ensuring its political respectability (*Hoffähigkeit*) under the new regime. Thereafter, Nazi authorities were forced to repeatedly admonish May's publisher for using the Party's endorsement in the advertisements for May's novels, and for assuring potential customers that May was a favorite author of not only Hitler but also of Goebbels, Göring, and the head of the Nazi Ministry of Culture, who called on young German men in 1934 to display "courage, decisiveness, love for adventure, and a spirit worthy of Karl May."[50]

Indeed, banning May's works would have proven grossly unpopular in Nazi Germany, given his enormous readership. The Nazi Party leadership in Saxony (where Radebeul is located) even paid their own visit to meet Patty Frank in late 1933. Frank gave them a tour of the museum, shared "firewater" with them, and concluded the visit by passing around a "peace pipe."[51] May's widow cultivated a cordial relationship with Nazi authorities, as well, publishing a series of articles in the regional Nazi Party newspaper entitled "Under the Swastika Around the World," which described her travels to May's Middle Eastern novel locations. She later joined the Nazi Party, was even greeted personally by Hitler at a public theatrical performance.[52]

Nazi cultural authorities still intended to oversee May fans' activities, however. Some of his less popular and most pacifist novels were often not available for sale during the Nazi period because they were allegedly "sold out," but most were read widely throughout the 1930s. Instead, the Party sought to piggyback onto and thus repurpose his popularity: May's German immigrant protagonists were celebrated in Nazi propaganda as victorious Germans and unbeatable warriors, who embodied authentic German characteristics. Nazi authorities also made use of the popular fascination with Westerns and Indian characters by supporting the publication of a popular new Western series about the historical Shawnee leader Tecumseh, which stressed the militarism and superiority of whites and demonstrated how Tecumseh's victories showed the efficacy of the "leader principle."[53]

Patty Frank and the Karl May Museum continued to function as usual throughout the Nazi period. Dressed as a cowboy, Frank was regularly photographed sitting next to the Western-style stone fireplace inside his log cabin, or at the bar of the Wild West themed "Smiling Prairie Dog Saloon," inside the museum complex. His anecdotes and exotic Indigenous artifacts continued to make good copy in German newspapers just as they had in the Weimar Republic, drawing both individual visitors and groups of fans throughout the 1930s. The museum became a popular destination for Nazi boys' groups' field trips, a testimony to the regime-transcending appeal for adolescents of weapons, exotica, and nature lore. Frank was photographed for one magazine spread, for example, with a series of visitors from the Hitler Youth, as he showed them May's rifle, and how to throw a lasso. The accompanying text asserted that the spirit of May and Winnetou both oversaw these visits, and gave their blessings to the Hitler Youth, and their Führer.[54]

Liberated from their original texts and recycled in other formats and contexts, May's characters could be made to stand for diverse positions. For this reason, Nazi authorities were more willing to allow fans to organize around derivative products and activities than to meet regularly to parse the potentially problematic novels themselves in group discussions. Nazi officials acted to suppress May literary societies, therefore, while allowing film and play productions and Karl May Museum tours. Cowboy and Indianist clubs founded in Weimar Germany continued operations after 1933 until all voluntary associations' activities were suspended during World War II.[55] Societies devoted to the study of Karl May's novels *per se* were not encouraged in Nazi Germany, however, since local authorities apparently viewed clubs that might discuss May's antimilitarist and pacifist themes with suspicion. One Karl May society founded in Thüringen in 1942 was dissolved two years later because "its goals are incompatible with National Socialism," and its leadership was put under surveillance.[56]

The National Socialist regime allowed and even endorsed commercial or amateur productions of May's stories in other media, however. The 1930s witnessed exhibitions, plays, movies, and puppet shows based on May's stories. Both the twenty-fifth anniversary of his death (in 1937) and the hundredth anniversary of his birth (in 1942) were widely commemorated, although Nazi authorities insisted that May's gravesite be made *Judenrein* (purified of Jews) before the 1942 graveside ceremony. They demanded that the bodies of May's widow's first husband, Richard Plöhn and Plöhn's mother (who had been Jewish) be exhumed from the family site and relocated before the ceremony took place. Karl May's widow, Klara May, was eager to gain the recognition and publicity that the ceremony promised. She therefore agreed to the relocation of her first husband's and mother-in-law's remains, since Nazi officials insisted that government leaders could not possibly give speeches in front of a family plot that included the grave of a "half Jew."[57]

Summer performances of May's stories on large outdoor stages or amphitheaters were first produced during the late 1930s, and attracted hundreds of thousands of spectators. The Hitler Youth helped to organize an early large-scale open-air performance of May's stories in Rathen, in 1938, and the production's program claimed that May's stories reflected "ideas of heroism, love for the fatherland, and racial awareness"; in 1940, over 450,000 came to a two-month run of performances about Winnetou in Werder, near Berlin. Performances given during World War II featured an elderly Indian chief in full regalia, introduced to the audience as "the last of the red men," who accused the English of using unfair treaties and lies to swindle his race, "and breaking the red man's will with firewater . . . but Germans offered us as brothers their hand . . . [and used] neither lies nor deception." Nonetheless, the English had slaughtered Indian warriors "to the last man."[58]

May's world continued to be a beloved one in German Western and Indianist hobbyist groups throughout the 1930s and 1940s, but some hobbyists were also increasingly aware that his depictions were romanticized. Enthusiasts continued to spend a great deal of time researching and learning specific Indigenous arts or skills in an attempt to make as real as possible a world that was inherently fictional, efforts that would intensify after 1945.

FIGURE 5. An Old
Manitou Club member,
photographed during his
military leave at home
near Dresden, 1942.
Courtesy of Karl May
Museum Archive.

World War II ultimately led to the suspension of club activities. Many of the
male club members were drafted, and resources to create costumes, artifacts,
performances, etc., became scarcer. One man active in the Dresden Manitou
club recalled that the club meetings gradually ceased altogether, since almost
all the men were drafted. The Old Manitou Club's collection of teepees and
Indigenous artifacts were all destroyed in the bombing of Dresden in February
of 1945, and the club then dissolved entirely.[59]

Cowboy and Indian clubs' collections were sometimes destroyed as German
cities were heavily bombed during the later stages of the war, and some members
who served in the German army were killed. Clubs nonetheless picked up and
resumed activities soon after the war's end, but now in a changed political and

social context. Germany was occupied and divided between the victorious Allied forces. Unable to agree about how to reconstruct Germany, the Soviet Union and the United States ultimately oversaw the creation of two separate German nations in 1948, dividing a nation that had been unified since 1871. The Soviet occupation zone became the German Democratic Republic (the GDR or East Germany); the American, British and French occupation zones were merged to establish the Federal Republic of Germany (the FRG, or West Germany). East Germany became a Soviet ally, a one-party state with a political system that took the Soviet Union as its model. West Germany was an American ally, and adopted a parliamentary democratic political system with a capitalist economy.

The postwar partition of Germany divided the German Western fandom, just as it had the nation itself. Over the next forty-five years, the two fan communities developed in somewhat different directions; Germans' strong engagement with Indigenous cultures, Indian characters, and the West continued unabated, but flowed through new and different political channels. The West German May scene was influenced by the steady growth of the West German consumer culture, which rapidly expanded the range of available Western commercial entertainments. West German fans were offered a host of new Western media productions to organize around and play with, and friends of Karl May were able to form a productive and long-lasting literary society.

In East Germany, the political playing field was quite different, and Western fans there had to maneuver around official disapproval of May's world and a different state approach to the political instrumentalization of Indigenous cultures. And in both Germanies, some Western hobbyists moved sharply away from a focus on Karl May, toward an increasingly strong focus on historical authenticity and reenactment.

# CHAPTER THREE

# A Wall Runs through It

## Western Fans in the Two Germanies

A fter 1945, Germany was occupied and divided between the nations who had formed an alliance to defeat her during World War II. Their alliance proved transient, and the two German nations established in 1948 developed against the backdrop of a Cold War rivalry between the United States and the Soviet Union that lasted until the fall of the Berlin Wall in 1989. During the early years of the Cold War, conflicts and showdowns between the United States and the Soviet Union sometimes took place in or over the two Germanies, since the boundary between the Soviet sphere of influence in Eastern Europe, and the American sphere of influence in the West, ran directly down the middle of Germany's prewar territory. For the first thirteen years of its existence, East Germany also lost a steady stream of its population to West Germany, as Germans voted with their feet and relocated from East to West. To stop these losses, East Germany built the Berlin Wall in 1961 and sealed off its border with West Germany, severing communities and families.

The German Western fandom was one of the lesser casualties of Germany's division into two nations. Throughout the early and mid-twentieth century, Western fans had been a pan-German phenomenon, with Radebeul one of their main hubs. Cowboy and Indian clubs from many German provinces were connected to one another by Patty Frank and maintained regular correspondences, arranging gatherings and cooperating in a microeconomy of materials and information exchanges needed to create their outfits and artifacts. Karl May novels and myriad spin-offs sold well across Germany, and Germans traveled from other provinces to see May theatricals at Rathen, Werder, and elsewhere. Fans came from across Germany to see Karl May's birthplace in Hohenstein-Ernstthal, and his home and museum in Radebeul. But Rathen, Radebeul, and Hohenstein-Ernstthal were now located in East Germany, and the publication of Karl May's novels would soon be banned in East Germany. The cowboy and Indian clubs located on both sides of the Wall were now in different nations, operating in very different economic and political contexts. Over the next forty years, Western fandoms in East and West Germany diverged, developing in different directions.

In West Germany, fans took up prewar activities soon after the war's end, and expanded them further. German Western hobbyists had researched and performed both cowboy and Indian roles from the very beginning, and were often simultaneously engaged with the story world of Karl May. Before 1945, the same person often had two sets of outfits and two club names, so that club members could perform roles as either a cowboy or an Indian, and might also have club activities that related to Karl May. After World War II, East German authorities now began to limit the roles available to hobbyists in their nation, largely suppressing fans' activities as "cowboys" by the mid-1960s. In West Germany, however, Western fans steadily expanded the repertoire of Western roles and reenactments to include a broad variety of white, Indigenous, and even Hispanic North American historical *personas* by the 1970s. The divergence after 1945 between the East German Manitou Club, located near Dresden, and the Munich Cowboy Club, which found itself after 1945 in the American-affiliated West German state, illuminates the ways that political regimes could shape hobbyists' options.

This chapter also explores a second divergence between the East and West German Western fandoms after 1948: the degree to which fans in each Germany could openly engage with Karl May's story world and characters. The East German regime wrestled for years with both the question of how to respond to hobbyists' desire to continue performing their cowboy roles after 1945, as well as with enthusiasts' desire to read and discuss Karl May. After some debate, East Germany shifted away from the policy of generally benign neglect (at least, for German fans who were not Jewish) that had characterized Nazi authorities' approach to German Western fans, and prohibited fan organizations centered on Karl May. These and other state interventions shaped the growth of Western fandom in East Germany. During the same period, the rapid growth of a consumer culture that emphasized commercial entertainments created the context for all fan communities in West Germany.

FIGURE 6. East and West Germany, as they existed between 1948 and 1990, with some of the most important Karl May or Western fan locations shown. The division of Germany meant that most fans found themselves on the opposite side of the Wall from locations or entertainments that were important in the May fandom. Map by William Nelson.

## Cowboys and the East German State

From the East German Cultural Ministry's point of view, the fundamental problem with Karl May's Western novels after 1945 was that they were set in the United States, which was now the opponent of the Soviet Union. The most beloved character, Winnetou, was of course a Mescalero Apache, but many of the other protagonists were white American citizens. There was simply no getting around this fact for most of East Germany's existence: Karl May's stories were set in a time and place that East German authorities refused to celebrate, and certainly did not want to direct scarce resources toward commemorating.

Stories that celebrated American settings and characters were therefore politically very sticky, since May's characters were associated with the "class enemy." Old Shatterhand and white cowboys in general could be and were painted as agents of American imperialism by East German cultural bureaucrats.[1] And whether May was read as a pacifist or not, the Nazis had not only tolerated but endorsed (while repurposing) May's stories and characters, which left them with a very tainted political pedigree in socialist East Germany. May's novels were also tarred by the fact that he was said to have been Hitler's favorite author, which further damned him in East German authorities' eyes. For the East German Ministry of Culture, therefore, May's novels had little redeeming social value.

East German cultural authorities debated the subject among themselves for a few years, but ultimately ruled that although ownership of May novels published before 1945 was not illegal, that scarce resources did not permit the printing of new copies, when there were so many more "worthwhile" stories for young people that the state preferred to support. May's books were purged from public libraries after 1950, as well. Used copies of May's books were still passed hand-to-hand among the hundreds of thousands of East Germans who owned prewar editions, however. They were also sometimes obtained surreptitiously from West German sources, since East Germans could visit stores in West Berlin until the Berlin Wall was built in 1961. But after the Wall was built, East German fans of May found it difficult to obtain new copies of his stories. Some traveled to other Eastern European nations (where May was still popular, and his novels available) and purchased them there, only to find that the books were confiscated by East German border guards, when travelers returned home.[2]

The East German authorities hoped that May's popularity would wane over time, and that East German fans would turn to story worlds that were more acceptable to the state. But May's fans did not accept the ban on publication and sought to evade the restrictions. Some fans mounted vociferous, impassioned letter writing campaigns to the Ministry, demanding the publication of his novels. For these readers, the fact that Hitler had liked May's stories and allowed their continued publication during the Nazi period was not *prima facie* disqualifying, and they certainly were not put off by the American settings and characters. Fans who wrote to the Ministry of Culture pointed out that many people from across Germany's political spectrum were May fans, including the Communist martyr Karl Liebknecht, one of East Germany's patron saints; they repeatedly noted May's themes of racial reconciliation and pacifism. But the Ministry was immovable, and the only outcome was that the most pugnacious fans were brought to the notice of East Germany's secret police.[3] In one East German province, a group of teenagers organized a Karl May reading group during the early 1950s to discuss the novels; their activities led them to oppose the emerging one-party political system, and all were given lengthy jail terms.[4]

The Karl May Museum, located in East Germany, was quietly renamed the Indian Museum. Its exhibits on white Americans like General Custer and Buffalo Bill disappeared, while Patty Frank wisely kept a lower public profile than he had during the Nazi period. He nonetheless continued to give tours to visiting fans, and the museum ultimately became one of the most visited (although little publicized) museums in East Germany. East German authorities refused to allow reprints of May's novels for thirty years until the cultural climate was somewhat liberalized during the 1980s, although East German derivative works like comics and films loosely modeled on May stories were approved earlier.[5]

May's novels therefore existed in a sort of cultural limbo for most of East Germany's existence: not illegal, but nonetheless disapproved of by the state, and increasingly hard to obtain. Certainly, no literary group devoted exclusively to the study of Karl May was allowed to openly operate in East Germany, although "circles of May friends" existed quietly in Leipzig and Dresden. As in the Nazi period, however, Indianist hobbyist groups were more acceptable to the regime than May literary societies because hobbyists could distance themselves from the text of the novels. Such groups could plausibly claim to be organizing around something other than just May novels, and they presented themselves as ethnologically focused groups, which indeed they increasingly were. And as in the 1930s, Indigenous peoples could also be made to stand for an array of values, some of which were acceptable to East German authorities. The values that Indigenous peoples stood for—and the ways in which they were instrumentalized by the state—were quite different from their political uses in Nazi Germany.

Indeed, one could argue that East Germany represented the high-water mark of German Indianist hobbyism, because the Manitou Club and other Indianist clubs ultimately received some financial and political support from the East German state. But this came at a price: club members had to drop their cowboy or other white American *personas* and any overt celebration of Karl May's story world and reframe themselves as "Indian friends" who were interested only in Indigenous American cultures. For the generation that had come of age before 1945, this represented an adjustment, although it was not a hardship for many of those born after 1945.

In both East and West Germany, Western fans picked up where they had left off before the war and refounded or resumed their club activities. In Radebeul, a drugstore owner named Johannes Hüttner survived the war; he had admired the prewar Manitou Club members (although he had been too young to formally join during the 1930s) and decided to refound the club. Hüttner became known to hobbyists by his club name, Old Powder Face, and his store soon became a hangout for younger Indianist enthusiasts in the region. Around 1950, Powder Face began to apply for legal registration as a club but ran into some resistance from East German authorities, who were taken aback by the emphasis on costumes and role-play set in the United States. Wouldn't it be better, one local official suggested, to study and re-create instead the lifestyles of the Indigenous inhabitants of Siberia, who now—under the inspired leadership of Stalin—were marching toward a brighter future? Hüttner and his friends disagreed, responding that they were interested only in American Indians. The Dresden area devotees persisted for six years in their applications, and were finally allowed to register legally in 1956 as "the District Cultural Group of the Central Project Bureau of the Glass and Ceramics Industry."[6]

While a club focusing on Indigenous peoples could—if its leaders were resourceful and willing to compromise—be politically rehabilitated in East Germany, cowboys were irredeemable in the eyes of the East German state and its security police, the Ministry for State Security, commonly known as the Stasi. One could hardly present cowboys as subjects of ethnological research. During the 1950s and early 1960s, therefore, most Manitou Club members had to be discreet about their cowboy costumes, and often only put them on in private, after the day's Indian activities were over. "After it got dark," three older Indian hobbyists reminisced after the fall of the Berlin Wall, "we would take off the feather headdresses and put on the cowboy hats."[7]

But cowboys needed guns—ideally, Colt revolvers. Since these were not for sale in East Germany, they had to make their own. Some club members simply retooled old Prussian revolvers to make them look more Western. An informer for the Stasi (evidently a Manitou Club member) reported on the secret weapons, which led to a Stasi raid of a club meeting and the confiscation of the weapons. One Stasi report concluded that Manitou Club members were unfortunately "very receptive to negative [antisocialist] influences." One member who lost his revolver in the raid recalled later that "we mourned for our Colts for a long time and carried mourning flowers in our [gun] holsters."[8] The younger generation of East Germany hobbyists who succeeded the "after dark" cowboys during the 1960s increasingly dismissed Karl May's stories as historically inaccurate, however. Avoiding conflict with the Stasi, they turned away from cowboy roles.

## In Pursuit of Authentic *Indianistik*

The next generation of Western hobbyists in East Germany, therefore, was generally content to focus on Indigenous *personas,* the more "authentic" (as they defined the concept) the better. The desire to perform white American roles continued to spark sometimes tense discussions within the East German Indianist hobbyist community, however, since fans were aware that cowboy role-play invited greater scrutiny and pressure from the authorities.[9] Cowboys remained a suspicious form of role-play for decades, until East German hobbyists were able to repackage them for authorities by the 1980s as members of the American rural proletariat, after which they became somewhat more tolerated.[10]

As soon as they were allowed to reestablish their club in East Germany, members of the Manitou Club worked hard to show their social utility to authorities. They organized an Indian culture exhibition at the Dresden Zoo soon after the club's successful legal registration. In more than fifty-five live demonstrations, club members performed lasso and whip tricks, archery, knife-throwing, and horseback riding, and also exhibited teepees and costumes to interested zoo visitors.[11] Indianist hobbyists thus replaced the traveling prewar circuses and other public exhibitions of Indigenous performers for the German public, and began to receive small subsidies from the East German state as "popular artistic collectives" in order to finance their public performances. The shows put on by Manitou Club members in particular were so successful that the club even mounted a small tour throughout East Germany in the late 1950s, with state support.[12] Other clubs were founded (or refounded) across East Germany after 1950, and many also received modest state subsidies for public exhibitions that state authorities saw as educational, and also as politically useful reminders of the American government's transgressions against Indigenous peoples.[13]

The Manitou Club and one other that was active during the 1950s were nonetheless in the earlier style of Western fans, one hobbyist from the next generation recalled after the end of the Cold War. These older groups:

> were related to this line of [prewar club] tradition, i.e. the cultivation of the lore of the Prairie Indians and the Old West, for which Karl May's books were initially more or less providing the inspiration. In the course of the years [especially after the 1960s, when this hobbyist became involved], the emphasis shifted increasingly toward a more intensive, ethnologically-informed occupation with the life, history, and cultures of the North American Indians.[14]

Beginning in 1958, East German Indianist clubs organized an annual national gathering during the long weekend of the Whitsun holiday. In 1973 these meetings were expanded to run for a full week each summer (called simply "Indian Week"), attracting as many as one thousand hobbyists for a week of games, sports, and costumed role-play. Like similar clubs from before 1945, hobbyist groups created feather headdresses, moccasins, and other accessories to show off at such gatherings. They performed re-created Indigenous dances to their own original music and practiced knife-throwing and using whips and lassoes. The Manitou Club's performances were so well regarded that they were even invited to perform in other Eastern European cities during the 1960s and 1970s.[15]

Even though their performances featured the same activities, e.g., knife-throwing and lassoes, that had engaged the prewar generation of hobbyists, Indianist hobbyists stepped up their game after 1960, and pursued "authenticity"—accurate mimetic performances and reproductions of artifacts from nineteenth-century Indigenous cultures—ever more seriously. Club members raised their craft skills to a new level, training themselves to create elaborate glass bead work, skilled leatherwork, and magnificent feather headdresses, moccasins, etc., using local materials in most cases. Some cultivated contacts with ethnological museums for this reason. Such groups strove for authenticity in their clothing and artifacts, gathering to practice the dances, songs, and crafts of their chosen Indigenous cultures. By the 1970s, some had founded newsletters that contained detailed instructions for other hobbyists about how to create artifacts and outfits that were close, or even perfect replicas of historic Indigenous North American clothing and objects.[16]

In both Germanies, craftsmanship was key to the pleasures of an experiential fandom and to hobbyist gatherings. As with groups of historical reenactors who emerged in other nations in later decades, German cowboy and Indianist hobbyists gained membership in their clubs and respect from other members by creating their own first outfit, a rite of passage that required study of historical clothing and artifacts, and the development of the club member's craft skills. As Petra Kalshoven, an ethnologist who spent time with German Indianist hobbyists after Germany's reunification, observed:

> Stepping back and experiencing the illusionist landscape of an Indianist tepee camp must be accompanied by the knowledge that, close-up, it is grounded in proper, tangible, material craftwork. The pleasure of Indianism lies in a play between distance (gazing at the camp from a hillock; wondering about a distant past) and close contact with materials and artifacts (gaining access to museum storage; becoming a skilled replica-maker).[17]

Craft skills were developed for their own sake, but also in pursuit of authenticity, which was seen as key to truly empathizing with and "touching" a historical culture (*Nachempfindung*). Authenticity, defined by accurate mimetic clothing and artifacts, and by mimetic performances, became increasingly central to many German Western hobbyists' activities and norms after 1960, as one segment of the German Western community drew away from the fantasy world of Karl May and genre Westerns and turned toward what they saw as a more authentic *Indianistik*.

The literature on authenticity—on its meanings, perception, and construction—is extensive. This literature is also linked to debates over cultural appropriation and representation of Indigenous cultures. The analysis of how authenticity is defined or deployed is important and quite varied in scholarly discussions of historical reenactors, heritage tourism, living history, and the work of Indigenous cultures to protect and preserve traditional skills.[18] How this concept is defined and deployed differs across these literatures.

German cowboy and Indianist hobbyists' understanding of authenticity largely resembled that of modern historical reenactors, as described by a leading

Australian reenactor and public historian, Stephen Gapps. In modern historical reenactment communities, he observes:

> Authenticity is a currency that confers status both within the reenactment community and on its relations with cultural institutions and wider audiences. It is not used by reenactors as a term for an original item or mentality; rather, it references a perceived proximity to an original. Ultimately, then, authenticity is critical for reenactors: it is a key term in our symbolic vocabulary and often thought of as being part of our "special responsibility."[19]

Similarly, their careful craft work and creation of replicas that displayed close proximity to the historical originals earned East German Indianists the right to perform publicly at cultural institutions. It was a key term, because hobbyists, and some East German cultural authorities, believed that accurate mimetic clothing and performances would, as one local reporter asserted in a report on a Manitou gathering, help to "replace the false and confused preconceptions about the lives, customs, culture, and beliefs of the Indians with a true understanding."[20] German hobbyism during the mid-twentieth century was an expression of nostalgia, of mourning something that was missing from their daily lives, and attempting to recapture it.[21] Hobbyists expressed this through their research and efforts to re-create aspects of cultures that they saw as endangered, and usually sought to honor these cultures and their representatives, actual Indigenous North Americans, whenever hobbyists had contact with them.

But authenticity had other values and functions for German hobbyists as well, which foreshadowed the concept's centrality among later generations of historical reenactors. Skillful, accurate re-creations of Indigenous clothing and artifacts brought respect from other club members, who might seek a skilled club member's advice on how to create their own outfits. And it was so central to the groups' mission that authenticity itself inevitably became a contested value, as hobbyists argued over what the rules for German Indianist gatherings should include, and debated the artifacts and behaviors that were truly authentic and hence appropriate, and later in the twentieth century, what might instead be dismissed as commercial and therefore inauthentic.[22]

Birgit Turski, who founded an East German Indianist club in the newer, post-1960s style and was active in this milieu for decades, noted that accusations of "rule-breaking" of guidelines meant to ensure authenticity was an evergreen and open-ended topic for dispute among East German hobbyists. Did a pair of moccasins, which were not waterproof and imperfectly suited to Germany's climate, have to copy historical models completely, or was it acceptable to line the inside with rubber soles? How much could one alter or adapt designs seen in a museum? Disputes between club members were often rooted in the tensions between the historical originals and the adaptations necessary to local circumstances, landscapes, and materials, along with the constraints imposed by East German state authorities.[23]

When disputes over authenticity and rule-breaking could not be resolved, factions within German Indianist clubs might break away to found their own clubs. Disputes over interpretations of what fans often refer to as "canon" (the original book or movie series, or other entertainment that fans organize around) are familiar to fans and all who study fandoms. Among German cowboy and Indianist hobbyists, these disputes revolved around what was an allowable historic re-creation, since historical cultures themselves formed the canon for this fandom.[24] Somewhat later in the twentieth century, parallel disputes among military historical reenactors would also revolve around authenticity of performances, costumes, and props. Among later Civil War reenactors, an entire vocabulary would develop to differentiate between those performances that were seen as extremely authentic and those reenactors who were, by contrast, disdained by their fellows as amateur or anachronistic.[25]

Inspired by an interest in North American Indigenous cultures, and sometimes increased by splits among existing groups, the number of hobbyist clubs engaged in the re-creation of "authentic" historical Indigenous cultures grew steadily during East Germany's history. Seven new clubs were legally registered between 1961 and 1970, joined by sixteen additional clubs by 1980, and ten more before the collapse of the East German regime in 1990, in addition to groups formed by break-away factions in older clubs.[26] Additional informal hobbyist groups formed as well by those who could not achieve legal registration, a paperwork-laden process in East Germany, nor the subsidies that could come with registration.

Indigenous visitors who came to East or West Germany were generally seen by hobbyists as the ultimate arbiters of authenticity; they felt honored when Indigenous individuals came to visit and sometimes admired the quality of hobbyists' handicrafts. Dresden area hobbyists retold a story for years that reflected both their pride in their meticulous craftsmanship as well as the mixed reactions that their hobby might provoke in Indigenous visitors.

South Dakota was the home of many Oglala Lakota performers who had worked for German circuses and shows before 1939; it was a community that had long-standing ties to German Western fans. One of their leaders came on a visit to East Germany and saw a replica of a traditional Lakota child carrier (sometimes called a cradle board), which had been made with great care by a local hobbyist who copied an original artifact in the Indian Museum's collection. The German hobbyist had worked for years on the project, collecting old beads and recreating historical styles of stitching to decorate it; he had even woven his own tiny American flag for the object, in order to match the decorations on a museum's historical example. The Lakota leader was very impressed by the child carrier and asked to borrow it for his own child, since his wife had recently had a baby. The hobbyist was deeply honored to have his work thus praised and used by a real Lakota. But there were great difficulties in getting it returned. Ultimately, the Lakota leader refused to return the object, claiming that it was a real historical child carrier and not one made by Germans at all. The story, still circulating decades later among East German hobbyists, reflected some of this community's core values: pride in their crafts and skills and a conviction that Indigenous people could bestow recognition of authenticity, but also a wry recognition of the discomfort that extraordinarily accurate mimetic performances could provoke among Indigenous visitors.[27]

Indianist hobbyists became even more acceptable to East German authorities after the late 1960s, when Europeans began to perceive Indigenous cultures even more strongly than they had before as victims of white Americans, and thus as subjugated peoples. The growth of the American Indian Movement (AIM) and its outreach to Indianist enthusiasts in both East and West Germany further supported this trend, and enlisted new German supporters for the AIM and Indigenous tribal leaders.

New novels presenting Indian characters in this light were published in East Germany, particularly the works of Liselotte Welskopf-Henrich, who enjoyed official approval and whose novels were promoted as an alternative to Karl May. A professor at Humboldt University in East Berlin, Welskopf-Henrich wrote a series of well-researched, highly regarded, and bestselling novels featuring Indian protagonists, beginning with the classic *Die Söhne der grossen Bärin* in 1951, which sold more than a million copies and was popular in both Germanies. She presented her Indian characters as people who faced pressure and poor treatment by white settlers and the American government, and sought to resist and escape such treatment, in language more explicitly political than the prewar tropes of the "last Indian."[28]

Welskopf-Henrich had an impeccable political pedigree in East Germany; she and her husband were Communists who had taken considerable risks to oppose and resist the Nazis, and chose to stay in East Germany. She was allowed to travel to the United States, where she built relationships with Indigenous Americans, including the AIM leadership. Welskopf-Henrich became a key figure connecting East German (and Eastern European) supporters to Indigenous activists. She developed good ties to the AIM in the 1970s, serving as a conduit to connect East German Indianist enthusiasts and hobbyists with Indigenous pen pals and AIM contacts.[29]

East German authorities continued to subsidize hobbyists' public exhibitions and equipment throughout the regime's existence, sometimes generously. Using its members' connections and resourcefulness, the Manitou Club was able to re-create a newer and larger set of club grounds, "Stetson City," outside of Dresden during the 1970s, expanding it after 1981. The new venue boasted not only the obligatory saloon and teepees found on almost all Western clubs' grounds but later expanded to include a trading post, a sheriff's office and jail, and (after the Wall fell) a shooting range and set of stables.[30]

One of the club's female members recalled later that she found great interest and pride in researching women's issues among Indigenous cultures, specializing in customs surrounding pregnancy, childbirth, and menstruation. She looked forward to East German hobbyists' annual summer gatherings, The Week, where she and others proudly displayed recently created handicrafts to Indianist hobbyists from other East German regions. Club members could see friends from clubs in other parts of East Germany and pursue a variety of pastimes: chatting and cooking together, swimming, attending workshops on Indigenous crafts or on the Lakota language, participating in skills contests, or joining more elaborate opening and closing rituals and ceremonies. The Week is still the highlight of the year for hobbyists in former East Germany today.

> In East Germany [she recalled], the hobby gave us the possibility, while remaining within the law, to distance ourselves from socialist daily routine. When we all gathered in the summer camp meetings, it felt at least a little bit as if we were in the far distant lands of North America ... sitting around a cozy campfire in the field where [Indian] dances were performed, or

gathering together in a comfortable circle of teepees, I am glad to sink into the romantic atmosphere [of the summer Week gathering]. Withdrawing from "civilization" for a few days, or even a week, can be very refreshing.[31]

Birgit Turski saw the attractions of East German Indianist clubs similarly, commenting that people were drawn to them by the hobby's combination of romanticism and ethnological interest. "There is romance," she recalled later, "in a lifestyle that is close to nature, which one could experience for a brief time in the relatively favorable conditions of the [hobbyists'] camp . . . there is also romanticism in the unconstrained social life of the camp which attracts many [members]."[32] Among this branch of Western fans, the allure of getting away from modern life and being part of a community with strong social bonds now replaced the attractions of Western fandom rooted in genre entertainment, where fans were fascinated by compelling fictional characters and their imagined world.

Club life had other attractions as well, offering a refuge that could underwrite a multigenerational community. Turski noted that outside social pressure promoted:

a strong sense of solidarity or fellowship [among club members] . . . only inside the club would you be sure that you would not be made fun of . . . Indianistik is often a family hobby. Problems always arise when only one partner [in a couple] is interested in Indianstik. The considerable amount of time and money required by the hobby will only rarely be tolerated by a non-hobbyist partner over the long run. Then [the club member] must decide between the hobby and the partner, and often chooses the hobby . . . romantic partners who met each other in the hobby are relatively common and are generally quite stable.[33]

Authorities allowed the growing number of hobbyist communities, even those who spent their free time withdrawing from East German social life, in part because they could be sure that most Indianistik clubs were being kept under surveillance and were subject to some influence by the Stasi and state authorities. The Stasi clearly had informants in the East German Indianist subculture, and was sometimes even able to influence these groups from within. The fact that the Stasi felt that Indianistik hobbyists were under solid surveillance, one leading member later argued, is "why the fans were increasingly able to pursue their hobby with such amazing generosity [on the part of the state]."[34] And those who informed on other club members were sometimes rewarded in currency that proved that—informers or not—they were also true fans: one informer was rewarded by the Stasi by being allowed to import Karl May's books from West Germany, and was even given an apartment in Radebeul directly across the street from May's old home, the "Villa Shatterhand."[35]

Indigenous cultures attracted new fans after the East German film authority released a series of very popular Indian films starting in the 1960s; some were based on Welskopf-Henrich's novels. West German filmmakers had released several blockbuster films based on Karl May novels starting with *The Treasure of Silver Lake* in 1962; although the May films could not be shown in East Germany, officials had become aware that many of their citizens were traveling to neighboring socialist Czechoslovakia to see these films. Soon thereafter, the East German film studio DEFA began to make its own Indian films, consulting with the members of an Indianist club founded in Taucha about the costumes. These films closely copied the look of West German Karl May films, and were sometimes even shot in the same Yugoslavian locations. The DEFA Indian films had scripts that were more socialist in tone, however, presenting the American "military as occupiers and historical baddies . . . [and] the fight between the good Indians and the bad cowboys in decidedly Marxist historical terms."[36]

The films were huge hits, as were movies made during the 1970s by Dean Reed, an American singer and actor who settled in East Germany in 1973. Reed, known as "the red Elvis," starred in a number of hit Western films. He possessed the allure of "the real thing" for Eastern Europeans and was also popular in the Soviet Union. Reed helped make cowboys more acceptable to East German authorities by portraying them with an anti-imperialist message.[37]

The films and the popularity of the American Indian rights movement, particularly after the occupation of Wounded Knee in 1973, inspired the creation of dozens more *Indianistik* groups in East Germany during the 1970s and 1980s. Unlike the members of the older clubs like the Manitou group, the younger people like Turski who were attracted to these new clubs were not interested in being cowboys, but instead pursued a dream of truly Indigenous lifestyles and customs that were more natural, and also more ecologically desirable and antiauthoritarian. The "young savages" (as the older club members called them) did their own ethnographic research, traveling to folklore exhibits and museums in order to photograph and copy costumes and artifacts. One member of the Taucha Club was employed by the Leipzig Museum for Ethnology and was able to get access to rare publications.[38]

Inspired by the AIM and buoyed by contacts with North Americans, *Indianistik* devotees in this generation became autodidacts of a high degree when it came to Indigenous North American dances and rites, learning about teepee construction, musical forms, and languages. Some focused their clubs on tribal cultures that had been largely ignored by German hobbyists in earlier decades, like the Iroquois and Pueblo Indians; these clubs gave lectures and put on exhibitions at schools and museums. By the late 1970s, they were making their own amateur films, too, to demonstrate accurate dances and techniques for creating costumes. Using their contacts with the AIM and Indigenous leaders, younger club members obtained ethnological literature from the US regarding teepee construction and other aspects of Indigenous culture, and they translated and distributed typewritten copies within East Germany so that even those German Indianists who did not speak English could get accurate information about how to make replicas.[39]

By this time, the range of possible interpretations of Indigenous roles had broadened considerably since the 1950s. Hobbyists who had been born and reared in East Germany were interested in linking their roles and groups to a more politically progressive critique of US imperialism, and in cultivating contacts with the AIM, as were some West German Indianist hobbyists. And finally, a third group emerged during the 1970s and 1980s: people who wanted to use an Indigenous *persona* and club to "drop out" and escape from daily life in East Germany as much as possible, and perhaps also to express a "green" critique of East Germany's poor ecological record. They, too, built "Indian settlements" outside of town, club grounds where they could live naturally on the weekend, as Indianists. But they abjured state subsidies, tried to escape state scrutiny as much as possible, and sometimes even built their weekend settlements in remote wooded areas, in order to keep them unobtrusive. A few of this last group sought out visiting AIM activists when they visited East Germany in the late 1970s. One Lakota visitor, Archie Fire Lame Deer, even trained some of the German Indianists in sweat lodge rituals and ceremonies and taught them about Lakota spirituality.[40]

Newcomers to East German *Indianistik* clubs could choose any of these approaches or seek out new modes of personal expression by modeling their activities on the Indigenous culture of their choice. They were using information about Indigenous American cultures in a performance of bricolage: focusing on interesting aspects of particular cultures (e.g., sweat lodges) and reworking them for their own purposes. One group might use "borrowed" rituals or objects from Indigenous North American cultures to mount an ecological critique while others sought connection with the AIM and its ideas in order to articulate a critique of the US government.

Harmut Felbers's club, founded in 1980 in Brandenburg, was an example of a group driven by a desire to find Indigenous models that allowed more activities for female members, rejecting what they saw as the "passive" roles allotted to women in some older hobbyist groups. Felber was twenty-two when he helped found the group, and he was the oldest member. He had read some novels with Indian protagonists while doing his mandatory military service after finishing school and organized a group of younger enthusiasts after his discharge to study and re-create Indigenous life, an escape from what members considered to be a gray sort of daily life. Felbers ran a small classified ad in a local paper, and twelve enthusiasts (most in their teens) responded, creating a group that lasted for more than a decade. The group chose the Mohawks as "their" culture for several reasons. "That was something special," Felbers recalled later:

> not every club chose the Mohawks ... and there were more pair dances to do [compared to other Indigenous cultures]. Among the Dakotas [clubs], the women just stood on the sidelines and chattered while the men played the role of great warriors in the center. We had a lot of girls in our group, and they weren't interested in that [the Dakota roles for women] . . . . They also liked the sewing and crafts a lot [which used leather, beads, and other exotic materials] . . . they really looked special [when costumed], and everyone in the school knew who they were.[41]

This club's choices were thus driven by the decisions of its female members, who rejected the more passive roles allotted to women in the older hobbyist groups. They may have also been influenced by the fact that the Mohawks were part of the Iroquois Confederacy, known for the leading roles played by women in Iroquois governance. Both the decision to join an Indianist group, as well as this club's choice of models, thus reflected a rejection of East German daily life, which paid lip service to women's equality but offered proportionately fewer leadership roles to women, while assigning them domestic labor.

At first, some of his neighbors thought that Felbers and his group were "nut jobs," he said. But after the group was invited to perform their Mohawk dances in full costume at a local agrarian fair to entertain some visiting Indigenous activists, and the performance was broadcast on TV, Felbers's standing with local townspeople rose considerably. "After that, they didn't call me 'crazy' again," he recalled proudly. "We had to be something special, they all decided, since we had been shown officially on TV and everything." Even better, Dennis Banks (a leader of the American Indian Movement) himself had been among the visiting Indigenous delegation, and afterward thanked Felbers's club warmly, calling them "our German Indians," a certification of authenticity that could not be surpassed. The event was clearly one of the high points of Felbers's adult life.[42]

Indigenous North Americans also assumed a mediating role in West Germany during the 1980s, although there they could profit more extensively from West Germans' interest in all things Indigenous, by opening shops to sell art or teaching classes in authentic Indigenous crafts. Many left-wing younger West Germans also supported the AIM during the 1970s, sympathizing with Indigenous Americans as an oppressed American minority. But West German fans didn't need Indigenous activists to provide political justification for their groups' existence in the eyes of the state, as was the case on the other side of the Wall, and so the function of Indigenous visitors in West German discussions was somewhat different. Nor did West German fans need to emphasize Indianist roles while downplaying cowboys or other white American *personas* in their role-play. Indigenous North American shops and classes were thus only one part of broader Western fandom in West Germany that included a more explicit celebration of Karl May and his works than could be the case in East Germany.

## At Home on the Range, Outside Munich

As in East Germany, prewar cowboy and Indianist clubs now located in West Germany resumed business within a few years of the war's end. The Munich Cowboy Club was able to use its long-standing connections to the owners of a local circus to obtain land to build its first "ranch" in 1954, converting a former German Army barracks for the purpose. The death of the circus owner a few years later forced the club to seek a new property to use, but the city of Munich offered them a lease in a forested area on the outskirts of Munich, and US Army engineers and soldiers stationed nearby helped club members to build the new ranch in 1961. American soldiers, particularly Indigenous American servicemen stationed in Germany after 1945, were encouraged by their superiors to attend German cowboy and Indianist club events, such as rodeos, to promote German-American friendship. The American government developed an array of "soft power" cultural initiatives to cultivate West German support during the Cold War, including American cultural centers called "America Houses," which organized exhibitions and offered books and information on Indigenous cultures and the West. This was tailor-made for German Western fans and hobbyists, and the America Houses were popular fan resources.[43]

The Munich club had counterparts in other West German cities. During the 1950s and 1960s the number of cowboy and Indianist hobbyist groups grew steadily across West Germany. In Munich alone, newly founded clubs included the Colorado Boys Munich (founded in 1957), the Arizona Boys (1957), and the Texas Boys (1955).[44] The Munich Cowboy Club began to acquire horses for members to use; by the 1980s, their ranch was boarding seven horses for members' use. Several hobbyist clubs were founded in West Berlin during the 1950s, and the city of Freiburg in southwest Germany ultimately boasted ten separate Western clubs. In Frankfurt, the "Hunkpapa" Club was able to build a "ranch" on the outskirts of town that included not only a saloon and sheriff's office but also stables and a corral, along with eight teepees and an "Indian Lodge" for the club's Indian hobbyist members, resembling a Mandan earth lodge. The entire ranch was surrounded by palisades, like a fort. As in Munich, the ceremony opening the club's expanded grounds in 1970 was attended by a local US army general and a representative from the American consulate.[45]

The rapid growth of Western clubs in postwar West Germany led to the first annual gathering of West German hobbyists in 1951 for a summer meeting, similar to those organized by East German Indianist hobbyists except for the inclusion of more cowboy role-play. West German hobbyists founded an umbrella organization to organize the annual gatherings, the Western Bund, which secured a permanent location for hobbyists' summer gatherings by the late 1980s.[46]

As in East Germany, Western hobbyists in West Germany became increasingly invested in the pursuit of authenticity in their costumes and performances during the decades that followed World War II. Like their East German counterparts, hobbyists cherished the summer gatherings that featured teepees and tents, dances and music, and the opportunity to show off their often meticulously researched, homemade handicrafts. But while East German hobbyists were constrained, or content, to focus overwhelmingly on the reenactment of Indigenous North American cultures and make their own artifacts, West German hobbyists developed a growing array of role-play and living history options, and they had new resources to pursue those roles. West German hobbyists could purchase their costumes and other goods commercially if they didn't want to create them; a West German company founded in 1974, the Hudson's Bay Indian Trading Post, offered a wide array of artifacts and clothing for Western hobbyists, and smaller vendors also attended hobbyist gatherings to sell their wares.[47]

Photos collected for a 2013 exhibition of the hundredth anniversary of the Munich Cowboy Club document the steady proliferation of roles for Western reenactors within the club after 1960. "Trappers" (fur trappers) and "mountain men" *personas* had been occasionally seen before 1945, but became more common in club life thereafter. The Munich club began to hold "trapper festivals," and "mountain men role-play" events. Perhaps influenced by the spaghetti Westerns of the 1960s, the Munich club boasted a "Mexican group" by 1970, whose sombrero- and blanket-wearing members performed "Mexican hat dances." Mexican groups became so well established in West German clubs that some ultimately added cantinas to their club grounds, along with the saloons. By the late twentieth century, the Munich club's annual calendar included: Victorian-costumed sewing circles and afternoon teas for ladies and balls with men dressed in cavalry uniforms; special performances of Hopi dances; and of course regular Indianist powwows, modeled on historical powwow formats. One new Munich club subgroup, the "buffalo hunters," who posed with buffalo rifles and authentic costumes, won the annual award given by the Western League for "best original [Western] group" in 1984. Members sometimes went beyond reenactment into what would today be called "cosplay," dressing and posing as particular historical individuals, like Annie Oakley or Buffalo Bill.[48] Indigenous cultures and role-play remained a central theme in members' activities in most West German clubs, but members had a variety of non-Indigenous roles to choose from, as well. One visitor to the 2003 annual summer gathering of the Western League (which consisted largely of clubs located in the former West German provinces) saw attendees costumed as Indians, mingling with hobbyists who came as trappers, mountain men, cowboys, and Civil War reenactors.[49]

## The Many Media Lives of Karl May

The most striking difference between Western fans in East and West Germany, however, was the steady diversification of the Western fan community in West Germany, and its rootedness in consumer culture. West German fans after 1950 were largely (but not entirely) organized around entertainments derived from Karl May's story world or other mass market Western stories. While there was a distinctly homemade, do-it-yourself flavor to Western fan activities pre-1945, by the late 1950s, West German fans could go shopping for what they needed whereas East German hobbyist communities had to scrounge for materials to create their own costumes and artifacts. West Germans could take advantage of a consumer culture that made it easy to find May-related or American Western costumes, artifacts, and Western entertainment spin-offs and other merchandise. By 1960, "Western Stores" found in many West German cities offered fans a large selection of Western clothing, including imitation Colt revolvers, cowboy boots and Stetson hats, and Mexican saddles. One store owner promoted sales by insisting that "true Westerners did not watch Westerns on television unless garbed in Western clothing."[50] Fans could also purchase a plethora of specifically May-related products: comics, records, posters, and every sort of fan memorabilia.[51]

West Germany after 1948 also offered fans a milieu where Karl May's stories and personal history were, at long last, not even slightly politically problematic. Moreover, the publisher's vigilant grip on the copyright over May's stories gradually eased, as the family that owned May's copyright became more comfortable with independent fan publications, and as the stories began to enter the public domain after 1962. The room for "free play," for a greater range of fan expression and experiences, thus expanded rapidly and the West German fandom became a spectrum of groups and hobbies that was best described as the "May scene": no longer centering only on cowboy and Indianist clubs but developing into a broader Western fan subculture among the most engaged fans. At the same time, it also became easier to be only a moderately engaged fan, since even those who did not belong to fan clubs could organize their free time or vacations around May-derived or other Western commercial performances and products that were offered to the public as a whole.[52]

The growth of Western fan activities and organizations, like other hobbies that depended on disposable income, kept pace with the expansion of West Germany's consumer society. West Germans increasingly had the funds and time to spend on travel and new consumer goods, and many of those who were May fans could now afford to celebrate May's world in varied ways. Indeed, they could indulge a taste for Westerns to a much greater degree than before the war. In the first five years after the West German Mark was introduced in 1948, offering once

FIGURE 7. A fan-made diorama of a scene from a Karl May novel, ca. 1970. Photo by the author, from private collection.

again a stable currency that was a prerequisite for a consumer economy, more than two hundred American Western films were released in West Germany.[53] A flood of cheap Wild West novels was published in West Germany, as well; in the early 1960s, for example, one study estimated that at least thirty-five to forty Western titles appeared on the market each month.[54]

West German fans also flocked first in the tens and then hundreds of thousands to revived and ever larger open-air performances of May stories held each summer. Open-air festival performances based on May's stories were first offered in Bad Segeberg, north of Hamburg, in 1952. The Bad Segeberg site became the largest of the annual Karl May summer open-air theatricals, drawing over nine hundred thousand visitors in its first ten years, and six million by 2001.[55] A stockade fort was built to screen the amphitheater where performances took place, and next door, a local group of Indianist hobbyists, the Apache Club, established an "Indian Reservation" in 1964 to re-create Indigenous customs and material culture for show visitors. Over time, hobbyists withdrew from running the "Reservation," which was later replaced by an "Indian Village," a commercial venture. The Indian Village grew to include a potpourri of sites familiar to viewers of Westerns like *Bonanza*: not only the obligatory saloon but also a jail and Chinese laundry, along with an array of souvenir shops selling Western and Indian gear, with American country western music playing over loudspeakers.[56] Like other Karl May summer pageants, the Bad Segeberg scripts were modeled somewhat freely on the author's novels. They rotated each year between the best-loved stories, and by including stars from the May films, drew audiences from both the book and movie fandoms. Scripts evolved over time, sometimes adding in characters familiar to audiences from other Westerns. For example, the 2006 Bad Segeberg production included a female doctor apparently modeled on the protagonist of the American television series *Dr. Quinn, Medicine Woman*.[57]

Bad Segeberg remains the largest of the annual summer open-air shows today, but other towns created their own performances over the following decades, both professional and amateur. The West German town of Elspe began to offer summer Karl May theatricals in 1958. Elspe's productions became known for taking wide-ranging artistic liberties with May's novels, even reviving Winnetou from his death bed if audience surveys requested an altered outcome for their hero. Elspe's Western town, next door to its stockade-surrounded theater, "Silverado," also gave (and gives) the Bad Segeberg Indian Village a run for its money. Silverado includes a saloon, hotel, nineteenth-century dry goods store, jail, and other Western sites. Wall paintings combine landscapes of Monument Valley in Utah and the Rockies, and the decorations include a miniature copy of the Statue of Liberty, collapsing and combining images from across the United States. In the saloon, visitors can order "trapper style" or "Mexican" schnitzels.[58]

Other towns offer smaller performances each year, often created by volunteers. Bishofswerda, a small town in Saxony in former East Germany, began annual productions featuring children or teenagers in all roles soon after the collapse of the East German regime; other local productions done by amateurs include the shows organized in the village of Pluwig in southwest Germany that began in 2000. The Pluwig group wrote a role into the Karl May performance scripts for one of their favorite *Gunsmoke* characters, Miss Kitty, who turns up to offer whiskey to the May characters.[59] Professional and fan-run May theatricals thus can choose between staying close to canon or mixing up the story lines to include appealing bits of other Western genre entertainments.

Available annually, and offering visitors their own local Western-themed infrastructure for food and housing, the summer open-air theatricals became a fandom within a fandom, and a gathering point for all Karl May fans and other Western hobbyists. Groups from other areas of Karl May fandom, e.g., those focused primarily on the films, could stage their annual meetups at Bad Segeberg or Elspe. Many fans arranged their vacations around the open-air theatricals each year, attending in costume; some memorized the scripts. The summer shows ultimately became not only a geographical focus and gathering point but also a source of endless subject matter for fans' own discussions and creative works during or around the summer performances. Fans created and create blogs, magazines, photos, and podcasts that included reporting on each year's productions.[60]

Western and May film fans were another growing segment in the postwar West German fandom. A few silent movies based on Karl May's stories had been made during the 1920s, but starting in the 1960s, a series of lush, beautifully scored color films based on the May Westerns were released to European-wide acclaim, helping to inspire the Italian "spaghetti Westerns" produced soon thereafter. The May movies were blockbuster hits in West Germany and in Czechoslovakia, where so many East Germans flocked to see them that East Germany had been pressured into financing competing Western films. In both Germanies, the 1960s Karl May films helped to "refresh" and expand the fan community, drawing in people who had not been attracted by the novels. In West Germany, the films were a huge part of the popular culture of the period; they and their stars received constant coverage in the media, for example in BRAVO magazine, popular among younger West Germans. As a result, new fans were attracted to cowboy and Indianist hobbyist groups, as well as to a variety of Karl May–related clubs.[61]

Some of the new clubs focused on the films themselves, while others were devoted to following the career of a particular actor; Pierre Brice, who played Winnetou in the 1960s films, and later in Bad Segeberg productions, had an enthusiastic fan following.[62] As in other fandoms, the production of new films and television shows also opens up new opportunities for fan tourism, since enthusiasts could now organize fan pilgrimage tourism to sites where May movies had been filmed, which supplemented older fan tourism to locations in the United States mentioned in May's stories. Besides the film location tourism popular among fans, Karl May films opened up other options for fan organization and activities: collecting and trading props, costumes, stills, and other objects associated with the movies; researching and discussing the films' scripts and production processes; and collecting and discussing the mountain of film spin-off publications and merchandising that by themselves, could and do fill a museum.[63]

In West Germany, "friends of Karl May" could also finally organize the sort of formal, well-established literary society that had eluded them under previous political regimes. May enthusiasts who were sophisticated in terms of literary scholarship and the canon had long been dissatisfied with the "popular," often expurgated editions offered by the publisher, and had circulated mimeographed newsletters that analyzed May's life and works in some detail. In 1963 they formed a working group to research a critical and scholarly biography of May.[64] The biography never appeared, but the project itself drew its members together so that in 1969 sixteen of them founded the Karl May Society, or KMG. There was only one woman in the founding group, which consisted largely of educated professionals, including several professors. The KMG became the most serious-minded and socially and culturally upscale of the postwar May fan organizations and became the largest literary society in Germany by 2000.[65]

Like contemporary literary associations in the English-speaking world, the KMG hosted an annual weekend and dinner, meeting annually in different towns, each site associated with some stage of May's career. The tone of its meetings tended to be earnest and scholarly, setting this segment of the May community apart from the reenactment cowboy and Indianist clubs or other gatherings of Western fans. The 1973 KMG gathering held in Regensburg was typical, in that participants gathered in a hotel for a good meal, followed by a lecture, music, sociability, and May-related presentations. Dr. Heinz Stolte spoke on "The Journey Within," which touched on the style and truths contained in May's Middle Eastern novels. The talk was followed by music, as a member played pieces by Debussy and Max Reger. In its account of the gathering, the *Süddeutsche Zeitung* noted dryly that "a large, somewhat darkened photo of the 'storyteller from Radebeul' graced the top of the concert piano—which resembled a sarcophagus—and which lent the meeting a suitable dignity." There were also tables where visitors could purchase KMG publications and other fan memorabilia.[66]

The social profile of the KMG was similar to that of early Sherlockian societies: the KMG was overwhelmingly male, although the percentage of women increased by the 1980s. Compared to younger fans' film clubs, the KMG was financially fairly secure. During the 1980s and 1990s, the KMG became more socially inclusive. But the KMG was only the most erudite end of a broad continuum of fan organizations and activities that revolved around May, Indian characters or Indigenous cultures, and Westerns in West Germany. At the less-serious end of that spectrum, many fans who also bought pulp Westerns, Western-style clothing, and joined less serious clubs were working-class or lower middle-class.[67]

The primary focus of the KMG was scholarship by and for "friends of Karl May," published analysis about the author and his story world. Like the body of work published by Sherlockians, such fan writing could range from the erudite to amateur, or the simply antiquarian and genealogical. Sometimes it drew on quite serious amateur research or even work undertaken as a labor of love by academics; or, it might be only an expression of the author's own interpretations. Running this gamut, fan scholarship became an area that the KMG cultivated with considerable success. In almost all cases, the KMG's publications aimed to illuminate and also to rehabilitate Karl May's literary legacy. In their eyes, Karl May was one of the greatest German writers, and they hoped to persuade the broader literary establishment of this as well.

Karl May's publisher had sponsored a *Karl-May-Jahrbuch* during the Weimar period, but its productions were far surpassed by the KMG's postwar research and publications. The KMG supported the publication of authoritative editions of May's many novels, since the publisher had issued abridged editions during the interwar period, which the society sought to supersede. The society also located and brought back into print his lesser-known works, as well as issuing a substantive yearbook packed with well-researched discussions of the author's life and analysis of his life and stories from every possible vantage point. It also circulated a newsletter for the entire fan community.

The KMG's political and cultural capital enabled it to do more than simply publish prolifically, however; after Germany's reunification, it amassed a fund of 3.5 million Marks in donations and state grants. This funding was used to purchase the entire contents of Karl May's dwelling from his publisher, which had inherited May's effects, in order to refurbish and furnish May's home, the Villa Shatterhand, in Radebeul, and restore it to how it had appeared during May's lifetime. May's papers remained in the publisher's hands, but the KMG pushed successfully to have them declared a "national cultural resource," which meant that they could not be sold abroad or divided up for domestic resale.[68]

Like the torrent of mid-twentieth-century Sherlockian scholarship, KMG publications were painstakingly exhaustive in their exploration of the author and his imagined world. They included analyses of the influences on May's novels;

philosophy and religion in May's works; a multitude of pieces on Indigenous cultures; various facets of the North American landscape; poems and other tidbits penned by May; articles on Arabian horses and the Middle Eastern settings of some May novels; defenses of May's literary value; weaponry in Karl May; Karl May's influence on other writers and on German culture; and many other substantive contributions to May scholarship. In its first thirty years, the KMG publications amounted to over 33,000 pages of material.[69]

To an outsider, this wide-ranging fan scholarship might seem like an eye-glazing obsession with minute details in May's stories. But for true May fans they were ambrosia, just as the summer theatrical performances "freely" based on Karl May or activities organized around May films attracted their own enthusiastic devotees. The attraction, especially for fictional source canons, was evergreen because the fan discourse was open-ended, since a multitude of readings were possible for each text. Writing about fans of other media, media scholar Henry Jenkins has argued that for fans, texts "assume increased significance as they are fragmented and reworked to accommodate the particular interests of the individual listener," an observation that also applies to Karl May fans.[70]

Thus, May fans mined the author's stories or details about his life, pulling out bits and details from various stories that they could knit together and use as a springboard for their own interpretations: speculation in essays about the origins of May's complicated worldview, or the sources of information he had used in describing an American West he had never actually visited, etc. Or a May fan might write his or her derivative fiction, which retold a plot originally given by May from the perspective of a different character, or help to produce a summer theatrical that brought Winnetou back to life, in defiance of the original novel's ending. Other May fans might publish pieces discussing cinematography, locations, and script adaptations, comparing the East and West German films. The published fan discourse on May, now free of restraint from both the publisher and state authorities, grew steadily over decades in West Germany until it almost rivaled the output of the Sherlockians. And as the East German regime liberalized its views on May after the mid-1980s, and finally collapsed in 1989, Western fans in East Germany also gained the freedom to broaden their own activities and discussions.

The novels and tales about May's life, almost as interesting to fans as the stories themselves, accumulated individual meanings for May fans through such use, reworking, and reinterpretation. So, one fan could develop and propound his theory about the complicated history surrounding May's convictions, while another might dispute that interpretation in the next issue of the society's journal. Other articles might discuss the uses of psychoanalytic theory for understanding one of May's characters, or where a particular scene in a May film was shot in Croatia. Amateur fan productions of May theatricals rewrote the original storyline in important respects, adding in beloved television series characters, or even Abraham Lincoln in one production. In the process of parsing and analyzing, these fans were "breaking up" canon texts into pieces just like their counterparts in other literary fandoms, pulling details out of stories and reworking them into new analyses of May's life or of the stories' world and characters.

In so doing, they made May's world their own, by creating their own analysis of the stories and characters, and thus blurring the line between consumption and production of entertainments. They became producers of new interpretations and extensions of the original story world and circulated these interpretations among other fans. The May fandom and German Western fan communities had always been participatory and often experiential. But after 1970, the work done by May fans became increasingly transformative as well, reworking the original story world to suit their own tastes.

Visits to the locations in Croatia used in the popular Karl May movies of the 1960s could also be deeply compelling for true fans, as one May film authority noted:

> for the uninitiated, it's sometimes hard to grasp why Insiders discuss the question of which granite cliff was the exact spot where Winnetou (Pierre Brice) and Old Shatterhand (Lex Barker) shook each other's hand [in the movie]. But actually we see here one of the most fundamental aspects of any Karl-May [fan creation] . . . the joy of research, of following up on clues and of discovery. And just as the reader [of the books] feels satisfaction when Old Shatterhand pieces together what the plot is of the tramps [he's tracking] from apparently meaningless small details, so too it fills the film scene tourist with awe to realize that he is standing exactly where the cameras captured Winnetou's death on film (which in fact can only be accomplished at some risk to life, since the area is ridden with landmines).[71]

In such discussions, the fan tourist tracked down clues, made inferences, and proposed theories to explain a small mystery. Here, and in other activities, deeply engaged fans became detectives of their canon.[72]

Fans' engagement with their object of fandom might shape not only their social relationships but also their households: a leading member of the KMG, Carl-Heinz Dömken, was an artist who put his professional skills to use in his fandom. He painted portraits of Karl May at different life stages that the KMG reproduced and distributed widely. Because of his attachment to the May novels set in Arabia, he also bred Arabian horses at his small property in the countryside outside of Celle. His home, where he sometimes hosted fan gatherings, was decorated with Western memorabilia. Dömken's fannish engagement thus influenced his home, social life, and other hobbies decisively, linking him to a cohesive community of Karl May fans.[73]

Fans who organized around Karl May's novels or films were only one part of the Western fandom in West Germany, however. After the collapse of the East German government, and the reunification of the two Germanies in 1990, East German fans could be more openly involved in both Karl May fandom, and in a Western fan community that included white North American role-play, country western music and dance, and culture rooted in an imagined Old West. For Germans in former West Germany, the reunification of Germany allowed easier access to the historic sites associated with Karl May's life, and Radebeul once again became an important center of Western fan gatherings and pilgrimages.

After 1990, German Western fans began to organize a variety of different celebrations that often involved more explicit Karl May focused role-play or costuming. "Karl May Gatherings," which would qualify as fan conventions in the English-speaking world, were organized annually after 1992, usually in conjunction with the open-air performances of May plays, in Bad Segeberg, Berlin, Radebeul, and in Karl May's birthplace, Hohenstein-Ernstthal, as well. Other costumed celebrations large and small became common in the 1990s, including the "Karl May Star Riders," a costumed horseback pilgrimage visiting several summer open-air theatrical sites across Germany organized by well-known May fan Renate Klücker.[74]

The tone of such costumed Karl May fan gatherings by the late 1980s was often droll, featuring a playful approach to staging characters and events from Karl May's world that was much less earnest than the KMG's scholarship and quite different from the cowboy and Indianist clubs' focus on authenticity. Rather than seeking to re-create a lost historical world, as most reenactment hobbyists were doing, costumed Karl May fans were engaging in an exercise of ironic imagination akin to role-play at an American Renaissance Faire. They tended to be younger than many cowboy and Indianist hobbyists, and approached their gatherings with a somewhat more tongue-in-cheek attitude. By the late twentieth century, May fans had long since come to terms with the fact that May had been a tale-teller. Because they knew he was a fabulist, some May fans were now more willing to see his as an imaginary world. Parts of the May scene became less concerned with minute details of authenticity, therefore, and their tone more playful.

As Michael Saler has observed of Sherlock Holmes fans, these fans "were not so much willingly suspending their disbelief in a fictional character as willingly believing in him with the double-minded awareness that they were engaged in pretense."[75] This ironic "belief" in the reality of Karl May's stories and characters gave these fans an imaginary, fictionalized world to immerse themselves in. The performative aspects of costume, artifacts, horses, playing with whips, lassoes, or knife-throwing, re-creations of scenes and activities from the novels, etc. (role-play and performance) created a sort of time-warp effect, as assemblies of costumed fans evoked a quaint, fun, and heavily fictionalized pocket of the historic American West.

The spectrum of Western fan interests in unified Germany—ranging from the playful to the painstakingly mimetic—were brought together annually in Radebeul starting in the 1990s for the "Karl May Days," an eclectic Western festival attracting Western fans and reenactors from across Germany. The Radebeul event offers an impressive array of activities, beginning with pre-festival lectures and performances at the Karl May Museum offered by the KMG, hobbyists, and others. The festival itself is set up on extensive grounds on the edge of town and includes fantasy re-creations of different aspects of nineteenth-century American cultures. In the "Little Tombstone" area, stunt cowboys demonstrate trick shooting and other skills, and sometimes performers dressed as Wyatt Earp and his group re-create the O.K. Corral showdown, while open stages host performances of an assortment of Karl May stories. The Star Riders have their own encampment elsewhere, while Civil War reenactors, both Union and Confederate, have their own separate "military camps." Children can pan for gold in a specially equipped stream or ride on a historical steam engine train, while a bluegrass and country western music festival takes place in another area. In the festival's early years, local Indianist hobbyists demonstrated their crafts and art forms, but after 2000, they were replaced by paid Indigenous North American artists and performers.[76]

With its mélange of American historical fantasy and Indigenous perform-ers, Radebeul festival attracts both casual and dedicated German Western fans. One observer was particularly struck by "its eclecticism that combines Native American performers and artists with representations of 'Indians,' reenactors with sports competitors, religious and ritual expression, cultural information with entertainment and commercialism, theater with dance and singing, earnest and comical role-play, artistry and artificiality.... [An] agglomeration of hybrid representations and festival elements and of playful and festive behaviors forms the core of the Karl May scene."[77]

But in a sense, the Radebeul festival and other, vibrant aspects of Germans' engagement with the American West—fan gatherings at Bad Segeberg theatricals and elsewhere, popular Western theme parks, or the "flag parade" performances of the Wild West Girls and Boys Club—represent the persistence and victory of historical fantasy over historical mimetic accuracy. As discussed in Chapter 6, German Western fans who valued historical authenticity were drifting out of Western reenactment by 2010, and instead were attracted to American Civil War or other military history reenactment groups. The Western fans who persist in the Karl May scene have become more tongue-in-cheek, and many consciously root their activities in a fictionalized setting.

Festivals like Radebeul's remind us that German Western fandom was in-spired over a century ago by *fictional* narratives of the American West: Buffalo Bill's *Wild West Show*, and Karl May's and other Western fiction writers' fantasy cowboys and Indians. Fictions often persist because they are, after all, inherently open-ended. They can be reworked and retold to fit the evolving needs of suc-cessive generations of Western fans. But the pursuit of authenticity, immersion in a painstakingly re-created historical mimesis that is rooted in current histor-ical scholarship, requires more research and effort, and thus has a higher entry threshold. And the claim to authenticity could sometimes leave fans open to challenges by others, discussed in Chapter 5, who see themselves as the owners of the historical culture that is being reenacted. By the late twentieth century, Western fans in several fandoms would be obliged to come to terms with the resistance and resurgence of Indigenous North American cultures, and the de-cline of Frederick Jackson Turner's frontier thesis narrative of American his-tory. The early twentieth-century consensus American history underlying the fictionalized histories that originally attracted fans, was itself under challenge, and was being rewritten.

# CHAPTER FOUR

# Little Houses on the Prairie

Pockets of the American Old West, developing over the course of the twentieth century, are strewn across Germany. During the same decades, reminders of another, more personalized frontier past were re-created or preserved across the American Midwest: the many farms and homes associated with a little girl whose family moved across the Plains in a covered wagon during the late nineteenth century. Laura Ingalls Wilder's first book, *Little House in the Big Woods*, begins with a description of the isolated log cabin not far from the Mississippi River where she was born in 1867: "the Big Woods stood all around the house ... as far as a man could go to the north in a day, or a week, or a whole month, there was nothing but woods."[1] The book tells how her mother grew vegetables and herbs and made their clothing, while her father hunted game for meat. The family preserved and prepared delicious foods and made everything they needed on a cozy, self-sufficient farm. But ultimately her father, land hungry and footloose, decided to sell the farm and take the family west. They would not come to rest permanently until they reached De Smet, South Dakota, ten years later.

The property in western Wisconsin where Laura's family built a log cabin, planted crops, and churned butter each week is still a peaceful and pleasant spot, a few miles outside of the small town of Pepin, Wisconsin. The original cabin is long gone, but the Pepin Laura Ingalls Wilder Memorial Society built a replica log cabin on the site in 1976, modeled on the description of its design given in the novel.[2] *Little House* fans come to see the replica from around the world, and many also visit the other Laura Ingalls Wilder "homesites," following a fan pilgrimage route across the Midwest that retraces the Ingalls's family journeys.

FIGURE 8. The homesites and museums established to memorialize Laura Ingalls Wilder and her family. The midwestern sites form a popular fan pilgrimage route. Map by William Nelson.

These are restored homes, or sometimes replicas of the original buildings, where visitors are drawn to see and touch the places where Laura and her family lived. A second replica log cabin built thirteen miles outside of Independence, Kansas (the setting of a later book in the series, *Little House on the Prairie*) is furnished with items like those described in the novel: a red-checkered tablecloth on the table and a china shepherdess over the fireplace. It's easy to imagine the Ingalls's daily life there.

Wendy McClure, who has visited most of the homesites, wrote that after reading and rereading the books as a young girl, the stories were so compelling and real that for her and her friends, Laura

> became a part of us somehow. She existed fully formed in our heads, her memories swimming around in our brains with our own . . . [the *Little House* books] gave me the uncanny sense that I'd experienced everything she had, that I had nearly drowned in the same flooded creek [Plum Creek], endured the grasshopper plague of 1875, and lived through the Hard Winter. . . . For a while I had a close imaginary friendship with the Laura of *On the Banks of Plum Creek*. . . . I daydreamed that she'd shown up in the twentieth century and I had to be her guide. I've discovered from talking to friends that this was a common desire.[3]

McClure is not unusual among *Little House* readers. In De Smet, South Dakota, I spoke with a local resident who told me about a friend who had moved to the town from another part of the country because Laura had lived there. Like many fans of the *Little House* series, this friend generally referred to the author simply as "Laura," and as with McClure, Laura was very real in her imagination. A woman who lived in a different midwestern homesite town and who had met many Wilder fans noted to me that "Most fans [who come here] have a heartfelt connection to Laura in the here and now and [some] feel that she's their best friend. When they come to [this town] there is a frisson of excitement because they can feel this energy that she left behind in this place."[4] For fan visitors, the stories they love and physical reality converge at the homesites, an experience that fuses history and fiction.

The first book in the *Little House* series was published in 1932; over the next decade, Wilder wrote seven more novels, concluding her story arc with her last book, published in 1943. A ninth book in the series (based on a draft manuscript found in the author's papers) was published after Wilder's death. The series follows the lives of a white settler family as it moves westward during the late nineteenth century. Since the books were written for the same entertainment "marketplaces of remembrance" of white settler–Indian relations discussed in Chapter 1, Wilder's story world generally aligns with the framework of other early and mid-twentieth-century Western genre fiction and entertainments discussed in this book. Indian characters or their communities are inevitably displaced in such stories, and replaced by white American settlers who build farms and small

FIGURE 9. The "Wayside" (replica) Ingalls Cabin near Pepin, Wisconsin. Photo by author.

towns in a wilderness. But unlike most Western entertainments of this period, Wilder's novels focus on the lives of white women on the frontier as embodied in the life of one family: *Little House* is thus a thoroughly domestic frontier series.[5]

The *Little House* fandom is also interesting for another reason: like its protagonist, a strong majority of its members are white women. Some are descended from frontier settler families, and they are all attracted to the fandom by their affection for and identification with Laura and her family. Like the German Western fans discussed in earlier chapters, this is an experiential fandom with many participatory activities, but the Wilder fandom is focused on the material culture and crafts of white female settlers, along with research and debate about their lives. Women make up the majority of the rank-and-file fans who visit the homesites or engage in other activities discussed in this chapter. The preponderance of women in the community is reflected in the term some fans use for themselves, "bonnet heads." The Mansfield Museum supervisor, Vicki Johnston, estimates that about 85 percent of their non-school field trip visitors are women with their friends or children, sometimes bringing their husbands with them. Some groups of visitors are multigenerational, with a grandmother, mother, and daughter who are all fans of the books. Groups of middle-aged female friends often travel to the homesites together on vacation, as well.[6] They come so that they can connect with Laura.

The "Laura" that fans are drawn to was the protagonist of one of the bestselling and most beloved series in American children's literature, and of the television series loosely based on the books, *Little House on the Prairie*. But Laura Ingalls Wilder (1867–1957) was also a real person, who wrote the *Little House* books. She was raised in a loving but economically insecure family, whose father (Charles, or "Pa" Ingalls) relocated the family repeatedly. As a result, Wilder's relics, memorial museums, and homesites are scattered across the Midwest, in the series of small towns where she and members of her family lived: Pepin, Wisconsin (the setting for *Little House in the Big Woods*); the farm property near Independence, Kansas (*Little House on the Prairie*); Walnut Grove, Minnesota (*On the Banks of Plum Creek* and also where the TV series was set); Burr Oak, Iowa (a sojourn omitted from Wilder's stories); De Smet, South Dakota (where four of her novels are set); and Spring Valley, Minnesota (where she briefly lived after the series ended).[7] The largest homesite (in terms of the annual number of visitors) is in the Ozarks, in Mansfield, Missouri, where Wilder lived for most of her adult life, wrote her books, and is buried. There is an additional homesite where the author's husband, Almanzo Wilder, grew up near Malone, New York (*Farmer Boy*).

Some of the homesites are solid examples of open-air museums, or even of the living history movement, offering heritage interpretations of the material culture associated with the Ingalls and Wilders. Living history, discussed in more detail in Chapter 6, was a growing trend in American museums during the same decades that the Wilder homesites were being established: living history sites that use interpreters, usually in costume, to simulate life in the past, often working with re-created artifacts in restored or re-created structures.[8] Colonial Williamsburg is perhaps the best known and most lavishly funded example of this type of institution. In Walnut Grove, the Wilder Museum offers a more modest set of experiences, geared to the period when the Ingalls lived in the town: visitors can walk through a dugout home and a homesteader's shanty, and see a prairie town post office, newspaper office, and dry goods store. Particularly iconic objects of prairie settlers' culture—a one-room schoolhouse and

FIGURE 10. A one-room schoolhouse built in 1871 near Independence, Kansas. The owners of the Kansas Wilder homesite purchased and moved the schoolhouse to their site in 1977, to show visitors what public schools looked like during Laura's childhood. Original nineteenth-century one-room schoolhouses can be found at several Wilder homesites. Photo by author.

a covered wagon—are found here and at most Wilder homesites, along with detailed explanations of the Homestead Act and the work and living conditions of the first white settlers.

The Ingalls's homestead site, just outside De Smet, is now a living history farm designed to engage visitors of all ages, with guides (in modern clothing) who explain or demonstrate for visitors the variety of skills, artifacts, and building types associated with homesteading of that era. The site includes a tool shop, a barn with live animals, a replica home modeled on the dwelling described in Charles Ingalls's homestead claim, and another dugout dwelling and settler's claim shanty. Visitors can ride in a covered wagon to experience a "lesson" in a one-room schoolhouse, or walk through a lovely small Lutheran church established in 1881 (now defunct) brought to the site from a nearby town. The Malone homesite, far distant from the others, contains the restored farmhouse that Almanzo Wilder grew up in, and replica barns and outbuildings comprehensively outfitted with mid-nineteenth-century tools and equipment. Tour guides and exhibits offer visitors lively explanations into the work processes and lifestyle of mid-nineteenth-century farming families like the Wilders.

In the town of De Smet, costumed guides offer visitors tours of two homes where the Ingalls actually lived, carefully furnished with objects that belonged to them, or their contemporaries. The attention to detail is meticulous, down to the painstaking restoration of the wallpaper patterns shown in photographs taken of the Ingalls in their final home. The De Smet buildings maintained by the Laura Ingalls Wilder Memorial Society also include the actual one-room schoolhouse attended by the Ingalls daughters, where visitors can reenact key scenes from one of the books, as well as a replica of the shanty schoolhouse where Wilder taught before her marriage, with a museum exhibit and separate learning center for children. The restored or replica buildings re-create and fuse both history and Wilder's stories for visitors. As at all *Little House* homesites, there is a gift shop offering a colorful array of Wilder-related or American history spin-off merchandise, including the ubiquitous, brightly colored calico "prairie dresses" and sunbonnets.

Both the De Smet homesite and the Mansfield homesite have cultivated close connections with their state historical associations and school districts and as a result are well-known regional history resources. Both are popular field trip sites for their states' schools, and receive a steady stream of schoolchildren through the academic year. The majority of their adult visitors, however, are *Little House* fans.

The tour guides in the De Smet buildings are not the only costumed participants. Some visitors come to the sites wearing long calico prairie dresses and sunbonnets (most are girls, but some are adult women), reflecting the fact that the homesites are a locus for both living history interpretations and fan pilgrimages. Participants at the "Laura Days" held annually by the Wilder homesite in Pepin, Wisconsin, also sometimes come in period dress complete with calico bonnets. For *Little House* fans, the homesites offer more than the usual attractions of living history sites. They house the actual artifacts that feature prominently in the stories, or that were used or even made by Laura herself: Pa's fiddle (prominently mentioned in every one of the books); the Spode china that belonged to adult Laura; clothing, quilts, and lace made by Laura or her family members; and the small china box that Laura received in *On the Banks of Plum Creek*. These are

FIGURE 11. A bread plate, mentioned in the final Wilder book, at the
Mansfield Wilder Museum. Photo by author.

storied possessions, which bring an imagined world into a material reality that
fans can see with their own eyes.

Beyond the Ingalls's household goods, the homesites offer fans the experience of walking in Laura's footsteps and being present at the places where
the books' events actually took place. Fans can wander across the homestead
land that Charles Ingalls filed a claim for in De Smet. Like Laura, they can and
do wade in Plum Creek, not far from Walnut Grove. They visit Laura's grave
in Mansfield, and those of her parents and sisters in De Smet. They explore
the kitchen and bedrooms of the same farmhouse where Almanzo worked and
played, in *Farmer Boy,* and pump water in the Wilders' pumphouse. In scholarly
literature, journeys to spaces where stories were filmed or took place are called
"fan pilgrimages." The term captures the deep significance of the experience
for some homesite visitors, since as with pilgrimages to sacred spaces, visits to
the homesites can "generate feelings of an extraordinary, authentic encounter"
with Laura and her world.[9]

In her study of North American colonial settlement living history museums,
anthropologist Laura Peers noted that "visitors respond strongly to the physicality
of historic reconstructions: their buildings, props, costumes, trade goods, and

food . . . [and to] the physical stimuli offered by these places: touching, tasting, smelling, hearing, drinking in the view. More than anything else, historic reconstructions are distinctive forms of communication and experience because of their rich materiality."[10] The Wilder homesites offer visitors the same sensory experiences of the past, but with the added fillip of knowing that these physical locations and objects are actually the same (or in the case of mass-produced items, sometimes identical replicas) as those that the Ingalls themselves experienced. Wilder homesite pilgrimages thus resemble both journeys made to celebrities' homes (like Graceland) and historical fictional pilgrimages (like those to sites where Jane Austen or Sherlock Holmes stories were set). One resident of a homesite town who has interacted with hundreds of Wilder fans commented on how they responded to being where Laura had lived:

> I sort of marvel at the people who travel great distances [to come here] and wonder what they're looking for, and whether they find it. For them there's this magical energy here. That's very important to people [that they can come to where the story took place].[11]

Fan pilgrimages are common in media fandoms; the Balkan locations where Karl May movies were filmed, for example, are perennial draws for May fans. But the Wilder homesites are interesting because they offer an unusual type of fan pilgrimage. No one can visit Hogwarts, of course, and the apartment at 221B Baker Street never really existed (although the house number was claimed by the Sherlock Holmes Museum in 1990). Nonetheless, Sherlock or Harry Potter fans regularly visit locations where the stories were set or where scenes were filmed. A unique aspect of the Little Houses fandom is that—to a degree that has no or few peers in other fiction-based fandoms—real locations are available to visit where the events described in the books actually took place, rather than just being imagined to have taken place there or filmed there. Real artifacts that were used, made, or worn by the "characters" can be seen. The cottonwood trees that Pa planted in 1880, described in By the Shores of Silver Lake, are still there. Fans can take home twigs from the same trees: fan relics. The homesite guides teach visitors how to twist hay or grind wheat, just as Laura did during The Long Winter, or show them how to braid rag rugs or make patchwork quilts, which Laura and her family made. Fans can therefore walk where Laura did, and experience the homesites in ways that are, for them, profoundly meaningful, because they can connect with Laura, surrounded by the setting and crafts of her life and those of her family.

Wilder's enthusiasts can do this because the *Little House* books tread a very fine line between history and literature, as fictionalized autobiography. Laura Ingalls Wilder always insisted that everything in her stories had really happened: "all I have told is true," she wrote, "but it is not the whole truth."[12] Some of her omissions of painful or embarrassing incidents could be explained by the fact that she was writing for children: for example, the fact that the Ingalls's baby son had died during one of their journeys; or that both parents and daughters had worked for over a year in a hotel in Burr Oak, which was demeaning work, by her contemporaries' standards. Sometimes the stories are skewed to reflect Wilder's own political convictions, or those of her daughter Rose, who was a leading intellectual in the mid-twentieth-century American libertarian movement.[13]

The omissions or evasions are unimportant to many homesite visitors, in any case. Most are not disturbed by the fact (if they know it) that Laura lived in Walnut Grove during two different periods and not only once (as the books lead us to believe) and omitted the family's stay in Burr Oak. Many *Little House* fans see the stories as classic literature that is rooted in historical reality, and the homesites and their artifacts as reflecting the American national biography and historical narrative discussed in Chapter 1. The experiential focus of the fandom, where fans can themselves see and experience the homesites, helps to reinforce that conviction.

## Fiction, Politics, and Historical Fact in the *Little House* Series

With the exception of *Farmer Boy*, the stories in Wilder's series are told from the point of view of Laura, and describe the journeys of her family and the events of her childhood and teenage years. The novels published in her lifetime end with her "happily ever after" marriage to Almanzo Wilder at the age of eighteen. Laura's father Pa is the moral center of the novels. His never-failing optimism, resourcefulness, hard work, good cheer, and affection for his family—along with the serenity and steadiness of Laura's mother, Ma—provide the children with a sense of security, even as their parents repeatedly uproot the family in search of a better life.

The novel begins in a snug cabin in the Wisconsin woods, full of good foods grown and processed by the family in a subsistence farming lifestyle. But her father moves the family in a covered wagon to "Indian territory" in today's Kansas, hoping for a better and larger farm once the Indians are compelled to leave by the government. The area is not turned over by the federal government to white settlers as quickly as Pa expected, however, and the Ingalls family packs up its covered wagon and moves to Walnut Grove, Minnesota about a year later. They live in a dugout by Plum Creek, a home dug into the prairie sod, partially underground. They later build a house, but their crops fail after an extraordinary plague of grasshoppers destroys everything that grows and devastates the surrounding countryside. Laura's sister Mary falls ill, becoming permanently blind.

Pa leaves to find work as a railroad paymaster (a challenging position) since a rail line is being laid to connect the Dakota Territory to Minnesota. He ultimately decides to move his family to the territory, which has been opened to white homesteaders, and where no Indian communities apparently remain. The landscape is enchanting but emptied of people or buffalo (the history of Indigenous peoples in this region and the historical context of settler relations with Indigenous cultures will be discussed in Chapter 5).

There, the Ingalls homestead a farm near De Smet, today in South Dakota. They endure hunger and great hardship there during the Hard Winter of 1880/81, as frequent blizzards and packed snow cut off the town (and much of the Midwest) for months from trains that brought in food. Many in the town lived on turnips and ground wheat, and only a dangerous journey by young Almanzo Wilder, who finds a farmer who has wheat to sell, saves some of the town residents from starvation.

De Smet later prospers, and the Wilder family was ultimately able to prove their homestead claim. Laura earns a teacher's certificate at the age of fifteen, and works as a teacher in a one-room shanty schoolhouse to earn money so that Mary can attend a school for the blind in Iowa. Almanzo begins to court her during this period and they marry in 1885, moving into the comfortable home that he has built for his bride on his own homestead. They have their own livestock and land, not far from her family. At the end of the last novel published by Wilder, their future seems full of promise.

The novels include a wealth of fascinating details about the material culture, lifestyle, and handicrafts of the settlers: how to make your own bullets by pouring melted lead into molds; descriptions of how to create a variety of clothing and textiles; information about diet and food preparation; the training and care of livestock; the design and building of homes; and how crops are planted and grown on the prairies. A typical and popular scene from the first book describes in detail how Ma makes butter with her daughters' help:

[Ma] churned a long time . . . [when she] took off the churn cover, there was the butter in a golden lump, drowning in the buttermilk . . . [and] salted it. Now came the best part of the churning. Ma molded the butter. On the loose bottom of the wooden butter-mold was carved the picture of a strawberry with two strawberry leaves. With the paddle Ma packed butter tightly into the mold until it was full. Then she turned it upside-down over a plate. . . . The little, firm pat of golden butter came out, with the strawberry and its leaves molded on the top.

Butter molds, particularly those with strawberry designs, thus carry meaning for Laura's fans; churns, too, are frequently featured in homesite displays. The stories convey a sense of how everyday production was carried on, in a setting where the beauty of the prairies and its wildlife are described in beguiling, often lyrical prose.

The stories also reflect the worldview of Wilder, and that of her daughter Rose Wilder Lane. Rose collaborated with her mother on the novels, editing each of them, rewriting some scenes, and offering advice. Both women loathed the New Deal policies of Franklin Roosevelt, and were deeply committed to a philosophy of individual self-sufficiency. As a result, the Ingalls family is depicted as being somewhat more isolated and self-sufficient than it actually was, and community organizations, communitarian activities, and government support for frontier communities, e.g., removing Indigenous peoples from their lands to make room for white settlement, are usually downplayed in the books. Rose Wilder Lane was one of the founders of the American libertarian movement, and she left the copyrights to most of the *Little House* books (and thus their royalties and television rights) to Roger MacBride, later a Libertarian Party presidential candidate. The *Little House* books therefore offer a vision of American history and culture in which each person and household is resolutely self-sufficient and does not look for help from the government.[14] Churches form the heart of community life in the stories, and Laura's parents help to found a Congregational church in both Walnut Grove and De Smet.

Another branch of the Little House story world and fandom is rooted in the very successful television series *Little House on the Prairie*, which premiered in 1974; it ran for eight seasons and is still shown in syndication. The television show was very loosely based on Wilder's books (arguably, not at all after the first season), and largely reflected the values and ideas of Michael Landon. Landon, who had previously starred in *Bonanza* (a globally popular Western television series), was one of the show's two executive producers. He directed almost half of the episodes, and played Charles Ingalls, Laura's father, in the series. Landon ensured that the series focused on cohesive, harmonious family life, and also included themes rooted in Christian faith and conservative values. It attracted a broad audience that included Ronald Reagan, and became popular with conservative and Christian organizations.[15]

Wilder's insistence that "all I have told is true, but it is not the whole truth" was surely made in good faith. She omitted some facts, and elided other calamities or failures on her father's part. Although she did not acknowledge it, some of the material had to be reconstructed from what her family had told her and contained inaccuracies. She was probably too young at the time to remember much that was described in *Little House on the Prairie*, for example, which was largely based on her own later research and her family's memories of the period. She and Rose also omitted additional details that conflicted with their political worldview, including the fact that Mary's tuition at her school for the blind was paid for by the state, or the significant role that the federal government had in subsidizing railroad building. But by and large, what she put into the stories probably matched up with her own memories and understanding of her family, childhood, and youth. Unlike Karl May, she had actually lived in the time and place she was writing about; but historians would still see the books as literature, rather than history.

Publications about Wilder's life that followed traditional historiographical standards based on a wealth of primary sources came later, and in abundance. We need not speculate as to the differences between the anecdotes in her books and the historical realities of her life, or what she chose to omit: Wilder scholars have done a tremendous amount of research in this area.[16] The core of this fandom's interest is the life of Laura Ingalls Wilder, the lives of her relatives and neighbors, and the culture she lived in: this engagement with Wilder's life and times drives the attendance at the homesites. But serious Wilder enthusiasts, including those who are professional academics, have gone beyond the homesites, creating a rich body of secondary literature, biographies, and other analyses about Wilder's life.

Wilder concluded her series at the very start of her marriage, with an implicit "happily ever after" ending. Doing so allowed her and her readers to easily fit her family's story into the "frontier thesis" narrative of American national identity and history promoted by Wilder's frontier-born contemporary, Frederick

Jackson Turner. There is no evidence that Wilder had read Turner's influential essay, but as one biographer noted, "she was certainly a Turnerian in the sense that she had imbibed many of his ideas from the culture around her and agreed with him on the central importance of the frontier to American life."[17] While Turner's research focused on the actions and accomplishments of white male frontier settlers, Wilder's stories complemented his narrative by including settler women's activities and points of view: building homes and families, planting gardens, and sustaining prairie communities. Both authors saw frontier communities as central to American democracy, and presented optimistic descriptions of American westward expansion.[18] Wilder's warm and loving descriptions of the Ingalls's happy family life, in particular, made homesteading seem more successful than it was for many who filed claims.

In fact, Wilder's adult life, and the later lives of her family and contemporaries, demonstrated the shortcomings and sometimes false promises of the Homestead Act familiar in recent historiography of the American West. The Plains were much more arid than the Old Northwest and unsuitable for the farming methods used on the typical acreage of farms in the Eastern half of the United States. The Plains and Rockies thus presented formidable challenges to homesteaders who arrived without a great deal of capital to help them develop their farms and stay afloat during hard times. White Americans' extermination of the bison herds and plowing of grasslands that had existed for thousands of years upset a delicately-balanced ecology, and recurring droughts could turn plowed land into dustbowls. Land speculation by East Coast investors and railroad companies was rampant, and only a minority of the lands claimed under the Homestead Act ultimately went to small farmers. Undercapitalized and unable to withstand the recurrent cycles of drought and other climate-related crop losses, less than half of those who filed for a homestead could persist long enough to "prove" the claim and receive title to it.[19] Wilder's own parents were able to prove their claim, but they could not succeed at farming over the long run. Charles Ingalls sold their homestead and moved the family into De Smet a few years after "proving" the claim; the Ingalls parents spent the rest of their lives in the town.[20]

Laura Wilder and her new husband faced "the same bleak reality as all farmers across the Plains."[21] Almanzo Wilder had gone into debt to purchase farm equipment and build the house. A hailstorm destroyed their wheat crop about a year into their marriage, when Wilder was pregnant with Rose. The Wilders owned their farmland but had not yet proven a second land claim filed by Almanzo, where he had built their home. They mortgaged their land to pay their debts and rented out the comfortable house that Almanzo had built for Laura on their second land claim, moving into a shanty where Rose was born in 1886. Their barn burned down; the next harvest was poor; and then both of them came down with diphtheria in 1888. Almanzo was left partially disabled, and they were forced to sell their mortgaged farm, moving to the second land claim, and planted new crops. As it had year after year, the next harvest failed, and the Wilder's second child, a boy, died shortly after his birth. A few weeks later, a cooking fire got out of control and burned down their home. Defeated, the Wilders gave up their second land claim before it was proven and moved in with Almanzo's parents in Spring Valley for a year.[22]

By that time, the drought and other climate-related setbacks in the Dakotas had been so severe and so long-lasting that, like thousands of other Plains settlers, the Wilders gave up on farming there. They ultimately moved their daughter and remaining goods in a covered wagon down to the Ozarks, where drought would no longer thwart their efforts. Both husband and wife worked hard for years to rebuild their finances. Almanzo drove a delivery wagon while Laura proved to be tenaciously entrepreneurial. She took in boarders, sold food at the train station, and developed a poultry business in order to purchase, expand, and improve on a farm near Mansfield, Missouri, where they spent the rest of their lives. They built a farmhouse there, full of the same thoughtful touches and clever design that Almanzo had put into the first house that he had built for Laura, in Dakota Territory. But permanent economic security only came late in life, when Wilder developed a career as a writer with her daughter's assistance, publishing the first volume in the *Little House* series at the age of sixty-five. By the time of her death at the age of ninety, royalties from stories about homesteading life on the prairie, (and not the farm itself) had made her affluent.[23]

The *Little House* series was popular from the start with American librarians and teachers, who shared the books with generations of American children during the twentieth century. Almost sixty million copies were sold by 2000, and the books were translated into thirty-three languages. The *Little House* books (particularly *Little House on the Prairie* and *Little House in the Big Woods*) were and still are ubiquitous on lists of all-time favorite children's books or lists of bestselling children's books. The role of teachers and librarians was crucial for both the books' sales and growth of the fan community during the first decades after they were published. Teachers made the *Little House* books (or excerpts from them) ubiquitous in school basal readers, read them aloud to their pupils, and many built both reading and social science curriculums around them during the mid-twentieth century. The support of librarians was equally crucial, since until the 1960s, children's librarians purchased 80 percent of the children's books sold in the United States.[24] The consistent promotion of the series in both children's libraries and public schools kept the books in print for forty years, remarkable for any type of literature, until the debut of the television series in 1974 and the publication of paperback editions by Scholastic books gave sales and the fandom a further boost.[25]

Even before Wilder's death, the books brought Wilder not only financial security but an honored place among American children's authors. Libraries and schools across the country organized celebrations of her birthday each February, and her local branch library in Mansfield was named for her. The Newbery Medal is the most prestigious annual award in American children's literature, and five of the *Little House* books were named Newbery Honor books. So many librarians came to feel that Wilder's work deserved special recognition that the American Library Association created a new, lifetime achievement award in children's literature in 1954 and named it for her, the Laura Ingalls Wilder Award. She was its first recipient.[26] The Wilders also welcomed fans who turned up at their farm almost daily (particularly in the summers), chatting with them and posing for photos, and Wilder received a large volume of mail from fans.[27]

## Walking in Laura's Footsteps: The Homesites' History

Soon after Wilder's death in 1957, notable local citizens in both Mansfield and De Smet formed organizations to memorialize Wilder. The Mansfield group, the Wilder Home Association, had to act immediately to forestall the sale of Wilder's home on Rocky Ridge Farm in order to preserve it for visits by fans, who continued to arrive, and whose numbers grew steadily. Wilder's daughter Rose donated some of the funds needed, and arranged for many of her parents' belongings to stay in the house, and the Association collected artifacts from the Ingalls and Wilder families and later developed a museum on the site. The Association advertised the fact that the building was still open, promising potential visitors that there was a "hostess on duty" daily, to show them around Wilder's home at Rocky Ridge.[28]

In De Smet, the local newspaper editor, Aubrey Sherwood, and two other well-known residents formed the Laura Ingalls Wilder Memorial Society. The

Society built up its homesite gradually over the next fifteen years, starting with a memorial plaque on the Ingalls homestead next to Pa's cottonwood trees, and acquiring the first home that Laura's family had lived in when they moved to Dakota Territory in 1967. In 1972, the Society purchased and restored the home built by Charles Ingalls in De Smet after the sale of the homestead, and later it did the same for the schoolhouse attended by the Ingalls girls. Near De Smet, the farm homesteaded and later sold by the Ingalls was turned into an attraction for visitors.

The number of annual visitors to De Smet and Mansfield grew in step with the attractions available in each town for Wilder enthusiasts. During the early 1960s, Aubrey Sherwood estimated that De Smet had several hundred visitors each summer. By end of the decade, over two thousand visitors came to see the first house acquired by the De Smet Society, and the numbers doubled, then tripled after the Society bought and restored the other buildings, and as the television series drew in fans who had not read the books, growing to eighteen thousand visitors annually by 1979.[29] The number of visitors has declined slightly in recent years, but De Smet (a town of about eleven hundred people) still welcomes roughly twenty-five thousand visitors each year. Located in a more heavily populated region and near the popular country western music mecca of Branson, Missouri, the Mansfield homesite attracts the largest number of visitors, although it has also seen a decline in recent years. In 2018, Mansfield (pop. 1,296) attracted almost twenty-eight thousand homesite visitors between March and November, when the site is open.[30]

Teachers and librarians were active supporters in the early Wilder homesites, and in 1961 a St. Paul librarian suggested that Pepin, Wisconsin (Wilder's birthplace, pop. 782) memorialize her. Leading citizens of Pepin formed a Memorial Society of their own, and did research to pinpoint the location of the log cabin where Wilder had been born, a few miles outside of Pepin. They, too, created a memorial plaque, and later built their replica cabin on the site where the *Little House in the Big Woods* had stood. Over time, the Pepin group developed a museum in town, as well. Walnut Grove, Minnesota (pop. 814) still had the collapsed dugout where the Ingalls had lived in *On the Banks of Plum Creek*, located on a farm near the town. Walnut Grove was not named in the book, and only began to attract significant numbers of Wilder fans once the television show began broadcasting, since Michael Landon chose to locate the series there. Although founded somewhat later than some of the other homesites, the people of Walnut Grove worked energetically to develop a regional history museum with many

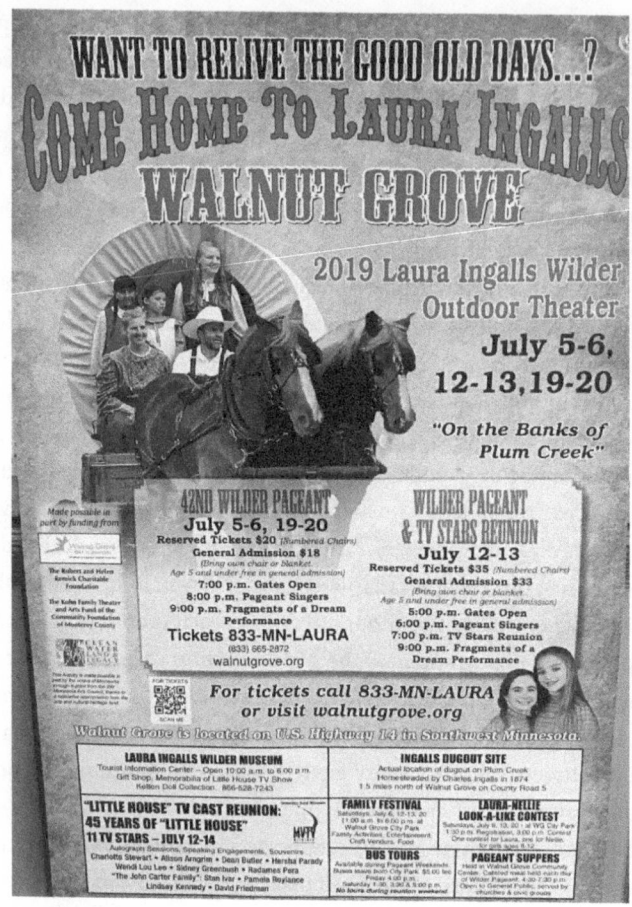

FIGURE 12. A flyer advertising the 2019 annual summer pageant based on Wilder's life in Walnut Grove, Minnesota. Photo by author.

period attractions, along with a successful pageant based on the Wilders' lives in Walnut Grove, which they began in 1978 and offered every summer thereafter.[31]

Additional homesites or museums were later founded near Independence, Kansas; Spring Valley, Minnesota; Burr Oak, Iowa; and Malone, New York. Collectively, the homesites came to form a Wilder fan pilgrimage circuit, particularly those located along the Laura Ingalls Wilder Historic Highway, which connects the sites in Minnesota, South Dakota, Wisconsin, and Iowa. Some fans took their families to a different homesite each summer, and tour guides organized homesite tours for groups starting in the 1970s.[32]

During their lifetimes, the Ingalls and Wilders had been well-respected citizens who had lived in Mansfield and De Smet for decades, and it is unsurprising that local elites acted to preserve sites associated with Wilder after her death. But in the other towns on the homesite circuit, the Ingalls had been transients, an economically marginal family residing in each location briefly before moving on. They had been long forgotten, before Wilder began to publish her series late in life; it then became clear that the most famous person to ever live in the area was a young girl whose sojourn there, long ago, had left no mark. But now she had tens of thousands of fans, interested in her life story. In small towns where the Ingalls or Wilders had lived a century earlier, enterprising small-town boosters saw their opportunity, and took it. Laura herself had been entrepreneurial: so were many of her fans.

For some homesite towns, Wilder tourism became a lifeline. Most small towns in rural regions across America have been under demographic and economic pressures for decades. Young adults often move away to larger cities, and many small towns struggle to maintain their population and important local services like schools, grocery stores, and doctors' offices. In Walnut Grove, pageant organizers sometimes invite the grandchildren of town residents to return to the town during the summer from their homes in larger cities, to fill the children's roles in the pageant.[33] But the development of the homesites bolstered local economies in towns where the Ingalls had lived, bringing visitors that allowed the towns to maintain restaurants and gas stations, even as other small towns in their region shrank, or even vanished. Erwin, South Dakota, the source of the defunct church relocated to the De Smet Ingalls homestead, currently has a population of forty-five; but De Smet's population has only declined modestly since its mid-twentieth-century peak. Some homesite town residents I spoke to were occasionally a bit weary of hearing about Laura Ingalls Wilder, but everyone acknowledged fan tourism's importance for their local economies. The homesite towns' strategies were hardly unique: analogous forms of heritage tourism and historical reenactment support regional economies around the world.[34]

Small town boosterism is only part of what drove the development of the homesites, however. Preserving buildings that are sometimes almost 150 years old and organizing pageants and other homesite festivals that rely on local organizers and cast members is an enormous labor of love for the participants (most of

FIGURE 13. Replica setters' dugout dwelling at the Walnut Grove, Minnesota home-site. Photo by author.

whom are volunteers), and offer rewards that go beyond material considerations.[35] The Ingalls were perhaps long forgotten, in some towns, but their ambitions, hard work, and lifestyle had mirrored that of many of their contemporaries. In memorializing the Ingalls's and Wilders' lives and homesteads, homesite towns-people were also creating exhibits that reflected their own families' histories, and the region's heritage. The Walnut Grove pageant organizers thus expressed the hope in 2003 "that visitors will take with them a sense of history and a deeper appreciation of the joys and hardships that challenged our ancestors when settling on the prairie."[36]

At the De Smet homesite, I spoke with a woman from North Dakota who had brought her daughter to see the homestead, school, and other buildings so laboriously restored and preserved by the Wilder Memorial Society. Like most people in her generation in the region, she had read the books as a child but had not come to De Smet because she was particularly a Wilder fan. She had brought her daughter to see the exhibits, she said, because "this is our heritage, this is my family's history, too." Regional school districts send thousands of children on field trips to Mansfield and De Smet each year for similar reasons. In a landscape where almost all buildings are relatively young compared to the East Coast (where eighteenth-century buildings are not difficult to find), the homesites also allow regional residents to see nineteenth-century historic architecture and objects that are "old," from the point of view of regional visitors.

For midwestern Wilder fans and many homesite visitors, the Wilder homes and farms are thus a point of pride because the homesites reflect their own regional history and values. But the homesites, and the festivals and pageants that are organized each year, also offer local volunteers and residents the opportunity to meet and interact with people from all fifty states, and from other nations. Groups of Japanese fans regularly visit the homesites, since the books were popular enough in Japan to inspire an animated Japanese television show, *Laura, the Prairie Girl*.[37] For some fans, the world of *Little House* is attractive precisely because it seems exotic, far from the reader's own life. "Growing up in Hawaii," Melody Miyamoto wrote, "I wanted to be Laura Ingalls. I wanted to run across the prairies, to live in a dugout, and even travel by covered wagon."[38] Like German Western fans, *Little House* fans who grew up in densely-populated or urban areas found the openness and space of the prairies alluring. Other fans I spoke to came from the Midwest themselves, and Laura's lifestyle did not seem so exotic to them. But they were drawn to her because she was a female protagonist who was "free" and had adventures in those open spaces—the Laura who explored ponds and creeks, roamed the prairies, and rode horses bareback in *Plum Creek* and *Silver Lake*—during a period when female characters in children's literature were usually more constrained.

The *Little House* series and the television show were global successes that appealed to readers for many reasons. For decades, these homesites have attracted fans from the rest of the world to small towns that might otherwise see few visitors from the East or West Coasts, let alone from other continents. The *Little House* stories have thus brought the world *to* Walnut Grove, and to De Smet, Pepin, and Burr Oak; most homesites keep careful tallies about how many of the fifty American states are represented among their visitors each year, and which foreign nations. In one small town after the other, I spoke to homesite volunteers or to midwestern fans who are active in the annual Wilder festivals and pageants, who expressed wonder and pleasure over meeting *Little House* fans from Japan, Argentina, or simply Americans from distant states, who were interested in learning how to make a nine patch quilt, to churn butter, braid a rag rug, or twist straw. Laura Ingalls Wilder connects them and makes them relevant to the rest of the world, allowing them to share their crafts and heritage.

To the homesite volunteers, the appearance of visitors from distant places is striking and interesting, and so most homesites carefully track the origins of their visitors. But at the same time, the bulk of those who make the trip to the homesites come from the same or neighboring states, and not from the East or West Coast or abroad. In the Wilder fan pilgrimage route, Americans from the Midwest, or states that border the Midwest, are heavily represented. This can be partly explained by the location of most of the homesites and their distance from either coast; it takes several days to drive from New York or Los Angeles to De Smet or Walnut Grove. Same or neighboring-state fans are probably also disproportionately attracted to the homesites because of their celebration of regional history and heritage; this is certainly true of the many school field trip visitors that some homesites attract. And if the homesites' visitors reflect the Wilder fan community as a whole, then it is an overwhelmingly white fandom, as well. While my own experience may not be completely representative, I visited six Wilder homesites during the summer of 2019. I saw hundreds of other visitors, and spoke to several dozen Wilder fans at the homesites. All of them appeared to be white.[39]

Like other open-air or living history museums discussed by anthropologist Edward Bruner, the homesites thus serve different needs for each of the groups involved. The Laura Ingalls Wilder scholars and memorial societies that created and maintain the sites have gone to considerable effort to present Laura's life "as it really was," ensuring that the buildings are historically accurate in every detail, down to the wallpaper patterns. The local volunteers who work at many of the sites as guides, or who produce the summer pageants about Laura's life, seek not only to preserve Laura's memory but to honor their ancestors and the region's early white settlers, while also promoting tourism and their towns' economic interests. Visitors to the sites come in order to escape to a time when life was allegedly simpler; to connect with Laura by experiencing the places where she lived; to see a lifestyle that is exotic (if they have traveled far to get there); or to see how their ancestors might have lived (if they are from the Midwest); to celebrate a particular narrative of the American dream; to educate their children; and to bring home personalized memories, souvenirs, and photographs. As Bruner observed of a living history site that memorializes Abraham Lincoln's early adulthood, "each of the parties involved has their own interests."[40]

## Experiencing the *Little Houses*

The homesites offer Wilder fans unique opportunities to see the settings and artifacts in the stories, but the crafts and hands-on activities that *Little House* stories inspired can be and are done elsewhere. As in other historically focused fandoms, *Little House* fans' activities were heavily weighted toward the experiential from the beginning, demonstrating a strong interest in hands-on activities that allowed readers to re-create aspects of Laura's life and work. Barbara Walker was introduced to the series by a librarian she knew, who had visited the homesites. "I got interested and so did my daughter," she said, "and here were lots of things to make [described in the books]: food and dolls and other things." Walker was inspired to research and create the award-winning *The Little House Cookbook*, which gave fans recipes for the dishes mentioned, along with broader social and cultural history of diet and food preparation in frontier settlements.[41]

A Pepin resident who helps to organize the Pepin "Laura Days" each year had a similar response: "When a kid reads the story of Sleeping Beauty, she can put on a pretty dress and lie down and pretend to sleep, but when she reads the [*Little House*] books, there are so many things she can do and make."[42] Teachers who taught *Little House* books often had pupils build log cabin models, make button lamps or butter, or cook foods mentioned in the books; adult fans could tackle even more elaborate projects.[43] It was easier for them to obtain fabric or items needed to make quilts and braided rag rugs or to churn butter, however, than it was for many East German fans to obtain Native American beads and quills and other raw materials for their costumes and artifacts. Both *Little House* fans and East German Indian hobbyists were rejecting modern consumer cultures by pursuing DIY crafts to replace modern products. But *Little House* fans living in a modern consumer culture could more easily obtain materials to do so than East German fans, who lived in a society where consumer goods (particularly imported products) were sometimes in short supply.

Quilting and patchwork, considered a particularly American folk art, are quite popular with some *Little House* fans. Handicrafters are active in many media fandoms, where fans often produce mimetic or playful reproductions of clothing or fiber arts seen in cult films or television shows. As Brigid Cherry, who studied fan handicrafts, noted, fans of historically focused entertainments are particularly interested in the "re-enactment of the crafting methods as a form of living history [because of what this] can tell us about making and the made in the past."[44] Some *Little House* enthusiasts practice textile crafts for the same reason, and also because these handicrafts have a strong presence in Laura's world.

The *Little House* books detail how Laura and her sisters gradually learned to quilt, doing beginners' nine patch quilts, and developing their needlework and quilting skills over the years. Wilder's daughter Rose was an enthusiastic quilter and needlewoman; late in life, she published a comprehensive reference work on the subject, the *Woman's Day Book of American Needlework*. Thus for fans, quilting carries strong associations with the Wilders, and it is also connected to regional heritage and arts. Julie Frances Miller, who volunteers regularly at the "Laura Days" festival hosted each September by the Pepin Wilder organization, manages the quilt displays and demonstrations each year at the replica Wayside cabin maintained by the Pepin homesite group. Wearing her own period costume, Miller teaches children and interested adults about classic American quilt block designs (e.g., rail fence, bear paw, friendship star, and maple leaf), patterns which can also be seen at the homesites in the quilts made by Wilder and her family. Miller teaches them how to make their own nine patch quilt (a beginner's form) or how to hand sew a quilt block. At the Laura Days, she teaches about 250 children (and interested adults) how to make nine patch quilts each year.[45]

One part of this fandom is thus engaged with skills, crafts, tools, and knowledge that have fallen out of use among most twenty-first-century Americans. The focus on nineteenth-century crafts and skills is an expression of the antimodernism that is intrinsic to almost all historically focused fandoms, but sometimes *Little House* fans are also deliberately pushing back on the "de-skilling" of housekeeping processes that accompanied the transition to a modern consumer culture in the United States. Compared to the period before 1945, relatively few Americans now sew or knit their own clothing and bedding; grow, process, or preserve their own foods; or do any of the other forms of household production described in the *Little House* books. Simply preparing entire meals from scratch is less common, in many households. For some *Little House* fans, preserving these skills is important in itself.

As Sarah Uthoff, a librarian who offers presentations and period-dress first-person performances as Laura at schools and other venues, commented, "This country is becoming divorced from the things that Laura did, and they don't understand them." Describing the loss of traditional crafts as a "divorce" is a resonant phrase, and one that conveys the importance that Uthoff and some

FIGURE 14. Calico sunbonnets and prairie dresses for sale at the De Smet homesite. Photo by author.

other historically focused fans assign to skills that render the possessor more self-sufficient. Uthoff noted that

> none of what she [Wilder] talks about [regarding] food production is intelligible to many readers, because they don't cook from scratch themselves so much. They don't know how to make their own clothes or that this can even be done (or the steps, like cutting patterns, stitching). They have lost the vocabulary of how things work today. . . . It's a danger for the country if you don't understand how things work . . . [and] these books do a great job of explaining how things work.[46]

Historian Anita Fellman argues that hands-on, experiential activities derived from the books serve other functions, as well. They build readers' faith in the stories as "true," and are history more than fiction, since readers themselves can perform the same tasks described in the books, which also enhances their sense of connection to the characters.[47] Julie Frances Miller's experiences as a *Little House* fan support Fellman's insight. Miller is a piano teacher as well as a skilled quilter; she is sometimes asked to play the pump organs that figure prominently in the books, and which are present at some of the homesites. At De Smet, Miller once played the pump organ used to furnish the Ingalls's home, and the fans present all sang Pa's favorite hymn, "In The Sweet Bye and Bye," sung at his funeral in 1902, a deeply moving experience for her. "The deeper you get into it [recreating aspects of the stories]," she commented, "the stronger the connection." Miller also volunteered at the Mansfield "Laura Days" festival one year as well, and played Wilder's own pump organ in her Mansfield farmhouse for visitors for six hours. "To hear it and to know that Laura played it [this same organ] and so did Rose," she said, "some people cried." Miller gains great satisfaction from her active role in many homesite events: "It's just so important to me to see that it's an important part of people's lives [when they come to the homesites] and can participate in these things and remember that for the rest of their lives."[48]

## Researching the *Little Houses*: Fan Scholarship and LauraPalooza

Like all aspects of social life and fan communities, the emergence of the internet after 1990 made it easier for Wilder enthusiasts to share information about crafts, homesite events, and experiential activities online. As in other fandoms, the internet made it easier to become engaged with the Laura Ingalls Wilder community; fans no longer had to go to the homesites or connect with each other via the homesite newsletters and events. They developed mailing lists and bulletin boards, and after 2010 (like other hobbyist groups) took their discussions to Facebook, Pinterest, and Twitter. The fans of the *Little House* television series also flocked to social media, which allowed them to share images from the show and of the show's stars.

Online discussions also broadened another longstanding focus of this fan community: research into the lives of the Ingalls, Wilders, and their neighbors and friends. Fan scholarship has become an important segment of the *Little Houses* fandom. Alongside the academic scholars who published on Wilder, deeply engaged enthusiasts and homesite volunteers had researched the Ingalls and their relatives for decades, sometimes publishing articles to present their findings in the homesite newsletters. But the growth of the internet, and the gradual digitization of federal and state records, made it increasingly easier for larger numbers of people to research the Ingalls and Wilders. Fans used online communities to share with one another their findings and discussions of the growing number of biographies and research published about the Ingalls and Wilders. The most successful and engaged researchers now not only publish books but can also maintain blogs, produce podcasts, and offer living history presentations about Wilder's life, dressed in period costume, to schools or community groups. Fan scholars meet with other enthusiasts at the LauraPalooza conferences (part scholarly conference, part fan meetup), which have been regularly organized by the Laura Ingalls Wilder Legacy and Research Association (the LIWLRA), a group of fan researchers, since 2010.[49]

Laura McLemore, a Kansas fan and scholar who has taught at both the college and elementary school levels in her region, described the origins of LauraPalooza and the LIWLRA. She had belonged to listservs where Laura Ingalls Wilder fans met and shared information during the 1990s, and over the years, developed a group of friends in the community who got together regularly at homesite celebrations to talk. After years of such meetups, six women who had met online decided to meet at the Independence, Kansas homesite for a weekend in 2008: "we sat in the kitchen of the farmhouse there," she recalled, "and we spent the whole weekend talking about Rose, the [Indigenous] Osage history there [in Kansas], and everything we could think about and decided that it would be great if we could have a place where people came together to talk about these things on a larger scale."[50] Several of the women present organized a mini-conference in De Smet in 2009, where they founded the LIWLRA, which organized the first large-scale LauraPalooza conference, held the following year at Minnesota State University at Mankato, Minnesota. The LIWLRA and LauraPalooza serve as a clearing house for fan research about Laura Ingalls Wilder and offer fans a supportive and attentive venue for their research.

One woman who has attended LauraPalooza described how fans bring their professional skills to hobby research on Laura and the Ingalls. "It's kind of a cheap thrill to delve into historical research," she commented. "With Laura as the portkey, you can go into history and see all of this documentation that supports her story; there is so much available in the Midwest into which amateurs and genealogists can delve."[51] Fans bring their own real-life expertise into their research in surprising ways; one leading member of the LIWLRA, a meteorologist, used her training to present research on the impact of nineteenth-century climate disasters on the Ingalls's lives and communities.

The LIWLRA and fan scholarship exchanges also offer participants something that would be immediately recognizable to people who are active in other fandoms: a connection to others who truly care as much as they do. Besides her scholarly research into Laura Ingalls Wilder's life and the presentations on Laura Ingalls Wilder that she has given at dozens of public schools, Laura McLemore's engagement with *Little House* includes a collection of objects that connect to the stories, which she stores in her "Laura room." When we spoke, she had recently located an antique butter mold with a strawberry decoration on it, similar to the one described in *Little House in the Big Woods*, to add to her collection. These antiques, she said,

> are meaningful to me. This is my collection and what I love, and these are tangible objects that connect me to the stories and to Laura Ingalls Wilder . . . [she was drawn to the LIWLRA because it offers her] a group of people who don't think I'm weird that I have a Laura room and they don't think I'm strange for it. Other people sometimes think I'm weird for going to LauraPalooza, but the other fans understand why I feel that way, and even though they don't all agree about politics or religion, it brings them together in ties of deep friendship.[52]

The pleasures of this branch of the Wilder community are similar to those offered by the online community that has developed around Ancestry.com, with its lively discussions of genealogy and sharing of historical records. A striking example of such research was that undertaken by one Wilder enthusiast, a former teacher named Margaret Clement, who went to enormous lengths to determine the exact location of the Ingalls's cabin in Kansas, the setting for *Little House on the Prairie*. Wilder herself had attempted to determine where her parents had briefly settled while she was writing her book, but the location she finally settled on was mistaken, and did not agree with other available records. Painstakingly sifting through land claims and the federal records of the 1870 census, Clement was able to determine the exact location where the Ingalls family had squatted land for over a year, including the well that Pa Ingalls had dug by hand.[53]

Wilder enthusiasts can (and do) research many topics related to Laura's life and times: the material culture or musical traditions of prairie settlement; family histories of the Ingalls's De Smet neighbors or contemporaries; the churches that Wilder's parents helped to found; and Wilder's daughter Rose, a successful writer in her own right who left behind substantial documentation in the form of dairies and letters, thus providing fodder for open-ended discussion and analysis by both academic scholars and self-taught hobbyists. They also organize online read-alongs of both the *Little House* books and recent scholarly work on Wilder.

The homesites themselves offer such engaging fan experiences that a visitor to this fandom might not immediately perceive the relative absence of something that is commonplace in most modern media fandoms: creative fan work that seeks to reimagine Laura's world along very different lines. The Wilder fan community is overwhelmingly more engaged by history than fan fiction. The focus on the historical reality of Wilder's life and times, and on connecting to her experiences through the reenactment of historical crafts and activities, in practice acts to marginalize the transformative works approach common in other modern media fandoms. Discussion of the author and the context within which a story world was created, which dominates the Wilder fandom, is found in most fan communities, of course. But the focus of fan discussions and activity in many media fandoms is on non-canonical alternative storylines, often expressed in fan fiction, vids, fan art, or other transformative works.

Most Wilder fans are motivated by a desire to connect with the real Laura and to learn more about her and her family. This focus works against interest in the alternative versions of the story, which fan fiction might explore. As one active Wilder fan, Sarah Uthoff, observed, enthusiasts are sticking pretty close to the background of the stories, and are "delving down, not out" in their activities. Roger MacBride, who inherited Wilder's copyrights, wrote his own authorized spin-off children's series about Rose's childhood, and her publisher later commissioned spin-off stories about Wilder's ancestor's childhoods. Neither series seems to have generated much discussion among serious Wilder fans, however. A recent, authorized novel for adults which retells the stories from the point of view of Wilder's mother Caroline received mixed reviews from fans I interviewed.

If authorized commercial add-ons to the series are largely ignored in fan discussions, non-commercial fan fiction is quite sparse: many of those I interviewed were not familiar with the concept. A search for fan stories set in the *Little House* world yields only slender results at two leading fan fiction archives, Fanfiction.net and Archive of Our Own: the second site hosts sixty-three *Little House* fan stories (for both the books and television series), compared to almost 220,000 Harry Potter fan fiction stories. Other children's classic novels from the same period as Wilder's books (that had *not* spun off long-running hit television series, which one would expect to have increased the number of *Little House* fan fictions) had several times the number of fan fiction stories posted.[54] The *Little House* books have inspired a deeply committed fan community, but they do not attract fan fiction writers.

This might also reflect the substantial respect, even deference, given to Wilder, compared to canon authors in other fandoms, which might produce less fan interest in "improving" on the canon. Indeed, it is difficult to imagine Wilder fans creating a playful and irreverent parody of the *Little House* series like the *Shoe of the Manitou* fan satire, in the Karl May fandom. Although the community itself has grown and changed during the decades since Wilder's death, it remains primarily an experiential fandom, focused tightly on one historic family and its community.

## *Little Houses* and the American National Biography

Barbara Walker, like many other Wilder fans, could re-create the activities in the books because they offer a treasure trove of engaging details about material culture: how to tap maple trees and make maple candy or syrup; butchering and fishing techniques; or how to survive in a blizzard. As a *New York Times* reviewer noted, these details are explained:

> in such a way that even a young child can understand the basis of how to build a log cabin . . . [or] make a button lamp . . . And these details are embedded so deep in the vibrantly felt spirit of place that the child reader experiences intimately the very feel and taste and smell and bite of being a settler's daughter in the brooding Wisconsin wilderness or in the midst of the endless prairie.[55]

This review also reflects how the wealth of specific period details not only engaged readers but also worked to sell the books as "authentic" history in a broader sense. In the community around *Little House*, "authentic" generally refers to a high degree of mimetic accuracy. Fans strive to determine the details of Laura's life as accurately as possible, and to re-create objects and replicas that are as faithful to the original as possible. This is a highly participatory and productive fan community, but it is not an audience that is particularly interested in transformative fan work, which might re-imagine or rework the original stories. Instead, fan activity is focused on obtaining accurate information and mimetic re-creation of the "real" Laura's world. Many readers and reviewers saw the tenacity, resourcefulness, independence, determination, skills, and family cohesiveness that form the core of the characterizations of the Ingalls throughout the series, however, as being just as authentic and representative of "real" American frontier history as the details about material culture.[56]

The stories were also seen as authentic accounts of the frontier experience because Wilder convincingly linked her own story to the national biography that most white Americans shared for much of the twentieth century. This was an understanding of American history in which Frederick Jackson Turner's frontier thesis played a central role, the replacement of Indigenous communities by white settlers was assumed, and white settlers were seen as fundamentally "innocent" in this process. The marketplace of commercial entertainments that she was writing for was rooted in this understanding of American history. Asked to speak at a book fair held in Detroit in 1937, Wilder described how as a child:

> I had seen the whole frontier, the woods, the Indian country of the great plains, the frontier towns, the building of the railroads in wild, unsettled country, homesteading and farmers coming in to take possession. I realized that I had seen and lived it all—all the successive phases of the frontier, first the frontiersman, then the pioneer, then the farmers and the towns. Then I understood that in my own life I represented a whole period of American history.[57]

Like "Buffalo Bill" Cody, another gifted American artist of the generation before hers, Wilder was able to present her story as that of a representative American frontierswoman, who was present for the "opening" of the frontier and some of America's formative history.[58]

Some of Wilder's readers were attracted to her stories because they reflected the reader's own family's heritage. But even those who were not descended from prairie settlers often saw them as fascinating stories that illustrated larger truths about American history. The homesite exhibits made these connections clear. An exhibit on "prairie heroes" at the De Smet homestead asserted that: "the pioneer men, women and children who settled the American West were heroes. Their struggle is a story of adventure, daring and courage. Laura Ingalls Wilder, her pa, Charles, her ma, Caroline, and sisters, Mary, Carrie and Grace were part of this great westward movement. Laura's "Little House" books describe her family's pioneer adventure." Similarly, the Pepin replica log cabin memorial plaque concludes that "the pioneer experiences she has shared in her books are a precious heritage," at least for those descended from white settlers.[59]

German fans of the American West—particularly in East Germany—had sometimes pursued their hobby against the prevailing political headwinds, but Wilder's stories and personal history easily aligned with a consensus understanding of the nation's history shared by most white Americans between the late nineteenth and mid-twentieth centuries. For decades after their publication, this alignment facilitated support for her books from libraries and schools, which in turn attracted new readers and made a television series spin-off (like other Western entertainments) more likely. During the first decades after their publication, the books were indeed often seen by reviewers as further evidence of American exceptionalism and the importance of the frontier legacy for American national character and modern American identity.[60]

When Indigenous people were mentioned in Wilder's books, it was against the same backdrop assumption that German fans of the mid-twentieth century had, along with most Europeans and white Americans: that the Indian characters belonged to a "vanishing" race, who inevitably made way for white settlers. But before the emergence of the New Western historiography during the 1980s, this did not affect readership levels. The frontier history that Wilder took as the context for her childhood enjoyed broad assent from white Americans across the political spectrum.

But Wilder's view of American history did differ from that of the Turner thesis and the historiography of her day in one important respect: its focus on settler women's experiences and points of view. As one of her biographers observed, Turner's frontier thesis focused "on male conquest, individualism, lawlessness, and the search for autonomy, while Wilder depicts a dual West, where men's actions are set off against women's interests in making gardens, building homes, and sustaining community, thereby providing an alternative vision of what the West was and could be."[61] The books devote more attention to the processes of frontier homemaking and to women's work than they do to men's roles, and follow the process of Laura's socialization as a young lady. And as Ann Romines notes, the very material culture and iconic objects that form part of the books' attraction for readers (the pump organ, quilt pieces or handmade lace, dolls, and the china shepherdess) are also domestic objects with strongly gendered associations.[62]

These qualities were almost certainly related to the demographic profile of the community, which—compared to German Western fans, and other mid-twentieth century literary fan communities like science fiction—was and still is overwhelmingly female. Some of the leading scholars in this field, such as William Anderson (among the first and most prolific researchers and authors on the Ingalls and Wilders), John Miller, and Donald Zochert, are men. But much of the academic scholarship and the overwhelming bulk of fan scholarship in the United States is done by white women. The small Japanese branch of the fandom, which revolves around the original books and also a Japanese animated show about Laura, is also heavily female.

## *Little Houses* and Homeschoolers

Before their marriages, both Laura Ingalls and her mother Caroline briefly worked as public school teachers in one-room schoolhouses. But since the Ingalls did not always live in areas where public schools were already established, much of Laura's early education was given to her by her mother, at home. A century later, some *Little House* fans began to homeschool their own children; their motives for doing so varied, however, and were not caused by an absence of local public schools. But the *Little House* novels, and hands-on activities inspired by the books, were incorporated into many mid- or late twentieth-century home-schooling curricula.

Homeschooling has become more widespread in the United States since 2000, and today attracts families who have quite disparate motives for educating their children at home. But when homeschooling began as a national movement in the 1960s, it was an uncommon choice. In its first decades, the homeschooling movement especially tended to attract people from two political backgrounds, who in very different ways were rejecting modernism and mid-twentieth-century American values and lifestyles: social reformers who were going "back to the land," and trying to live off grid, on the one hand; and conservative Christian parents who rejected the secular nature of public schools and the values taught in them, on the other. The *Little House* books were a surprisingly good fit for both types of families, perhaps because the stories could be aligned with different versions of antimodernism.

For political progressives who were experimenting with anti-consumerist, off-grid communities in the 1960s and 1970s, the *Little House* stories offered an

FIGURE 15. A 1905 Lutheran church (out of use since 1969) at the De Smet Ingalls Homestead. It was built in nearby Erwin, SD, a town that is now almost entirely depopulated, and was moved to the De Smet Ingalls Homestead in 2009. The church is meant to offer visitors a sense of the Ingalls's religious life and community. Photo by author.

example of a family that did an impressive amount of its own household production. Going far beyond handicrafts and macramé, the Wilders had grown and processed most of their own foods and created many of their own household goods. They could be read as embodying a model of economic self-sufficiency whose practitioners lived in close connection with the natural world. For Christian conservative homeschoolers, the *Little House* stories, which describe communities in which most settlers (including the Ingalls) are believing Christians, are active in church life, and champion the values of familial self-sufficiency and limited government, align well with a conservative Christian worldview, and thus also easily fit into a Christian homeschooling curriculum.

The number of homeschooled children in the United States grew from approximately 250,000 children to over one million between 1985 and 1999, and an estimated 90 percent of those who homeschooled their children in that period were evangelical Christians.[63] Homeschooling families have become more diverse in their motives and demographics since 2000, as parents who are dissatisfied with school safety, bullying in schools, the special education services offered for special needs children, or other aspects of public education have turned to homeschooling in increasing numbers. But evangelical Christians are still strongly represented within the American homeschooling movement, supporting Christian homeschooling conventions and Christian homeschool curriculums.[64] Read from these fans' point of view, Wilder's books can be used "as a primer for traditional values such as religiosity, patriotism, and the traditional [male-headed, nuclear] family," and can be used to socialize their children into the conservative Christian culture that these fans are part of.[65]

But the stories easily support other readings as well, and are also popular with secular homeschooling families. Even a brief survey of the thousands of homeschooling pages on Pinterest shows that field trips and hands-on activities for experiential learning based on *Little House* stories are frequently suggested for homeschooling curricula in the elementary grades. The books can be used for both history and literature homeschooling curriculum on "westward expansion," or "pioneer life." The flexibility of both homeschooling content and Wilder's books means that homeschooling curricula that include the books can reflect diverse political viewpoints, as well.

During the summer of 2019, I surveyed sample homeschooling curricula for homeschoolers on a variety of platforms, but particularly those posted on Pinterest, a popular site with homeschoolers and those marketing teaching materials to homeschooling parents. I also examined the websites of companies and nonprofits that create learning materials for homeschoolers, and websites of homeschooling conventions (there is a circuit of such annual conferences and conventions, both religious and secular). I found a variety of deeply conservative religious curricula online for American history homeschooling that included *Little House* books, based on an almost Turnerian view of white settlement, with cursory attention to a few famous Indigenous leaders. Some of these materials aimed to support an "inerrant" evangelical Protestant approach to teaching children. But I also found curricula including *Little House* books that were rooted in the more critical, multicultural view of American history that became widespread after 1990, discussed in Chapter 5.[66] Today, homeschoolers who use Wilder's books seem to span the current American political spectrum.

At the same time, the use of *Little House* books (and other children's novels) has diminished within the public school curriculum since 2001, after the implementation of the "No Child Left Behind" Act, which encouraged a move away from literature-based curriculum toward a focus on phonics, vocabulary building, workbook drills, and frequent tests. But the decline of the use of *Little House* books in public school curricula after 2000 was also influenced by the late twentieth-century political and cultural changes discussed in Chapter 5. Widely used in public school curriculums across the country during the mid-twentieth century, the *Little House* series is now primarily used only in homeschooling curriculum, and for private leisure reading.[67]

## Memory Work and National Identity

German cowboy and Indianist hobbyists argued during the early and mid-twentieth century that they were doing ethnological work to preserve the memory and culture of Indigenous cultures on the other side of the world. The antimodern allure of those cultures and the landscapes they inhabited lay precisely in that temporal distance and exoticism, in how different those (imagined) lifestyles were from German fans' daily lives. A similar fascination may draw Japanese or other non-American fans to the *Little House* stories and to the Wilder homesites, or appeal to Americans who have no familial or personal connection to the project of frontier settlement or the Midwest.

Many *Little House* fans and homesite staff or volunteers do see their hobby or work (correctly) as linked to their own families' histories, however, or to the history of their hometowns or regions. The memory work that such fans are doing is rooted in their own cultural history, and the *Little House* books clearly resonate strongly with white midwestern American society, as evidenced by the children's field trips that school districts across the Midwest organize to the homesites.

At the same time—like the first book reviews of the series and the mid-twentieth century teachers and librarians who were among the earliest Wilder enthusiasts—the fans I interviewed almost universally believed that the *Little House* books and the historic regional cultures preserved by the homesites are important because they are central not only to regional but also to American national identity and history.[68] Both the books and the homesites memorialize and emphasize a time when white frontier settlement was important: when it was the leading narrative in American national biography, and small towns and farms in the Midwest were the arena within which settlement unfolded. In these narratives, small frontier towns took center stage (as they did in TV Westerns and still do in the homesites' summer pageants), although nowadays inhabitants of such towns might feel more marginalized in American politics and culture. During the early and mid-twentieth century, the national biography that Wilder's stories were rooted in was widely shared by white Americans from all regions and most political persuasions. But as will be discussed in Chapter 5, this consensus understanding of American history and identity began to fragment after 1990.

One scholar of historical reenactment, Anne Brædder notes that:

> the very process of making and using replicas of [historic material cultures] engenders reflections about the relationship between past and present at many levels; and reenactment, because of its performative character, remains an essentially "open-ended" endeavour, an "unfinished business," that makes a fruitful contribution to political and cultural memory work in society.[69]

The memory work done by homesite volunteers, fan scholars, and hobbyists like Miller and Uthoff, who are active in experiential fan activities, support Brædder's observation. Their engagement provokes their ongoing reflections about American history, and sometimes about their families' or community's place in that history, which they shared with me in interviews. But their memory work is rooted in Laura Ingalls Wilder's own, edited memories and stories, which included a particular view of white settlement and Indigenous peoples common in her generation, which many Wilder fans no longer support. As the political culture around the homesites has changed in recent decades, Wilder fans' memory work has also been forced to grapple with changes in how historians, and many Americans, understand the history of the West and Indigenous cultures.

# CHAPTER FIVE

# "And Then the American Indians Came Over"

## Fan Responses to Indigenous Resurgence and Political Change after 1990

*For 500 years, you know who was on the right side of history? Christopher*
*Columbus. From 1492 to 1992, you never heard a bad word about that guy.*

—COLIN QUINN, RED STATE, BLUE STATE

B efore the early 1990s, the first Monday in October was celebrated solely
as Columbus Day in the United States, commemorating Christopher
Columbus's arrival in the Americas. A huge Columbus Day parade was
held each year in New York City, and the day was observed as a legal holiday
across the United States. But after 1990, an increasing number of Americans,
led by Indigenous activists, began to argue that the same date should be observed as Indigenous People's Day instead, a counter-celebration that would
commemorate the histories of Indigenous American cultures. Today, the first
Monday in October is still celebrated by many Americans as Columbus Day, but
a growing list of American municipalities and states honor Indigenous People's
Day instead. The tensions created by competing celebrations is one example of
conflicts that arose as a result of the reevaluation of American and Indigenous
history by some parts of American society during the late twentieth century,
and conservatives' reaction to these changes.

The history of Columbus Day is echoed in the development of Western fandoms after 1990. Like Columbus Day parades, fan communities rooted in the history of the American West had the wind at their backs for much of the twentieth century, in both public historical and popular culture terms. Western genre entertainments readily found large audiences around the world, and an understanding of American history heavily influenced by Turner's frontier thesis and other early twentieth-century narratives shaped the cultural marketplaces for popular Western tales. But the prevailing cultural winds were now shifting.

In both Germany and the United States, quite different but substantial changes in larger political configurations took place after 1990; these changes on both sides of the Atlantic brought challenges, in different ways, to some members of the Western fandoms discussed in this book. In the US, some segments of the American population began to critique the romanticized narratives of "Westward expansion" that formed a crucial part of American historical narratives before the late twentieth century. The resulting historical disputes became one site for the "culture wars" of the 1990s, as Americans became more divided and politically polarized over many issues, including (and perhaps especially) how they saw their past. As a result, the cultural marketplace for historical fictions of the West changed substantially by the end of the century, and the *Little House* stories now carried different, and less positive meanings for many American readers. First, Indigenous American activists and then some white Americans began to critique Wilder's books and challenge their honored position in the canon of American children's literature.

In Germany, the opening of the Berlin Wall, followed by the collapse of the East German state and German reunification in 1990, led to even more rapid and fundamental political change than American culture wars and political polarization did in the United States. *Die Wende* (German reunification) was a political moment that rapidly altered the social and economic playing context for German fandoms. The East German state had suppressed some types of fan organization and activities, which were now allowed again in reunified Germany. But the East German state had also offered a social function and political rationale for *Indianer* hobbyists, and the role they played in East German society tended to shelter them from particular types of pressure (e.g., accusations of cultural appropriation).

Fans in former East Germany now had a broader array of options for their hobbies. They could organize openly around Karl May's story world to form public May literary societies and pursue role-play and reenactment of white American Western roles, along with a broader array of Western fan activities. Their exposure to Indigenous North Americans—sporadic before the opening of the Wall, and deeply valued by East German hobbyists—greatly increased as well. In former West Germany, too, Indigenous artists and entrepreneurs marketed their services more frequently than before 1980. The encounters produced mixed results from fans' point of view, as some Indigenous visitors disputed German fans' representation of Indians and mimetic reproduction of Indigenous arts and handicrafts. At the same time, *Indianer* hobbyists were no longer the only performers available to audiences in the former East Germany who were interested in Indigenous cultures: Indigenous artists could now be hired from across the Atlantic for a variety of performances and services.

The political changes that influenced fans' activities in both the US and Germany played out quite differently, but there was one common thread: the increased presence and self-assertion of Indigenous North Americans, some of whom now critiqued or confronted Western fans in both nations. The critiques offered by Indigenous activists and scholars in both nations affected Western fans on both sides of the Atlantic. In addition, different outside political forces now bore down upon fans' activities in both nations, forcing many to learn to steer against political crosswinds. All of these changes took place within a context of changing popular understandings of the American West and increased Indigenous activism.

## Indigenous Resurgence in the New West

The US government's push to "terminate" its remaining treaty obligations to Indigenous American tribes and to eliminate tribes' limited remaining sovereignty on their lands inspired broad inter-tribal activism and resistance during the 1960s and 1970s. The Indigenous resistance organization of this period best-known in Europe, the American Indian Movement (AIM), challenged both conservative tribal governments and federal authorities by occupying San Francisco's Alcatraz Island in 1969, and by occupying a church at the site of the 1890 Wounded Knee massacre in 1973. The FBI hounded the AIM relentlessly in the aftermath of the occupation (which ended after seventy-one days) but the event was a public relations disaster for the US government. People across the United States and around the world (and particularly in both West and East Germany) sympathized with the AIM. In Europe particularly, AIM became the public face of Indigenous American activism, and received broad support from Western European left-wing parties and activists.[1] AIM leaders Russell Means and Dennis Banks visited Indianist hobbyists and German AIM supporters in both Germanies during the 1970s, establishing connections with both hobbyists and other German supporters.[2] The East German state supported AIM, since the group's critique of the American state aligned with the regime's anti-Americanism, and East German Indianists greatly valued the contacts with AIM leaders.

Over the next three decades, tribal governments in the United States had some success at regaining lost lands, treaty rights, and in fostering economic development on tribal lands, for example, through casinos as well as natural resource development and other industries. Inhabitants of reservations and Indigenous Americans who lived outside of reservations continued to suffer from much greater poverty, lower life expectancies, worse educational and social services, and higher unemployment rates than white Americans. Nonetheless, Indigenous American cultures achieved considerable resurgence after 1980. They pursued a strategy that some referred to as "survivance," a term that denoted Indigenous cultures' survival, resistance, and cultural revival.[3] By 2000, so many more people self-identified on the US Census as "American Indian or Native Alaskan" that this group became one of the fasting growing ethnic categories in the United States, at least in term of the census head count.[4]

Indigenous activists also began to challenge both historical and popular cultural representations of their history. At the same time, the New Western historiography was increasingly the basis for new approaches to public history education, as articulated in school textbooks, museums, monuments, and other popular historical sites. Both developments called into question what historians refer to as the "master narrative" of American history, in which Turnerian concepts like "pioneers," "westward expansion," and "the frontier" had long played a central role.[5] American academic historians began to approach the story of the West quite differently, as a multicultural narrative of encounters between varied national, social, and ethnic groups. The New Western historiography readily acknowledged cross-racial violence, conquest, and settler colonialism, along with the costs of economic exploitation of natural resources.

As Mario Carretero and Floor Van Alphen have observed, the objectives of history education can be classified as "romantic" or "enlightened." Both types of objectives have existed since the very beginnings of history education in public schools around the world and other popular educational institutions, e.g., museums or patriotic celebrations.

> In a romantic vein, history education is a fundamental strategy used to achieve (1) a positive assessment of the past, present, and future of one's own social group, both local and national and (2) an identification [of citizens] with the country's political history. In an enlightened vein, history education has aimed at fostering critical citizens' capability of informed and effective participation in the historical changes happening nationally and globally. This can involve a critical attitude toward their own local or national community.[6]

"Romantic" and nationalist approaches to public history education were dominant in the United States through the mid-twentieth century, and still are in many nations today. A classic example would be the Fourth of July celebration described in Wilder's *Little Town on the Prairie*, which was centered on a positive, celebratory narrative about the origins of American democracy; the history education described in Wilder's books is typical for the late nineteenth century. But after the 1970s, public history across Western Europe and the United States took a turn toward the "enlightened" approach, which stressed multiple points of view and a more critical history of the nation and state. Overall, late twentieth-century historians became increasingly aware of the limitations of historical education that was centered on the nation-state, and which focused primarily on the nation's birth, struggles, expansion, and values, rendering other actors marginal to the main narrative.[7]

In teaching the history of the American West, an "enlightened" approach drew on the research of the New Western historians—more critical of settler colonialism and of violence against Indigenous cultures—which was introduced into public school curricula and museum exhibitions during the 1980s and 1990s, including at the National Park Service's Homestead National Monument. At the same time, Indigenous Americans drew on their own experiences to begin offering alternative versions of the official history taught in American public schools, and critiques of the depictions of Indigenous Americans offered in children's literature and public education.[8]

As a result, the consensus narrative of American history—the "national biography" that had dominated public history education and American popular culture for most of the late nineteenth and twentieth centuries and helped define white American identity—was fractured and remade during the late twentieth century. Americans on the political left tended to accept a more multicultural approach to the teaching of American history, and the sometimes bleak assessments of white settlers' impact on other cultures and the environment offered by the New Western historians. The new histories questioned, or even dismantled, the older historical narratives' portrayal of white settlers as heroic pioneers who were generally "innocent" in the story of US-Indigenous violence. But other Americans, including cultural conservatives and Ronald Reagan, did not accept the New Western historians' findings. Politicians, school boards, and academic historians were all drawn into what became known as the "culture wars." Conservative critics of the new history curriculum argued that it presented the United States as a nation of oppressors, ignoring what they saw as the promise of American exceptionalism.

A 1991 Smithsonian exhibit, *The West as America*, became an example of this cultural divide. The exhibit used the paintings of well-known artists of the nineteenth-century West like Frederic Remington and George Catlin to show how art had romanticized and promoted the doctrine of Manifest Destiny. The exhibit thus problematized the premises of white settlers' westward expansion. *The West as America* provoked considerable controversy, foreshadowing the firestorm ignited by new public school history curricula and history standards released during this period, such as New York City's *One Nation, Many Peoples: A Declaration of Cultural Independence*, which emphasized American pluralism and the oppression of ethnic and racial minorities. The New York model was not widely copied, but other revisions of public school history curricula such as California's 1988 *The History-Social Science Framework* (which other states adopted as well) and the 1994 *National History Standards*, had a substantial impact on public history education. Both of these standards greatly increased the amount of time and material devoted to world history and also incorporated a multicultural approach to US history that sought, as the *National History Standards* noted, "to engender a critical perspective on conventional interpretations of the American past."[9]

Conservative historians and politicians rejected the new historical pedagogy. Commenting on the New York curricula, historian Raymond Carr fumed that the new approach crossed "the fatal line between a legitimate cultural pluralism and a divisive ethnocentrism, committing the historical absurdity of denying America's historical heritage."[10] Conservative author Lynne Cheney, who as head of the National Endowment for the Humanities had initially supported the development of the *National History Standards,* attacked the finished document; she argued that "by not teaching young people the traditional American narrative ... Americans no longer had a shared sense of the American past."[11] Conservatives objected to the new historiography's penetration of public history education, but generally with modest success.

Local and state school authorities did retain discretion in textbook adoptions and curricula, which meant that in states where conservatives were politically dominant, textbooks were somewhat less critical of white settlement and the treatment of Indigenous cultures than they were in liberal states.[12] But overall, there is little doubt that the new historiography was broadly adopted in American public schools, and was ultimately reflected in the influential Advanced Placement US and World History tests, which shaped American high school history teaching. By the early twenty-first century, most American schoolchildren were being taught a version of the American past that differed substantially from the one offered to their parents and grandparents. This development continued to provoke considerable resistance among cultural conservatives, who sometimes responded by placing their children in conservative private schools, or by beginning to homeschool their children. Indeed, this battlefield of the culture wars was revived and given new life by the Trump campaign in 2020.[13]

## The Imagined New West

During the same decades, Western genre entertainments lost their commanding position in both American and global media, although the causes were complex and varied. Literature focused on the West saw substantial changes after the late 1960s. Paralleling the growth in Indigenous American activism in the political realm, Indigenous writers like Pulitzer Prize winner N. Scott Momaday, Leslie Marmon Silko, James Welch, Louise Erdrich and others led a flowering of literary publications during the 1970s and 1980s that became known as the Native American Renaissance. Western genre literature written by white authors began to question the "heroism" of Western protagonists, and even—in Thomas Berger's *Little Big Man,* E. L. Doctorow's *Welcome to Hard Times,* and especially in Cormac McCarthy's *Blood Meridian*—to subvert the values and forms of the genre altogether, leading some to refer to these novels as anti-Westerns. These novels rejected traditional Westerns' claims to express core American values, and instead they portrayed the often mindless violence at the heart of white Americans' westward expansion.[14]

American Western films had reflected changing cultural concerns and sometimes negative evaluations of white settlement of the West earlier in the century. As early as 1956, one of John Ford's last films, *The Searchers*, questioned earlier depictions of Indigenous cultures and explored the devastating consequences of white hatred toward them. *The Man Who Shot Liberty Valence* (1962) and *Cheyenne Autumn* (1964) sympathized with each film's Indian characters and depicted white conquest as corrupt and violent. These films were successful, but the genre as a whole, and particularly Western television shows, generally celebrated white settlement of the West and quintessential "American values" through the 1970s. By the late twentieth century, this had largely changed; *Dances with Wolves* (1990) flipped the traditional Western perspective, and showed the arrival of whites as a disaster, while Clint Eastwood's revisionist *Unforgiven* (1992) was a bleak meditation on violence and "honor" in Westerns, without a hint of romance.[15]

Hollywood Western films thus began to reflect more critical late twentieth-century popular understandings of the white settlement in the West. At the same time, more traditional Western fans could continue to find niche programming based on earlier Western tropes on the Turner Broadcasting Network's TNT channel, founded in 1988. TNT became the main producer of Western films, made for TNT instead of theater distribution. TNT Western films were often remakes based on classic Western genre novels by Zane Grey, Louis L'Amour, and other early twentieth-century genre writers, and catered to audiences (often older viewers) who had flocked to Western series and novels in previous decades. These made for television films centered on courageous, individualistic heroes, who championed a traditional moral code against lawless opponents, with stories that took a Turnerian understanding of the American frontier and pioneer settlement as their context. David Pierson, who has studied TNT Westerns, concluded that "TNT productions evoke a deep-seated, nostalgic desire for Western myths and heroes, and for mythically well-defined gender roles for men and women ... TNT's audiences appreciate the traditional values expressed by these male leads."[16] Early and mid-twentieth-century Western entertainment tropes and historical narratives thus lived on, but were no longer predominant on network broadcasting or Hollywood films, instead aiming at niche cable audiences.

Late twentieth-century Western films and television could still be quite broadly successful, e.g., the 1989 miniseries *Lonesome Dove,* but the genre had lost its previously dominant status in popular entertainments. Western fans no longer had a huge array of primetime network series to choose from, but they did have their own cable channels in addition to TNT, devoted to constant Western programming. Arcade and video games also included popular Western games, and Western theme parks were created in both the United States and Germany.[17] But by 2000, most fictional genres had dedicated cable channels and popular video games. Instead of representing the preeminent form of American entertainment, the Western was now one of several popular genres on all media platforms, following what one Hollywood historian refers to as "the generic diaspora of the 1980s."[18]

Western genre entertainments had become fractured, inverting earlier popular tropes in a fashion that paralleled the changes in public history education pushed forward by the New Western historians and Indigenous activism. High-quality historical research is accurate research, which takes into account all the available evidence in order to explain change over time. By this standard, New Western historiography was unquestionably superior to Turner's paradigm and publications. Its analyses were more broadly based; they accurately captured the experiences of an array of historical actors in the West and explained historical change better.

Americans on the left, younger Americans, and members of ethnic minorities (sometimes overlapping groups) were often supportive of this paradigm shift. But for many others, the developments in both public history, public education, and popular culture were disconcerting. Pioneers were now acknowledged to be colonizers, and the frontier was now recognized as Indigenous homelands, where Indigenous peoples had been subjected to forced relocations or unprovoked attacks. This was an inversion of older understandings of national history and white settlers' identities that some Americans found to be uncomfortable historiographical terrain. Like the late twentieth-century histories of slavery and racism in American history, the New Western historiography probed something that was deep and painful for many Americans, and prompted often defensive responses. It represented a challenging, even unacceptable engagement with American national identity for conservatives in particular, whose identity was rooted in pride about their heritage and ancestors' accomplishments.

## Little Houses in the New West

While the decline in the popularity of Westerns during the late twentieth century affected all of the Western-based fan communities discussed in this book, the paradigm shift in public history education posed a more direct challenge to admirers of Wilder's stories. German Western fans had always deplored the treatment of Indigenous cultures by white Americans, and public education in both East and West Germany was been clear-eyed about the costs of white expansion and settlement in the West to both Indigenous peoples and the environment; these views were politically uncontroversial. The first generations of German Western fans had also subscribed to the overall view, however, that Indigenous North American peoples were a "vanishing race," and that white westward expansion was inevitable. But Wilder's books were very much creations of early twentieth-century American popular history in their depictions of white settlers, westward expansion, and American Indian characters.

Popular narratives and entertainments based on the history of the American West were shaped by the expectations of nineteenth- and twentieth-century audiences and entertainment markets, where entrepreneurial artists like Buffalo Bill and Laura Ingalls Wilder sought recognition and fortune. Before the late twentieth century, those markets were rooted in a shared understanding among most white Americans during those decades that their nation was fundamentally justified in its treatment of Indigenous Americans, and in the overall project of white settlement of the West, which had been rooted in the appropriation of Indigenous lands. This shared understanding was reflected, for example, in Buffalo Bill's famous staging of Custer's Last Stand, and his *Wild West Show's* recurring performance of Indian warriors' attack on an innocent settler family's log cabin.

Wilder's stories had crucial differences from Buffalo Bill's show, and from the late nineteenth century mementos and entertainments that retold (and reshaped) the stories of settler's encounters with Indigenous American cultures, like the souvenirs and popular narratives based on the Pacific Northwest Modoc War studied by Boyd Cothran. Wilder was memorializing her beloved family and their lifeworld on the Plains, and she was not recounting any particular historic battle or cultural engagement between whites and Indigenous Americans.[19] Above all, she was writing for children, and not adults. Nonetheless, she was also writing for a 1930s commercial market that had a shared understanding of American history in which white American settlers had followed their destinies to cross a continent, and had established farms and built democracies in the wilderness. But by the late twentieth century, the cultural marketplace for narratives of American history had changed substantially, and Wilders' stories now carried different meanings for many readers.

Most of Wilder's books either omitted local Indigenous cultures entirely (even when they had been there, historically), or depicted them briefly, in sometimes positive ways. The first book in the series, *Little House in the Big Woods*, presents the Wisconsin woods that the family settled in as nearly empty, with only a few white families in the area who had moved into what were apparently "empty" lands. "As far as a man could go to the north," the book opens, "there was nothing but woods. There were no houses. There were no roads. There were no people."[20] In fact, a variety of Indigenous cultures could be found in nineteenth-century Wisconsin and Minnesota, although at the time Wilder's book was set, most were in the process of being forcibly removed by the federal government in the ethnic cleansing that followed the US-Dakota War.[21]

In 1862, the Dakota people, incensed by years of treaty violations and starvation, and because federal payments for their ceded lands had not arrived, attacked white settlers in New Ulm and the surrounding region, killing between 650 to 800 whites over a several month period. In response, Minnesota's governor declared that "the Sioux Indians of Minnesota must be exterminated or driven forever beyond the borders of the state." The treaties were abrogated and the Dakotas' land was seized; thirty-nine Dakota were publicly hanged in the largest mass execution in US history. Most of the remaining Indigenous peoples in the state (including the Winnebago, who had not joined the uprising) were shipped off to Dakota Territory and Nebraska.[22] Wilder's mother undoubtedly remembered the panic that seized white settlers in Wisconsin during the months before the Dakota were defeated, and the *Little House* books make it clear that Ma feared and disliked "Indians."

But Wilder's books were intended for children, and the Dakota War ended years before she was born. Indigenous Americans are erased in the story world of the first book and when the family moves on to Minnesota and then to Dakota Territory in later volumes, the land is similarly "empty" of both buffalo and Indigenous communities, with no discussion of how that came to be. Except for *Little House on the Prairie*, Indian characters appear only fleetingly in the other books, usually depicted in positive terms. An elderly chief appears suddenly in De Smet in one scene in *The Long Winter*, to warn the settlers that the coming winter will be extraordinarily harsh; Laura's father takes the warning seriously, which helps to save the family. In *By the Shores of Silver Lake*, a mixed-race friend of Pa's, Big Jerry, protects the family from a threatened robbery.

Indian characters (no tribal affiliation is given) are a substantial presence and threat to the family only in *Little House on the Prairie*, the novel that caused the most controversy among Wilder's readers by the late twentieth century. Laura was less than three when the family squatted land on the Osage Diminished Reserve in what is now southeastern Kansas. The territory was not open to white settlers and the Osage people had a reputation for fiercely defending their lands; in deciding to move his family there to establish a farm on land that belonged to the Osage, Charles Ingalls must have known that he was taking a considerable risk. The Osage also believed (with some cause) that the government was not living up to its treaty obligations, and owed them payments for other, previously ceded lands. But Charles Ingalls and other whites were convinced that the government would soon forcibly remove the Osage from what remained to them of their homeland, and sell their land cheaply to any settlers who had already established "facts on the ground." The Osage were off at their hunting grounds when the Ingalls family arrived, but they later returned.

Relations with the Osage were tense over the next year for the white settlers who had squatted land. The book describes Indian characters as "naked wild men," who entered the family's cabin without invitation—as if they owned the land—who forced Ma to cook for them, and stole Pa's tobacco when they left.[23] On another occasion, two Indian characters enter the cabin and attempt to take all of the furs that Pa has stockpiled, their food, and their tobacco; but in the end, they leave the furs behind. With no explanation as to why the Osage might have felt aggrieved toward white settlers who were squatting on their lands and using their resources, the book simply depicts the Indian intruders as frightening thieves: "Their eyes were black and still and glittering, like snake's eyes....Their faces were bold and fierce and terrible."[24]

Later in the novel, the family hears "war cries" and "terrible yells" for days and nights on end, and fear that the Indians will massacre all the settlers. Although Wilder did not know this, the cries and conversations the family could overhear were probably the Osage's deliberations regarding a new and somewhat more generous federal treaty offer for their lands, which they were ultimately compelled to accept. Toward the end of the book, the Indian characters ride past the cabin in a long and solemn procession, clearly vacating the area; Laura abruptly demands that her parents obtain an Indian baby for her, a bizarre demand that both parents reject sharply. Nonetheless, the Ingalls family leaves Kansas at the end of the book, blaming the government, which Pa claims is going to clear the white settlers from Indian Territory. In fact, the Ingalls left Kansas because the farmer they had sold their Wisconsin farm to had defaulted on his payments, and had asked to return the land to them.[25]

The book's characters express a range of attitudes toward the "Indians." Ma clearly dislikes and fears them, and some of the family's neighbors claim that "the only good Indian is a dead Indian," arguing that the Indians deserve to lose their land, because they don't develop it as white settlers would.[26] Pa, who consistently acts as the moral center of the stories, repeatedly argues that the Indian characters are "perfectly friendly," and that "Indians would be as peaceable as anyone else if they were let alone. On the other hand, they had been moved west so many times that naturally they hated white folks."[27] On two occasions in the book, he has respectful and amicable interactions with Indian men. But Pa also believes that "an Indian ought to have enough sense to know when he is licked," and tells Laura that "when white settlers come into a country, the Indians have to move on."[28]

Like the marketplaces of remembrance that Wilder was writing for, Pa has no doubt that white farmers have a right to settle in the territory, even if they homestead before the government has legally acquired the land. In the end the Osage, a vanquished people, retreat quietly from the scene, leaving the land to the settlers. The book presents the white settlers as having a right to expect that the land that they have developed as farmland would become theirs, when in fact the Osage were the legal owners of the land, at the time when the book was set.[29]

Some of the earliest research done by Wilder scholars (both amateurs and professionals) after her death established the actual location of the Ingalls's farm, something which Wilder and her daughter had been unable to do with their research during the 1930s. Once the location was established, it was clear that the Ingalls had moved into Osage lands. One of the earliest and bestselling biographies of Wilder, published by Donald Zochert in 1976, noted that the 1870 census taker who had visited the Ingalls's homestead wrote on the Ingalls's census schedule that "the Lands [their farm stood on] belong to the Osage Indians and Settlers had no title to said Lands."[30] Later biographies also made it clear that the Ingalls had settled on Osage lands, and that the Osage were affronted by the fact that "the lands promised them by the United States government were being invaded" by settlers, who were damaging or taking Osage game and crops, and they responded by attempting to intimidate the settlers into moving away.[31] All of these biographies also noted that the family had returned to Wisconsin because of their purchaser's default on the Wisconsin farm, and not because they had concerns about squatting land, or because the federal government was clearing out the settlers by force.

These facts were widely understood among the many amateur and professional scholars in the Wilder fandom by the 1970s, who by this time had established a historical context and corrective to the novel's claims. But the aspects of the book that caused the most controversy beginning during the 1990s were not only the land squatting but rather *Little House on the Prairie*'s descriptions of the Indigenous characters' appearance and behavior. Wilder's books were popular with American school teachers throughout the mid- to late twentieth century, and they often read them aloud in class or assigned class projects based on the books. *Little House on the Prairie* was a common choice for teachers, and thus many schoolchildren of all races were exposed to the novel's descriptions of "Indians."

## *Little Houses* in the Classroom

By the early 1990s, Wilder scholars and Indigenous scholars began to publish critical evaluations of Wilder's books, particularly *Little House on the Prairie*. In a few school districts, Indigenous school employees and parents began to question the book's place in elementary school curriculums, where exposure to it was mandatory for all children. Attempts to remove the book from school curriculums or even libraries failed in Louisiana and Sturgis, South Dakota in 1993. In Sturgis, the school board temporarily restricted teachers from reading the book in class, but left copies available in the school library; the ban was later rescinded. One white parent's response to the Sturgis request previewed the arguments that would appear in later defenses of the book's place in elementary schools. Sam Hurst, a white rancher in the Buffalo Gap area, wrote to the *Rapid City Journal* in November 1993 that:

> When I read that Sturgis school officials were considering a ban on the reading of Laura Ingalls Wilder's prairie classics in the classroom, I did what any red-blooded American parent ought to do. I pulled *Little House on the Prairie* off the shelf and read it to my children. A committee of parents and

teachers will now begin the contentious process of trying to decide what's appropriate for elementary school students and what's not, a slippery slope indeed. My 9-year-son was very indignant about the many references to Indians as "savages"... what I find baffling is the notion that if we ban books like *Little House on the Prairie*, Indian children will somehow be protected from racism. It's absurd on its face; Indian children have their own life experience to set Wilder's writings in context. They know European civilization has a problem with racism. They don't need to be sheltered from Laura Ingalls Wilder, or 19th century racial attitudes. It's white children who need to read the book and understand their own history. It's the white community that needs to examine our history of settlement. Like all good literature, Wilder's work should be read in its historical context.[32]

Hurst marshalled the same responses that many white parents and grandparents had toward later requests that the book be removed from elementary school curriculums. He saw it as "book banning," which for him was intrinsically indefensible. Hurst and others also felt that the book contained many "teachable moments" about the history of white settlers' racism, and felt that in any case, it was best to acknowledge the uglier aspects of whites' westward expansion during the nineteenth century.

A Lakota parent, Angela Cavender Wilson, mounted a more sustained protest against the book in 1998, which inspired much broader discussions and reporting throughout Minnesota. Cavender Wilson was a member of the Upper Sioux Community near Granite Falls, and her daughter Autumn was a third-grade pupil in the Yellow Medicine East school district in 1998. Cavender Wilson was also a graduate student in history (she earned her PhD from Cornell in 2000) and was already an Indigenous rights activist.[33] When Autumn's teacher, Bev Tellefson, a fervent Wilder fan, read aloud *Little House on the Prairie* during the fall of 1998, Autumn went home in tears. The mother of another Lakota child in the class later told the school board that her daughter told her that she was not bothered by it, but then explained, "I just pretend that I'm not Indian."[34]

Cavender Wilson subsequently submitted a complaint to the district that listed and cogently analyzed the many negative descriptions of Indian characters in the book, along with its overall endorsement of the doctrine of Manifest Destiny. "The underlying message in this work is that the white settlers are the heroes and the Indians are the villains," she concluded.

I do not believe that any child should have to be made ashamed of who they are while attending school. The bottom line is that my daughter was hurt and embarrassed. I believe it would be difficult for any native child to finish the book and not feel a sense of humiliation, degradation, and sadness because of the way Indians are portrayed.

Cavender Wilson requested that the book be pulled from the school's curriculum, pointing out that while children could avoid reading a book kept in the library, that no child could avoid exposure to a reading that was part of a mandatory curriculum. In the form she filled out to submit her complaint, she was asked "In its place, what book of equal literary quality would you recommend that would convey as valuable a picture and perspective of our civilization?" In response, Cavender Wilson circled the words "our civilization," and wrote in "who is 'our'?"[35]

Cavender Wilson presented a thorough, persuasive critique of the book to her local school board and persuaded all but one member. The school board temporarily removed it from the curriculum and appointed a committee to evaluate what types of materials would be appropriate for each grade level, but it did not remove the book from the school library. One school board member perceived Cavender Wilson's proposal as "book banning," however, and this was how her proposal was subsequently framed in the discussions that followed.[36] For the next two months, the local and Minnesota state press reported on (and contributed to) a lively and generally quite civil debate, in which both sides discussed the book's impact on the children who read it, and the role that it might play in elementary school curriculums.

Like Sam Hurst six years earlier, many white residents of Granite Falls saw the book as a "midwestern classic" that was part of their cultural heritage, and objected fiercely to "book banning" on principle. The racist descriptions of Indian characters in the book were widely acknowledged, but some argued that these could be used to teach pupils about the history of racism, and that this was a more honest accounting of American history. Autumn's teacher, Bev Tellefson, responded to Cavender Wilson's complaint. She wrote to the school board that she used the book in her classes to teach her pupils about

The lack of understanding between cultures at that time in history . . . [and how the family] return[s] to Minnesota when Pa learned that the government had jumped the gun in allowing resettlement on Indian territory [Tellefson seems to have taken the book's explanation at face value, which was not accurate]. This was and is history! . . . This is history and literature coming alive for them and not just literature . . . This book is used as a tool to not discriminate [*sic*]. It was a reality of the times and with the discussion of what is and is not appropriate behavior in the past it is our hope to not repeat it again . . . [Tellefson mentioned other historical instances of injustice, e.g., treatment of Chinese migrants during building of railroads and the Holocaust, concluding that] people must be aware in order to make progress in human relations. Hiding the history is not the answer to the opportunity to learn from the mistakes of the past.[37]

The community around Granite Falls was clearly deeply divided on the issue, but two local newspapers, the Granite Falls *Advocate Tribune* and the *Central Tribune* of Willmar, Minnesota, ultimately published editorials recommending that the book should be removed from the school curriculum (which pupils could not avoid) but that it should also continue to be make available for children to check out individually from the school library, if they wished. The most important newspaper in the state, the *Minneapolis Star Tribune*, had more mixed commentary (seeing the books as offering "teachable moments" regarding racism in American history) but its reporting also gave a full airing to Cavender Wilson and her allies in the Upper Sioux Community.[38]

The school board might have agreed with the compromise solution endorsed by the local newspapers, but the issue was so widely discussed that it attracted the attention of the Minnesota State Civil Liberties Union, which weighed in very strongly against any form of censorship. Informing the Yellow Medicine East school board that removing the book from either the curriculum or library (two entirely different propositions) would violate previous Supreme Court decisions, the MCLU threatened a lawsuit against the district if it acted on Cavender Wilson's complaint. Fearing an expensive and protracted lawsuit, the board voted to rescind their decision that the book should not be read in the classroom to all students. Cavender Wilson left the board meeting in tears when this was announced. But in order to avoid continuing divisions, the teachers at her daughter's schools were asked to take down classroom displays that featured Wilder's books, and in other ways apparently lowered its profile in their classrooms.[39] Cavender Wilson's daughter was transferred to a different teacher's class.

The use of Wilder's books in American public schools declined after 2000. Historians and teachers alike attributed some of the change to the impact of the No Child Left Behind Act of 2002, which introduced far-reaching changes in how reading skills and social studies were taught in public schools across the United States. The Act worked to diminish the role of novels in elementary school curricula, and to discourage the practice of reading aloud from novels to pupils. In reading textbooks (basal readers) given to elementary school students, the use of excerpts from Wilder's books declined; in their place, some districts adopted passages from historical novels that were told from the point of view of nineteenth-century Indigenous children, such as Louise Erdrich's *Birchbark House* series.[40] Changing evaluations of Indigenous cultures and white settlers in American history no doubt played a role in individual teachers' choices, as well, although Wilder's books continued to be used by many homeschoolers.

Across the Midwest, some of the small-town elites and board members of the Wilder societies which had created the homesites during the mid-twentieth century began to take into account their contemporaries' changing views of Western and Indigenous history. The Laura Ingalls Wilder Museum in Pepin, Wisconsin, made substantial changes to its displays on the local history that formed the backdrop to its focus on Wilder's birth and early childhood in the area. The new displays wrote Indigenous history back into Wilder's original narrative of Wisconsin woods that were "empty" of people other than white settlers. Relying on research done by archeologists and other scholars, the displays now trace the history of regional Indigenous cultures between 10,000 BCE and 1650 CE, discussing changes over this period in local climate and Indigenous cultures' food sources, technologies, arts, architecture, trade networks, and political systems. The small museum devoted a relatively large space to regional Indigenous histories, but the display's narrative ends around the time of first contact with Europeans. In 2007 the Pepin homesite organization also updated the "Laura Contest" held at the town's annual Laura Days celebration. Winners had been previously selected based on their ability to create costumes and conform their appearance to those of the book's character, which of course advantaged those who could resemble white settler children; thereafter, the contest was based on an ability during a verbal quiz to show an understanding of Wilder's novels, and on contestant's ability to analyze them, thus rewarding analysis rather than mimicry.[41]

In Mansfield, Missouri, the homesite's leadership convened a series of meetings in 2003, inviting public history and humanities scholars and experts from across the United States to brainstorm the future of the site, as the basis for a new master plan. Completed in 2008, the new plan included a fundraising for a new museum complex and a larger set of displays on the Ingalls and Wilders, which was opened in 2016. It also noted that "the impressions of an ancient road still in use until at least 1894 are clearly visible on Rocky Ridge Farm. Worn down by many centuries of Native American use prior to the arrival of settlers, it was also used by the settlers, and was even an alternate route taken by one of the last contingents on The [Cherokees'] Trail of Tears. The Master Plan honors the location of the former road by leaving it undisturbed and viewable to visitors from newly created walking trails."[42] The educational programs offered by the Mansfield homesite for children also began to incorporate information about Indigenous cultures and history. Some of the sites associated with Wilder have not changed how they present the history of white settlers, however, and elide the history of local Indigenous cultures.

Outside the community of Wilder fans, however, the depiction of Indigenous Americans in Wilder's books faced much stronger scrutiny and criticism from scholars and librarians after 2000. Children's librarians—the professional group that had promoted and supported Wilder's original success—now distanced themselves from her work. Some members of the American Library Association began to argue that the organization should change the name of its lifetime achievement medal for illustrators or authors of children's literature, which had been named for Wilder in 1954. The Wilder award was administered by a branch of the American Library Association, the Association for Library Service to Children (the ALSC, which represented children's libraries), which also oversees the prestigious Newbery awards for children's literature and other awards. In 2017, the ALSC's Board of Directors established a task force to evaluate whether the organization should change the Wilder award's name, since (as the Executive Director wrote to the Board) some members were concerned that Wilder's

> place in the canon of children's literature is not universally consistent with ALSC's [core] values . . . The Wilder Award began in 1954 when the ALSC Board gave Wilder an award for lifetime achievement, and later established the ongoing award in her name. Today, this award elevates a legacy that is not consistent with [ALSC core] values of diversity and inclusion—something that we did not fully understand as a profession when we created the award . . . A member wrote me: "the Wilder [award] is a monument that says something about our profession's history, but every year that it is given out it also says something about our present."[43]

The task force created by the Board surveyed the ALSC's members and those of affiliate organizations and asked them to vote for or against changing the Wilder award's name; it also asked for input by literary scholars and well-known children's authors.

The results of the ALSC vote were lopsided: members voted to change the award's name by a 2 to 1 margin. But the task force's survey also revealed complex, deeply held positions among the ALA's membership. One librarian who voted to change the award's name wrote that

> I grew up loving Wilder's work. I am from Kansas, the descendant of homesteaders and my parents gave me the book with an idyllic story about how similar our family's story is. I now live far away and am married to a tribally enrolled Native man, raising tribally enrolled biracial Native children. These are hard legacies to reconcile. I have a lot of nostalgia and lingering positive feelings for Wilder, but I am more worried about what her legacy could mean for children like my daughters. And even for children like me who never stopped to consider that when my great-great-great grandparents "won" their land, from who did they win it?[44]

Another librarian agreed, arguing that "Wilder's books, while treasured and important, convey negative and harmful images and ideals about indigenous people ... another author's name might better represent a lasting positive impact on children's literature," which is what the award recognized.

But many members came to very different conclusions, seeing the name change as a form of historical erasure of unpleasant truths and the imposition of current values on past cultures, like the midwestern parents who had opposed the removal of the books from their children's curricula. Others again argued that the books had a plethora of "teachable moments," like the librarian who responded that: "The Wilder books are still seminal children's literature in the US. They had an impact on me personally in my youth and they helped me question and interrogate some of the treatment of Native Americans. The books are incredibly powerful in opening critical conversations." The role that Wilder's books could play as a conversation opener with children regarding white settlement and Indigenous peoples was widely cited by defenders of the *Little House* books.[45]

Given the membership's vote tallies, the outcome could not have been in doubt: the Wilder Medal's name was changed in 2018 to the "Children's Literature

Legacy Award." The reaction among librarians (both those who were critical of Wilder's books, and those who loved them) and Wilder's admirers was immediate and heartfelt. When the ALSC Board's vote to change the award name was announced at ALA's 2018 annual conference, Dr. Debbie Reese—a Nambé Pueblo educator and librarian who founded the influential American Indians in Children's Literature blog—tweeted that, "a motion is being made to change the name of the award." "All in favor! Nobody opposed. Lot of tears!" "Tears of joy."[46] The majority of public reactions among ALA members mirrored Reese's. Although clearly in the minority of ALA members, some members nonetheless strongly disagreed with the decision; a few even donated to the Mansfield Wilder organization in protest. One commenter on the *Library School Journal's* announcement of the decision wrote that:

> Sadly, this confirms my suspicions that the decision is rooted in politics. Conservative opinions are excluded more and more in education and literary world [sic]. This decision represents the opinions of only one portion of literary leaders ... preserving and learning from our history tends to be a more conservative view. The latest craze is to change the name of anything that is tied to racism, inequality, injustices of the past. An attempt to erase the history rather than understand and learn from the evolution of our country—mistakes and all."[47]

Members of the Wilder fan community also disagreed with the ALSC's decision, offering the same perspectives that had informed earlier debates. The Laura Ingalls Wilder Legacy and Research Association issued a response that argued that although Wilder's books are "encumbered with the perspectives of racism that were representative of her time and place, also includes overwhelmingly positive contributions to children's literature that have touched generations past and will reach into the future ... [her books'] perspectives are teaching moments to show generations to come how the past was and how we, as a society, must move forward with a more inclusive and diverse perspective."[48]

This chapter has summarized the debates among parents, teachers, librarians, and Wilder fans about the depiction of Indigenous peoples in her books at some length, because these discussions exemplify the ways in which historical fan communities are affected by historiographical and cultural changes in their own, present-day cultures. In this case, changes in Western historiography and public history narratives challenged and fragmented the consensus understanding of

American history that had predominated among white Americans for much of the nineteenth and twentieth centuries. At the same time, historical genre entertainments, particularly Westerns, declined in popularity with American audiences.

These changes meant that the fictional world and values of the *Little House* books remained attractive to cultural conservatives, reinforced by the values presented in the *Little House on the Prairie* television series, which frequently stressed conservative and religious themes. But in the process, the books became less appealing to liberal Americans (e.g., the majority of the members of the ALSC), some of whom distanced themselves from the series. The *Little House* stories and television series still have fans across the political spectrum, but as Wilder scholar Pamela Smith Hill noted, "Laura Ingalls Wilder's reputation is crumbling," among liberal and progressive readers, because of what Hill sees as "a superficial understanding of Wilder's work."[49]

The *Little House* fan community and some of the homesites, like the culture they are part of, have begun to work through the process of reevaluating and including Indigenous Americans into the historical world where the stories are set. The fact that the stories are seen as "Midwest classics" and that the homesites offer the experience of white communities' regional histories, along with ways to visualize and experience the story world, means that the fandom and its organizations will continue to draw an audience among white midwesterners and cultural conservatives nationwide. But changes in school curricula and methods, along with the shifts and fragmentation in Americans' understandings of their history and the decline in the popularity of Western genre entertainments, make it unlikely that the books will ever regain the popularity and widespread classroom use that they once enjoyed. As a result, the *Little House* fandom is aging, a trend noted by most of the Wilder fans I interviewed.

## German *Indianer* and Indigenous Cultures after the Wall

In Germany, membership in the cowboy and Indian clubs is also aging, although the causes there were somewhat different from the changes that affected the *Little House* fandom and American Western fans. The changes in Germany's political culture and state policies were more fundamental than the US culture wars, and the underlying causes for political upheaval were unconnected to German Western fans' enthusiasms. But the rupture of the *Wende*, which transformed the laws, economy, demographics, and space for cultural expression in eastern Germany, in many ways produced more knock-on effects for German fans than *Little House* fans had experienced. Unsurprisingly, the greatest changes were seen in the provinces that had been part of East Germany, but Germany's reunification affected all Germans, and the region's absorption by West Germany in 1990 sharply changed the playing field for German fans of the American West. And in Germany, as in the United States, Indigenous resurgence and criticisms offered by Indigenous activists affected fans' activities, and sometimes put fans on the defensive. In this respect, the experiences of German and American fans were parallel, as both communities grappled with the fact that the Indians had not "vanished," as their foundational stories had envisioned.

Western fans had faced many obstacles to the pursuit of their hobbies in East Germany. Karl May fans could not organize openly in literary societies or publicize book-related activities, nor were the other platforms for telling May-related stories (open-air theatricals, Karl May movies, etc.) allowed until the last few years of East Germany's existence, when cultural policies began to liberalize.[50] Before the 1980s, Western fans risked retaliation from the East German secret police if they developed role-play *personas* based on white American roles, and were effectively redirected by the secret police to focus on Indigenous cultures and *personas*. Thus only one form of Western club life could receive permission to organize and even (perhaps surprisingly, from an American point of view) could receive financial support from the state.

State support for Indianist hobbyists' public performances was one example of East Germany's sponsorship of cultural events that were intended to offer their citizens a window on the outside world. Few East Germans were allowed to travel outside of the Soviet Bloc, and the regime attempted to compensate for travel restrictions by sponsoring a wide variety of cultural events featuring music, dance, and other forms of expression from other nations and cultures, generally framing the entertainments in ways that aligned with Soviet Bloc politics. Thus, East German *Indianer* performances gave their fellow citizens exposure to mimetic versions of Indigenous cultures—cultures that Germans had long felt an affinity for and profound interest in—but that very few East Germans could ever experience in person. An additional advantage, from authorities' standpoint, was that hobbyist performances also aligned well with the regime's critique of US imperialism and the oppression of Indigenous Americans.

East German fans had also worked around consumption constraints that were found in all Soviet Bloc cultures. Since few East Germans were allowed to travel to the United States or order goods from there, fans faced challenges in obtaining the raw materials needed for making *Indianer* outfits and artifacts; they displayed impressive resourcefulness and dedication in solving those problems. They cherished the rare contacts that they could have with Indigenous North Americans, particularly the AIM, which cultivated contacts with both West and East German supporters.

The constraints on East German fans' consumption were only one small example of the problems faced by East German consumers overall, and the failure to satisfy consumers was one (but not the only) cause of East Germany's collapse. Their nation's political and economic systems were interconnected with those of the Soviet Union, and both nations struggled with economic stagnation and internal political challenges during the 1980s, which resulted in rising discontent. Growing popular political protests mounted by East German citizens compelled the Politbüro to open the Berlin Wall in November 1989. A few months later, East German citizens voted for parties that supported their nation's unification with West Germany as new provinces within the previously-existing West German nation-state, which took place in October 1990.[51] In a short space of time, East Germans lived through drastic economic and political changes. These changes left some East Germans feeling that their region ultimately became a colony of West Germany, suffering from persistently high levels of unemployment and the steady loss of younger East Germans to the "older" provinces in the west, where economic prospects were brighter.[52]

For East German fans, the regime's collapse transformed the social and political context for all fandoms, and for every type of leisure activity. Western fans could now organize any form of club they desired, and soon began to play with white Western roles.[53] If they could afford to travel to the United States, they were now able to do so. The merger with West Germany also meant that larger numbers of Indigenous entrepreneurs and artists could more easily visit the Eastern provinces, offering the same handicrafts, services, and performances that they had offered in growing numbers during recent years to West German consumers.[54] The museum in Radebeul was renamed yet again, as the Karl May Museum, and the author's former home on the museum grounds (used by the state for other purposes in East Germany) was refurbished and reopened to fan visitors. As in West Germany, fan groups in former East Germany soon began to mount their own summer open-air productions of Karl May performances. The *Wende* had changed and broadened Western and indeed all East German fans' range of expression and activities.

At the first gathering of leaders of *Indianistik* clubs from former East Germany after the Wall was opened, one long-time hobbyist noted a sudden change in how those present had dressed for the meeting. Previously, she wrote, "most of the Indianists came to the meetings wearing Stetson [hats] and Indian artifacts like necklaces, amulets, etc. Doing so expressed playful opposition to daily life [in East Germany]." But at the first gathering after the regime's collapse, only one person attended wearing a Stetson. Instead, many of the younger members were wearing Palestinian scarves, a clothing accessory that was popular among West German political progressives and which they saw as a similar symbol of opposition to the authorities. Many of the homemade (i.e., German fan made) pieces of Indian outfits had now disappeared, and in their place "people proudly wore newly acquired original Indian turquoise jewelry."[55]

The rise in the value of the German Mark compared to the dollar after 1980 and the end of travel restrictions on East Germans after 1990 meant that many more ordinary Germans traveled to the United States during the 1980s and 1990s than before, and thus more were exposed to modern Indigenous Americans. Germans' perceptions of the Indigenous peoples they met challenged their earlier, historic or fictionalized images of "Indians," offering Germans more modern images, which included lifestyles not as different from their own as some might have hoped to see. The growth of internet sites in the 1990s gave Germans a second point of entry to encounter Indigenous North Americans, constituting a second wave of international contacts and exposure to the "real thing."

In this sense, the collapse of the Wall served as a sort of transnational wake-up call, allowing some Germans to perceive the romanticized or outdated aspects of their former interpretations of *Indianer*, while others persisted in earlier views of Indigenous peoples. Some German hobbyists and other fans were disillusioned by the reality of American reservation life, where they witnessed poverty, alcoholism, and also how Indigenous Americans had "unIndian" lifestyles that included pickup trucks and refrigerators. "They aren't real Indians anymore," a few older members of the Old Manitou Club assured visitors in 2007. "Anyone who wants to know what the 'real' Indian life is like would be better off coming here."[56]

This quotation points to the fact that for some German Western fans, actual Indigenous visitors to Germany failed the test of "authenticity," which for them was rooted in historicity. For these fans, "real" Indigenous people did not wear modern dress or have modern lifestyles. Some hobbyists requested visiting Indigenous people who wanted to join hobbyists' summer camps to wear handmade historic clothing styles, which Indigenous visitors might perceive as the erasure of their modern identity. Other Indigenous visitors were made to feel inadequate by Western fans because they did not look or dress like Plains Indigenous peoples, which remained the "gold standard" for Indigeneity in many Germans' eyes. This led Drew Hayden Taylor, a visiting Anishinaabe writer from Curve Lake First Nation, to conclude that "they're [the Germans] obsessive about Plains Indians. Tipis! You never see a longhouse, you never see a wigwam, it has to be Plains, and, of course, Lakota if at all possible. You know, I think the Lakota had a better publicist or something."[57]

That said, other Indigenous North Americans who visited Germany after 1990 had positive experiences and were treated with respect by German fans who wanted deepen their understanding of Indigenous cultures and sought mentoring from Indigenous elders. Renae Watchman, a Diné (Navajo) scholar who visited German fans' powwows, had mixed feelings about the gathering she observed. But she also commented that other visiting Indigenous people in recent years had educated German participants in the correct songs, dances, and format for powwows, teaching Germans to approach "powwow as a diverse, vibrant celebration of song and dance rather than as a kitschy, romanticized Plains display."[58] Other Indigenous North Americans were impressed by the skilled handicrafts that German fans had mastered.

Overall, Indigenous North Americans became less interesting to many younger Germans, since their representations were more modernized; as Glenn Penny noted, "many lost their interest in playing Indian once they were confronted with 'the real thing,'" which worked to reduce the number of new members joining cowboy and Indian clubs across Germany. At the same time, more Indigenous people visited or settled in Germany after 1980, taking control of "the authority to mediate representations" of Indigeneity; they claimed the role of selling "real Indian art," of teaching "real" crafts classes, etc. for those who were still interested in "the real thing."[59]

Indigenous Americans who lived in Germany formed their own organization in 1994, the Native American Association of Germany (NAAoG). The new organization offered Germans education about Indigenous dances, music, regalia, and culture, and in its early years, organized powwow meetings that non-Indigenous people could take part in.[60] Hobbyists simply could not compete with Indigenous artists and performers in entertainment marketplaces by the early twenty-first century. In East Germany before 1989, Indianist hobbyists had provided a cultural experience—exposure to carefully studied and re-created handicrafts and performances—for other Germans. But now, Indigenous performers were also available for localities and organizations that could afford them, while public subsidies for hobbyists' performances dried up.

In Radebeul, city authorities used the presence of the Karl May Museum and the city's long association with May and his fans as a springboard for a new Karl May Days festival, held annually. The festival served as an annual "big tent" gathering for the entire spectrum of German Western fans after German reunification, with separate areas on the grounds and events for a variety of Western-related activities. German Indianist hobbyists were active in the festival during the 1990s and through the first years of the twenty-first century. As they had before the fall of the Wall, Indianist hobbyists in their outfits performed dances and provided entertainment during the Karl May Days, but they generally did not mix with the Karl May fans because they saw May's depiction of the West as sheer fantasy. After 2000, however, Indigenous North American performers contacted the festival organizers and offered to perform at the festival, and have now become an established part of the entertainment. Indigenous performers displaced the older East German hobbyists, who stopped participating. Many no longer attend the Karl May Days, or if they do so, dressed in street clothing.[61]

Indianist hobbyists across Germany have declined in numbers in recent years. In the former East German provinces, hobbyists no longer had to register with the state and find official sponsoring organizations in order to meet, and many found the West German regulations for "registered clubs" to be burdensome and avoided registering at all. Those who continued their hobby did so as a "private matter" instead of offering public performances, and some hobbyists in the eastern provinces only met with larger numbers of fellow hobbyists at the summer Week camp for all Indianist hobbyists, which continues to be held.[62] The Brandenburg Mohawk group also declined steadily after German reunification; out of the twenty-four members it had at its peak, only nine still remained in 2005. A parallel decline among German Indianist hobbyists seems to have taken place in former West Germany, although the participation of cowboy and other role-players continued; as one leader of the Munich Cowboy Club lamented, "we don't have more than three [Indians] anymore."[63] German hobbyist meetings are held in fenced or otherwise restricted locations, which are guarded by patrols of hobbyists who turn away outsiders, except for limited "open" events when outsiders are allowed to attend, in the hope that new members might be inspired to join.[64]

East German Indianist hobbyists had developed a form of cultural tourism for the audiences who attended their public performances, without being indigenous to the cultures that were being performed. Over generations, these fan communities had developed into separate subcultures, increasingly pursuing "authenticity" in their handicrafts and performances after 1960, while also creating their own histories and subculture identities, marrying and raising children in these communities. But after the *Wende*, the increasing presence of Indigenous North Americans in Germany, changing attitudes in the West and criticism from some Indigenous people about fan activities that were now widely seen as cultural appropriation, and the increasingly contested question of who had the right to represent Indigenous cultures, meant that the contradictions entailed in such a hobby became difficult to navigate. This was particularly true after hobbyist communities received increased attention from academics, filmmakers, and journalists (some of them Indigenous) after 1980.[65]

As we saw earlier, throughout the twentieth century German Indianist hobbyists had sought contact with Indigenous peoples, and gladly deferred to their authority and expertise about Indigenous cultures. Some Indigenous North Americans who met German Indianist hobbyists (either in Germany or during hobbyists' visits to the United States) responded positively to hobbyists' empathy and engagement with their cultures, and acknowledged a mutual affinity between Germans and Indigenous cultures. Glenn Penny's work persuasively demonstrates that many Indigenous activists appreciated the support they received from East and West German supporters of Indigenous cultures' rights and that "some American Indians grew to tolerate and, on occasion, even appreciate the hobbyists' other activities [creating replicas of tribal regalia or handicrafts, and reenacting Indigenous ceremonies]."[66] Members of Lakota communities that had maintained contact with German hobbyists for decades, and who had supplied performers for German circuses, were more accepting of German tourists' interest in participating in sacred ceremonies and of their sincerity, as were some Navajo communities. Other Indigenous cultures, like the Hopi communities that German tourists sought out, perceived the visitors' intense interest in sacred spaces, artifacts, and rituals as rude and disrespectful.[67]

German tourists to North American reservations were thus welcomed and appreciated by some tribal cultures, while being regarded warily by others. Within Germany, however, tensions sometimes developed after 1990 between hobbyists and Indigenous visitors or permanent residents. Some Indigenous visitors perceived German Indianist hobbyists as inappropriate and disrespectful, and said so. Marta Carlson, a Yurok scholar who researched and filmed a documentary about German hobbyists, *Das Powwow*, initially preferred the approach of the East German hobbyists she met to the West Germans, seeing East German fans as respectful and more informed about Indigenous cultures. Over time, however, she became uneasy and puzzled by what she saw as cultural appropriation. She concluded that "if these groups had a true appreciation and respect for Native Americans, they would cease their appropriation of Native American culture altogether."[68] Indigenous scholar and activist Ward Churchill came to the same conclusion. He dismissed the fact that "hobbyists are quick to cite a long history of German-Indian contact as the foundation of Germans' interest in and knowledge about Native American cultures," and instead argued that German hobbyists' activities were a "postcolonial continuation by cultural and spiritual means."[69]

The refurbishment and expansion of the Karl May Museum in Radebeul also brought increased contact with Indigenous visitors. Some were impressed by the museum's holdings, while others were critical of the ways that the displays were framed and presented. Indigenous visitors were particularly offended by the display of scalps allegedly from Indigenous people, given to the museum by Patty Frank. In 2014 the Sault Ste. Marie Tribe of Chippewa Indians, supported by the National Congress of American Indians, sent a delegation to the museum and requested the repatriation of a scalp said to be from a Chippewa. The museum investigated the provenance of the scalp, which was difficult to document, and ultimately refused to turn it over to the Sault Tribe; the scalps were, however, removed from public display and some displays were updated and reframed. In 2020, the Museum agreed to repatriate the scalps to the US.[70]

The Native American Association of Germany originally allowed non-Natives to join them in powwows and dances, often dressed in their own homemade outfits and regalia. But one of the organization's founders, Lindbergh Namingha, came into conflict with German hobbyists, who were sometimes critical of modern Indigenous Americans:

They [the hobbyists] are like a living museum and I find it very offensive, especially when they refuse to let true American Indians [such as himself] participate in their events. They say we're too modern [or inauthentic] and believe we've lost our Native Americanness. They can't seem to understand that our culture, just like theirs, has evolved from the 17th century to the 21st.[71]

In the first years after its creation, the NAAoG allowed Germans to dance in their powwows, wearing Indigenous regalia. By teaching Indigenous dances and music, the members of the NAAoG "envisioned a future of non-Native Americans dancing with a great deal of respect to the meaning of Native American powwow dancing." But conflicts arose between the organization's leadership and Germans who participated:

We recognized the Europeans who take this very seriously and want to understand what dancing really means beyond the beautiful regalia. On the other hand, we cannot dismiss non-Native American dancers who perform Native American dancing as a hobby. A hobby which allows an opportunity to display themselves in traditional regalia to reflect their ability to dance in terms of a big show. Their action exposes them as not possessing the understanding or true concept of the Native American dancing. They have had knowledge of powwows, but lack the spirituality & pure purpose that is associated with Native American dancing. . . . While some [hobbyists] were very respectful, others did not even want to listen to Native American elders' direction or wisdom. Those who did not take heed to the Native American elders continue to do as they wish thus fully disrespecting a culture they have no understanding. Simply, non-Native Americans have no right to act like this, because this is not their culture![72]

The group's leaders had come to see some Germans' powwow performances as reflecting expertise regarding Indigenous outfits and artifacts ("head knowledge") but perceived them as disrespectful, and thus committing cultural appropriation, when they rejected Indigenous Americans' own interpretations of their dances and rituals. Many German members left the group as a result of the dispute, and instead gravitated toward an emerging German-run "powwow scene." The powwow scene (which includes some former German Indianist hobbyists) includes a calendar of regular gatherings devoted to dance, singing, and drumming, which draws primarily European participants.[73] In the "Pow-wow scene," German participants tend to define "authenticity" as using regalia, songs, dances, and formats modeled on modern Indigenous American powwows held in North America, whereas German Indianist hobbyists are interested in replicating historic Indigenous cultural practices.

Globally, however, there was less toleration of racial cross-dressing by the late twentieth century, since this was increasingly seen as insensitive cultural appropriation at best, or at its worst, as the reproduction of racist tropes about Indigenous cultures. The argument that Indianist hobbyism could be a form of living history or public education was increasingly difficult to sustain in the face of Indigenous North Americans, now resurgent, who claimed the right to self-representation. Many Indigenous Americans, such as the Lakota communities surveyed by historians Roy Rosenzweig and David Thelen, felt that their survival as a culture depended on their own mastery and preservations of their dance, music, and handicrafts, seeing these as "essential to group and individual survival."[74] German hobbyists interviewed by ethnologist Petra Kalshoven were aware of these arguments and expressed a variety of responses, which sometimes reflected discomfort with dressing as *Indianer*. Some stopped wearing their handmade outfits at gatherings, but continued to practice storytelling, crafts, and other traditions that German hobbyist communities had developed. Other hobbyists simply withdrew from public performances, and continued their gatherings in private. After generations of evolving practice, Kalshoven suggests that these communities' activities are no longer strictly mimetic but have developed "beyond representation in becoming its own thing, where something new is at stake."[75]

Changes after 1990 thus increasingly brought German Indianist hobbyists into face-to-face contact with Indigenous North Americans. Sometimes the encounters were positive and amicable, with both sides acknowledging a mutual affinity.[76] But as a whole, hobbyists began to withdraw from the public sphere, and in some cases, to redefine their hobbies. Rather than create their own mimetic historic Indigenous outfits and artifacts, some hobbyists are now active in the German "powwow" scene, or choose to engage in other forms of historical reenactment, discussed in Chapter 6.[77] In both Germany and in the United States, the increasing presence and voices of Indigenous people were changing how fans engaged with their hobbies, although the changes in the *Little House* community after 1990 were quite different than developments among German Indianist hobbyists.

Cowboy and other white American *persona* role-play, and other forms of fantasy celebration of a mythical American Old West, however, still continue across Germany. The difference in the recent histories of the Munich Cowboy Club and the Radebeul Old Manitou Club are instructive, in this regard. The Munich club currently defines its activities as a form of living history and historical reenactment. This *raison d'etre* is a substantial shift from earlier generations' view of their hobby, which justified their hobby as preserving "dying" cultures. As the earlier justification became untenable after 1970, Munich fans began to rework their performances, shading into cosplay by the late twentieth century, when they created costumes as actual people like Buffalo Bill and Annie Oakley. The number of club members has declined in recent years, and the membership is aging, but the club continues to put on a lively calendar of annual events.[78]

But like other West German clubs, the Munich group had always offered members a wide choice of historical North American *personas* to play, and continued to maintain its club grounds and annual calendar of events, presenting them in recent decades as living history to the public in regular "open days" and events. During the same decades, the Old Manitou Club members withdrew from public contact and Indian performances after 2000, and no longer appear to hold any events that are open to the public, although members continue to attend the annual summer Week for eastern German Indianist hobbyists.[79] The Munich club, and other Western clubs, also overlap with an array of Western-themed hobby groups, like the German country western music and line dancing "scene," and the type of Western music and performance groups exemplified by the Wild West Boys and Girls Club, discussed in Chapter 2.

Indianist hobbyism appears to be withdrawing from the public sphere and diminishing overall, with some members instead participating in the Civil War reenactment groups discussed in Chapter 6, but the Karl May fandom is still active, more than one hundred years after the creation of the first Western fan group before World War I. These communities revolve around collective discussion, play, and interpretation of May's life and stories, as told in an array of media forms: picking them apart, recreating them, and reworking them according to the interests of the moment. One factor contributing to the vitality of this branch of the German Western community is the fact that fans continue to receive and can interact with new "canon" (new versions of the story world) in several forms. The German RTL network produced a remake of the Winnetou novels in 2016, *Winnetou, the Myth Lives On*.[80] Much like BBC's 2010 *Sherlock* series (which remade the Conan Doyle stories), the RTL version updated and revised the 1960s Karl May films with grittier, less fanciful details in filming locations, costumes, etc., while also changing the ending of the Winnetou story series, provoking divided and lively reactions among fans. In one key respect, the new RTL version resembled earlier plays and movies: the producers deliberately cast an Albanian actor for the role of their lead Indian character, Winnetou. The new movie's creators considered many Indigenous actors for the role, but decided ultimately that they didn't fit the producers' own expectations for what an "Indian warrior" would look like.[81] Their expectations in casting the production were shaped by the fact that Karl May's "Indians" had always been fantasy characters; the change was that May fans were now fully aware of this, something that Indigenous scholars and visitors had always known.

At the same time, May summer theatricals offer new productions annually to growing audiences; the 2019 season broke the record for Bad Segeberg's production, with over four hundred thousand visitors.[82] The Wild West of Winnetou and Old Shatterhand thus continue to be available as ever-present fictional refuges from the routines of daily life; and yet at the same time, fans are constantly remodeling and reinterpreting both worlds through their collective debates and discussions. Their appeal is still partly the nostalgic one of a "lost world," although all of those involved are aware that the nostalgia is for a world that never existed.

Over the last century, the options and forms of expression open to Karl May and all German Western fans could be narrower or wider, depending on the political regime they were operating under, the general economic circumstances they were operating within, and the consumer goods and media forms available to them. Among twentieth-century fandoms, the German Western fan spectrum is thus interesting because it demonstrates how changing political cultures can influence and shape the expression of fans' devotion to their object of fandom. Western fans also demonstrate the ways that role-playing can offer fans both an escape from daily life as well as a menu of symbolic shorthand to choose from, which they can use (as East German Indianists and Civil War reenactors do) to express personal values and identities.

After more than a century of fan activities, the celebration of the May books and films themselves remain attractive to fans, along with a broader Western set of hobbies and activities, while the pursuit of "authentic" *Indianer* lifestyles through the re-creation of Indigenous North American arts and crafts has diminished. Perhaps the May story world and the mythical American Old West as a whole remain compelling precisely because of this imagined world's romantic, "inauthentic" content, and the open-ended nature of fictional narratives. The summer open-air May-themed theatricals provide annually refreshed focal points for fan gatherings and discussions, since the performances offer new interpretations and story lines each year; and fan pilgrimages to locations mentioned in the novels, or where films and television shows were filmed, continue to draw substantial participation.

Karl May and related German Western entertainments do not claim to be historically accurate, or to present living history. They may be (and often are) offensive to Indigenous people and are criticized for racist tropes; but it is difficult to see their fantasy performances as cultural appropriation in the sense that Indianist hobbyism represents. Instead, they are unabashedly fictional, sometimes bordering on whimsy, and often tongue in cheek, characteristics which are clearly part of their appeal. The ahistorical "history" of Karl May's world might also explain the fact that it has proven robust in successive periods. Being purely fictional may help to insulate the May fandom's imaginary world from each generation's tendency to revisit its own history, which in the case of less fictionalized, historically focused fan communities, can result in reevaluations of the past that challenge or even overturn the premises of the historical world that fans play in.

# Indians into Confederates

## Historical Fiction Fans, Reenactors, and Living History

*Let us then admit that there are two histories: the actual series of events*
*that once occurred; and the ideal series that we affirm and hold in memory.*
*The first is absolute and unchanged ... the second is relative, always*
*changing in response to the increase or refinement of knowledge.*

—CARL BECKER, "EVERYMAN HIS OWN HISTORIAN"

Carl Becker, a leading early twentieth-century historian, emphasized in the lecture quoted above a distinction that is often made by academic historians: the difference between the past itself and history, as that history is understood and remembered by living people. The past has its own reality, although the amount of surviving evidence to tell us about that past might vary. But historians' understanding and interpretation of that past is always a work-in-progress.

Amateur historians and historically focused fan communities often seek to recapture the past "as it really happened," meticulously reconstructing historical artifacts and material culture. These concerns are sometimes labeled "antiquarian" by historians, to distinguish them from their own approach. But like academic historians' understanding of past cultures, historical fandoms' understandings of the past are always evolving, developing through each group's research and debates. This book has argued that fans' interpretations and activities change as the world around each fan community alters, adapting to the needs and circumstances of successive generations. But fandoms can also decline and diminish for a variety of reasons: if the fictional genre that the fandom's source canon is part of declines in popularity; if no new remakes or updates of the source canon appear over decades; or if the prevailing political and national culture that the fans live in is such that the canon no longer appeals to many readers in that culture.

This book has traced the histories of particular Western fan communities. They are rooted in a fictional and historical understanding of the American frontier, although each recalls the history of American white settlement quite differently, focusing on different actors and processes. All of these fandoms were affected by changes during the twentieth century in *how* the history of the American West was remembered and by the resurgence of Indigenous activism. Western fandoms were also strongly influenced by broader historical changes: the politics of the early to mid-twentieth century in their respective nations (e.g., the divergent views of the United States in East and West Germany); the political movements of the 1960s and 1970s, which ultimately altered how history was taught in American public schools; the decline of genre Western entertainments that occurred after the end of the Cold War; the culture wars of the 1990s; and (for German fans of the American West) the *Wende*, the reunification of Germany and the transformation of Germans' social and political worlds that followed. As we have seen, these fan communities were also affected by late twentieth-century debates over who had the right to represent and retell those histories: whites or Indigenous people.

The cumulative effect of the changes in the world around them influenced the activities of the members of these fandoms, their available options, how they were and are seen by their contemporaries, and whether new and younger fans come to join these communities, so that they could persist over decades. Broader cultural changes during the twentieth century in the United States and Germany also shaped how each fandom imagined Indigeneity ("Indians" in the imagined West) and white American identity. The fandoms that this book has explored imagined whiteness and Indianness quite differently at the start. How they negotiated and thought about race changed over decades, partly in response to both the presence and resurgence of Indigenous activism after 1970, and sometimes because of changes in how the history of the American frontier was remembered.

When it came to "Indians," for a good part of their histories, all of these fan communities were discussing purely imaginative constructs. The Indians characters presented in Karl May novels, the *Little House* books, and other Western genre entertainments were fictional creations embodying nineteenth-century Germans' and white Americans' concerns and fantasies, both fearful and romantic, about Indigenous cultures. Early and mid-twentieth-century German fans largely internalized the depictions of Indian characters they had been offered in Western genre fiction and entertainments: Karl May novels, those of James Fenimore Cooper and his German imitators, in Cody's *Wild West Show* and traveling circuses, and in early Western films.

German Western fans sometimes saw Indians as violent and threatening, but they were also often depicted as brave, noble, and virtuous, living lives that were closer to nature than modern Europeans, evoking parallels to the Teutonic tribal ancestors of modern Germans. Above all, representations of Indians were compelling and fascinating for early German fans of the American West. Their cultures were said to be rapidly declining, or perhaps already extinct. This was a loss that German fans mourned sincerely, condemning the American federal policies and greedy white settlers who were the cause. They began to revise their elegiac views of Indigenous cultures after coming into contact with AIM and Indigenous activists after 1970. As popular attitudes toward cross-racial identification and dressing, and critiques of cultural appropriation, changed after 1990, German hobbyists also gradually withdrew from public performances as Indianists. Some went into other forms of historical reenactment.

Compared to German Western fans, *Little House* fans never uniformly mirrored the views of Indian characters offered in their fictional canon. This probably had several causes. First, German fan groups organized the earliest cowboy and Indian groups fairly soon after seeing the *Wild West Show*, admiring Indigenous performers in traveling circuses, and reading Karl May and other Western fiction: there was little time gap between canon and the foundation of the fandom. Laura Ingalls Wilder, by contrast, wrote about white settlers and Indians more than sixty years after she first encountered the Osage people as a young child; her stories reflected the attitudes common among white Americans during her childhood.

A second reason that *Little House* fandom had more varied responses to their canon's depiction of Indian characters is that Wilder herself offered a range of white characterizations of Indians and views of settler-Indian relations. Some of her characters argue that "the only good Indian is a dead Indian," and the descriptions of Indians in *Little House on the Prairie* are biased and pejorative. But Pa (Laura's moral compass) shows respect and empathy for the Indians he encounters, and goes to some lengths to avoid violence in his dealings with them. While the *Little House* characters vary in their assessment of Indians, however, they are nonetheless united in their agreement that Indians must "move on," and surrender their lands to white settlers, who will allegedly make better use of the lands. And except for *Little House on the Prairie* and one scene in *The Long Winter*, the rest of Wilder's books generally overlook the existence or history of Indigenous Americans in the territories where Laura lived, resulting in their near-complete erasure.

In their first decades, the fandom and homesites largely followed suit. Local Indigenous communities were not mentioned at homesite museums before 1990, and were not much discussed in fan publications. Rather, the focus of the fandom was on the celebration of white settlers, and their role in American history. The plaques, statues, and homesites that the Wilder community created were intended to memorialize Wilder and white settlers, and also served to codify and "freeze" public memory in ways that reflected mid-century American national identities.

But the fandom changed and broadened its view of Laura's world when it was challenged by Indigenous activists, and as the New Western historiography was absorbed into popular cultural understandings of the West after 1990. By 2019, some homesites had begun to incorporate current understandings of Indigenous history into their exhibits and activities. For some fans, the homesites and Wilder monuments now served as an entry point to understand and question the national biography that Wilder's story world was rooted in. This awareness permeates the activities of many of the fans I spoke with. Pamela Smith Hill, a fan and scholar who has published on Wilder, summarized this position:

> The brilliant accomplishment of the books is that the LIW stories encompass the central contradiction and conflict of the history of the American West, which is the conquest of native peoples—and we need to find meaningful ways to teach children about this painful subject. *Little House on the Prairie* encapsulates the confusion a child feels about pioneer attitudes toward their rights versus the rights of native people. . . . This is a subject we need to see and talk about honestly as Americans.[1]

Hill's interpretation would have been an outlier among Wilder fans fifty years earlier, but it accurately reflects how the books are now seen by many white fans, particularly those who would identify as politically liberal. In a general sense, fan scholarship and discussions also began to give more attention to two extremely helpful but minor nonwhite characters who had appeared fleetingly in the books: Dr. Tann, a Black doctor who appears in one book, and an elderly unnamed Indian man in *The Long Winter*. One fan who is a leader in the home-schooling community commented to me that, "I feel the heroes of two of her books were POC. The elderly Indian man who came to De Smet to warn them [about a series of approaching blizzards] ... without that, there certainly would have been much loss of life. The other example is of Dr. Tann, saving the family by finding and treating the family for malaria .... or there very likely wouldn't have been an Ingalls left to write about."[2] Overall, the bulk of the *Little House* fandom has thus now taken steps to write Indigenous people into its historical vision, but it still cherishes the life worlds and legacies of white settlers, along with the undoubted beauty and quality of Wilder's writing.

In 2021, the Laura Ingalls Wilder Legacy and Research Association respond-ed to the broader national discussion within the US about racism, inclusion, and equity that had developed during the previous year by announcing a new commitment to diversity in its work. The LIWLRA acknowledged that Wilder's books "have racist depictions ... the norms that were accepted in the 1930s about the 1870s and 1880s should not have been tolerated then and are not tolerated today by our organization. We share the pain that is palpable across the Little House community." The organization pledged to support diversity among its membership, board members, in its conference presentations, and in its outreach to audiences.[3]

But *Little House* fans' politics run the gamut from progressive to conserva-tive, and the stories themselves can be read and used to support a variety of worldviews, as Hill's observations make clear. Among Christian conservative homeschoolers, the books can and sometimes do support a "doubling down" on the centrality of white colonial settlement to Americans' history and national identity. Conservative fans are attracted by the books' emphasis on individual self-sufficiency, their hostility toward government institutions, and the impor-tance of religion in the Ingalls's lives, which they see as aligned with conservative Christian antimodernist analyses of current American society and politics.

Some of the politically centrist or progressive fans I interviewed noted with bemusement modern conservative Christians' embrace of the series, since they interpret the role of Christianity in the Ingalls's lives quite differently. Pamela Smith Hill commented that "I've always been puzzled at the way conservative homeschoolers embrace [Wilder], because the Ingalls family prized public education for their own daughters. [Wilder's] brand of Christianity for its time was much more liberal [than modern evangelical Protestant denominations]."[4] Hill and several politically liberal or centrist fans repeatedly mentioned to me a key scene in *Little Town on the Prairie*, when Laura and her parents encounter (and clearly distance themselves from) an evangelical Christian revival meeting led by Rev Brown:

> Chills ran up Laura's spine and over her scalp. She seemed to feel something rising from all those people [attending the revival meeting], something dark and frightening that grew and grew under that thrashing voice. The words no longer made sense, they were not sentences, they were only dreadful words. For one horrible instant Laura imagined that Reverend Brown was the Devil. His eyes had fires in them.[5]

When we discussed this scene, Hill said: "This quotation feels especially timely now; it could be a liberal's description of President Trump and his influence over conservative Evangelicals."[6]

Yet conservative Christian fans I interviewed saw the religious views of the Ingalls quite differently and embraced the *Little House* stories as part of their own interpretation of American history and national identity. The Wilder fandom thus mirrors the challenges mounted against and fragmentation of earlier, Turner-influenced views of Indigenous cultures, white colonial settlement, and American national identity that have emerged in the United States since 1990. Like German Western fans, the Wilder fandom has reevaluated its canon repeatedly, in ways that reflect broader, sometimes polarized contemporary political debates.

The homesite towns themselves today are embedded in landscapes that reflect the political polarization that characterizes modern America. Driving from one midwestern small town to another during the summer of 2019, I was struck by the ubiquity (compared to my Northeastern home region) of billboards championing pro-life arguments and images on highways, and by the groupings of towering Christian crosses on hills outside some towns. Driving into Mansfield, Missouri to visit Wilder's homesite, I noticed a green field full of tiny white crosses. When I stopped to see what sort of cemetery this might be, I saw a sign proclaiming it to be "the field of the fallen unborn": a piece of religious and political protest art. Christian conservatives in many states still hold fast to older American narratives in which white Christians form the foundation for American national identity, and the conviction that they now form a declining percentage of the population has radicalized some. This means that some conservatives champion the *Little House* books as their cultural heritage, while many American liberals and scholars distance themselves from the celebration of American exceptionalism present in Wilder's books.

The diversity of political worldviews and interpretations of Wilder's work were captured in fans' responses to a long series of performances posted on Facebook during the 2020 pandemic by actress Alison Arngrim. As a child actress, Angrim had portrayed Laura's nemesis, Nellie Oleson, in the *Little House* television series; she remains popular and active in the Wilder community today. During the 2020 pandemic, she offered long readings from a series of books on her Facebook page several times each week. Sporting a rainbow-colored array of calico prairie bonnets and including her own frequent side comments, Arngrim read aloud not only Wilder's novels, but as the pandemic wore on, also an array of modern spin-off fiction, as well as novels written by Wilder's daughter, Rose Wilder Lane. The readings reflected a full spectrum of political views, ranging from a prairie girl story in which the protagonist was biracial, which challenged nineteenth-century racism, to Lane's deeply conservative stories. Fan comments on the readings discussed historical foods and lifestyles, but they also interpreted the readings from a broad range of political viewpoints.[7]

But historically focused fan communities in both the United States and Germany were influenced not only (and perhaps even primarily) by scholarly debates, "culture wars," or new historiography, but also by broader changes during the same period about how the past—not only that of the American West, but globally—is remembered or presented. As anthropologist Edward Bruner noted, academic historians focused on scholarly research have faced increasing competition for authority over historical interpretations since the late twentieth century. A variety of new ways of "doing" history as a public hobby or educational activity became increasingly important in how the past was remembered in both Europe and the United States. These approaches had not existed as widespread popular cultural practices when the Western fan communities that are the subject of this book were originally founded, but both the *Little House* and the German Western fan communities were influenced by these practices, with which their own activities overlapped and increasingly converged, in many cases.

These late twentieth-century trends included the rapid growth of hobbyist military reenactment communities. The best-known community here focused on reenactment of the American Civil War, but many other types of historical reenactment also developed after 1970. Military historical reenactments had roots in the nineteenth century, in the historical pageants, parades, and reenactment spectacles staged by authorities in several Western nations to commemorate important events in the history of the nation-state.[8] But the emergence of amateur groups of historical reenactors during the 1960s and 1970s was a grassroots development of hobbyists, which came to replace the historical spectacles organized by elites for patriotic and pedagogical purposes. Reenactment was now organized by small amateur groups, who often focused on the histories of other cultures. As Stephen Gapps, a museum curator who holds a doctorate in history and is also a long-time reenactor noted, after 1970:

> As more people gained the time and access to the means to stage history themselves, they began to immerse themselves in the re-created artefacts, costumes and personas of the histories prominent in the social imaginary ... social groups and classes historically excluded from conceiving and organizing public histories enthusiastically embraced history as an enjoyable performative *experience*. Public and private theatres of working blacksmiths and medieval knights at re-created "Pioneer Villages" and "Medieval Fairs" spread rapidly through Europe, North America and Australia.[9]

Gapps notes that amateur historical reenactors were initially overwhelmingly male, and characterizes the proliferation of military historical reenactment groups as (among other causes) "a masculine response to second wave feminism" that itself underscored the essentialized nature of the masculinity that reenactors were performing.[10] But within a generation, increasing numbers of women joined Civil War and other military history reenactment groups, first in "civilian" roles and later performing as *personas* of women who dressed and fought as men. Like German and American fans of the West, the new amateur military historical reenactment groups did their own research in order to create costumes and artifacts, "committed to doing unsanctioned history work."[11] They re-created the past for themselves and for spectators at their performances.

Historians have generally been bemused by historical reenactors, and sometimes critical. Reenactors attempt to recapture a single historical moment, privileging individual sensory and emotional experience. Academic historians, however, are concerned with social and political structures, events seen on a larger scale, and explaining change over time: processes that historical reenactment cannot shed light on. Vanessa Agnew, in a cogent critique of how reenactment can mislead audiences, argues that reenactment "elegize[s] certain aspects of the past and elide[s] what remains uncomfortable and troubling . . . this approach [to understanding history] is tantamount to an act of mastery, not one of confrontation with the past. These reenactments promote a form of understanding that neither explains historical processes nor interrogates historical injustices."[12]

But the growth of "reenactment," as it is discussed in scholarly discourse, now goes far beyond military historical hobbyists' gatherings. By the late twentieth century, the types of "reenactment" studied by scholars included the depiction of historical material culture and lifestyles in new types of historical reenactment "reality" television shows, like the British series *Edwardian Country House*, and the development of a large number of "living history" sites or "open-air museums," such as the popular American Colonial Williamsburg. Compared to traditional museums, "living history," as one British curator observed, is when institutions use living, costumed people to simulate life in the past, often working with re-created artifacts in restored or re-created structures.[13] Besides costumed interpreters, "reenactment" in museums also included new ways of educating and entertaining museum visitors through other types of performances, sometimes referred to as "museum theater." The term could also refer to performance artists whose work reenacts history, often using sly humor and subversion, like the Canadian Cree artist Kent Monkman, aka Miss Chief Eagle Testickle; and the emergence of "experimental archeology," which re-created ancient technologies, architectures, and lifeworlds in order to better understand historical cultures.[14] In all of these venues, "reenactment" can offer viewers "tours of the past," describing and interpreting history for the public.

The focus on individuals' physical, psychological, and emotional responses to all types of historical reenactment has been called the "affective turn" in scholarship about historical reenactment, broadly defined.[15] Scholarship on the affective turn in reenactment examines how these projects explore the past in ways that stir audiences' emotional connections and personal engagement, focusing largely on "reenactment" in a very broad sense, often as created by museums or television productions.[16]

The emergence of a broad array of historical reenactment genres, including museums, living history sites, open-air museums, and monuments, also reflected the growth of "public history" as a subfield among academic historians during the late twentieth century, a branch of the discipline that focuses on public history education delivered through a variety of non-classroom sites and institutions. Many public historians began to argue that the academic history teaching offered in schools and universities did not meet the interests of most laypeople, and was not the venue that most Americans used to engage with their nation's or family's histories. In an important study that drew on surveys and interviews done in 1994 with 1,453 Americans from a broad variety of ethnic, social, and regional groups, a team of historians found that 20 percent of those interviewed "took part in a group that studies, preserves, or presents the past. And about two fifths said that they had a hobby or collection related to the past." Projecting their survey results nationally, they estimated that "20 million Americans pursue historical hobbies and collections" in at least a moderately serious fashion.[17]

But although an impressive number of Americans had pastimes that involved history, the study found that formal, academic instruction in history was not well-regarded by those who were interviewed. Nonwhite participants often saw classroom history instruction as biased and selective in its depiction of their communities' treatment by white Americans, and almost all respondents would have agreed with one man, who described his history education in school as "just a giant data dump" of names and dates.[18] Although those interviewed in the study sometimes admired and respected their history instructors, for them, history courses were not nearly as trustworthy sources on "real" history as accounts passed on to them by family members, or the "real" artifacts and accounts presented at museums and living history sites. Museums, rated as highly trustworthy by 80 percent of respondents, were the most highly regarded of all sources of historical information.[19]

The percentage of survey respondents who were seriously engaged with history during their free time was nonetheless striking, as was the array of historically connected hobbies that they pursued, which provide a broader context for thinking about historically focused fandoms. The project's respondents included people who belonged to military historical reenactment groups, but also genealogists, people who designed and played military history board games, and a dizzying array of historical hobbyist collections, including collectors "of old barn paintings, Christian art, needlework, quilts, stamps, coins, World War II relics . . . liberty bells, fire equipment . . . Victorian wreaths, arrowheads, folk art . . . early American glass, railroad schedules . . . Indian artifacts, comic cards, old LPs, baseball cards, and Pete Rose items." Some respondents pursued their hobbies alone, while others belonged to historical associations of people who collected and repaired or reconstructed such items, such as the National Association of Watch and Clock Collectors, who collect, repair, and discuss antique watches.[20]

Few of the historical hobbyists interviewed by the survey's organizers were focused on historical-fictional or media entertainments, but they often overlapped with the Western fans discussed in this book in their pursuit of "authentic" material culture as a key to touching the past. The role that their hobbies and hobbyist communities played in their lives would also be recognizable to many media and fiction fans. When asked about the importance of his hobby in his life, one collector of antique motorcycles said simply "It is my life," and others appeared to the [academic historian] interviewers to be constantly preoccupied with their hobbies. These hobbyists often create "nurturing subcommunities," with other collectors, the survey noted. One Ohio teacher who collected antique folk art (and whose husband collected Civil War objects), met regularly with other collectors and told interviewers that "it's also like a counterculture of people . . . a different breed of people. It's just a very comfortable group of people. You never feel like you don't belong there."[21] The Ohio teacher would probably have appreciated Dr. Laura McLemore's "Laura room," which held her collection of nineteenth-century artifacts connected to the *Little House* series.

Hobbyist reenactment done by independent amateur historians developed connections to and sometimes overlapped with the emerging field of public history and other forms of popular reenactment. Reenactor hobbyists, particularly military history reenactors, are commonly used by historical television series or films as skilled "extras" on the set to fill the ranks of soldiers in the background of a scene, for example. Historical reenactors are even consulted by actors in such productions, since they are (often correctly) seen as authoritative resources on how to dress and move in historical productions.[22] Reenactors are also regularly invited as "guest" performers or historical interpreters at special events hosted by living history sites and open-air museums. One manager of a living history site noted that skilled hobbyist reenactors, either groups or individual performers, could greatly increase the number of visitors to a site, and help raise funds that could be used to save or renovate historical structures.[23] George Washington's Mount Vernon property, for example, is now a historical site with a professional staff of costumed interpreters, like Colonial Williamsburg. Mount Vernon also hosts several special events each year that feature outside hobbyist reenactors:

The largest of these events hosts dozens of American Revolutionary War reenactment units and individual reenactors, equaling hundreds of additional reenactors on the property. . . . Reenactors can provide hands-on demonstrations of period skills and trades for the public and demonstrate the use of working period/reproduction items at the site such as spinning wheels and looms, blacksmith tools, or cooking tools . . . [they can be] wildly popular and good money-makers [for living history sites].[24]

But the collaboration of fan groups with public institutions is not a new development; it had been pioneered decades earlier by some of the fans discussed in this book. Since the 1930s, German cowboys and Indianist clubs (and later, Indianist hobbyists alone, in East Germany) had mounted public educational demonstrations of crafts and skills from the American West. As we have seen, starting in the 1930s, cowboy and Indianist clubs gave craft and skills demonstrations, and in East Germany, Indianist hobbyists were invited to perform at a variety of public gatherings by the authorities. Even after 1990, Indianist hobbyists in East Germany continued to offer public demonstrations and exhibitions for some years, and the crafts and costumes exhibited during "open days" of cowboy clubs in western Germany continue to draw the public today.[25]

In the United States, *Little House* homesites, originally founded as memorials to one set of settler families, the Ingalls and Wilders, grew over time to present the larger context of their regional historical cultures, in ways that foreshadowed the growth of open-air museums. Special events like the "Laura Days" discussed in Chapter 4, offer visitors similar types of craft demonstrations seen at other living history sites. Like German Western fans, *Little House* fans sometimes pursued their hobbies in ways that resemble experimental archeology: working to reproduce food, textiles, and objects mentioned in the novels and common in white settler communities.

But although the Western fan groups studied here sometimes foreshadowed late twentieth-century trends in reenactment and public history, Western fans (like other groups rooted in a genre of historical fiction) had the added layer of affective connection with a particular fictional world and its characters, as well as with the past in a broader sense. Historically focused literary fan groups like those discussed here thus found a different entry point into historically focused fandom well before the rise of military historical reenactment: an entry point that was organized around a focus on the performance of the processes of historical daily lives, crafts and culture, and households.

The Western fans discussed in this book nonetheless resemble and during the early twentieth century sometimes foreshadowed modern nonfiction-based historical reenactors in their focus on "authentic" material culture. Both types of reenactors—those rooted in a fictional historical world, and those who were simply historical reenactors—sought the closest connection possible with the past in the sense described by Carl Becker, "an actual series of events that once occurred," rather than as academic historians define history: how the past is now remembered by living people. For all of these groups, one key to the "actual" past is to seek the highest degree of authenticity possible, in the costumes and material artifacts that reenactors create. Gapps argues that reenactors see what they do as historical interpretation in its own right, paralleling academic historians' publications, and that their pursuit of authenticity is central to their interpretations:

> Ultimately, then, authenticity [in material culture] is critical for reenactors: it is a key term in our symbolic vocabulary and often thought of as being part of our "special responsibility." Like historians, reenactors not only tell stories but also cite evidence: the footnote to the historian is the authentic (recreated) costume to the reenactor. . . . If historians do two things—compose elegant paragraphs and pursue erudition—reenactors craft a theater of history through authentic props and costumes.[26]

The expansion of public historical sites and reenactment in a broader sense has resulted in Western fans' increasing connections to and participation in other types of historical reenactment, not rooted in any fictional world. This is especially true for German fans from cowboy and Indianist clubs, although I spoke with a few *Little House* fans who were also active in other types of historical reenactment. German cowboy and Indianist club members have always sought "authenticity" in material culture as a way to connect with the past, even as Western genre entertainments declined in number, and public Indianist role-performance became less tenable after 1990; performance of white American Western roles, however, continued in many clubs. In addition, some German Western fans joined American Civil War reenactment groups, or other historical reenactment hobby organizations.

The number of German reenactment clubs organized around other themes, such as medieval historical re-creation or even playing "Huns," grew during the late twentieth century, complete with horseback riding, weapons, and early medieval costumes. One advantage for Germans in choosing the Huns for reenactment is that Attila the Hun (or his descendants) are unlikely to move to Germany and challenge such hobbyists' notions of what the "horde of Huns" was really like, or their right to represent Hun culture.[27] Going that far back in time, moreover, offers a past that is seen as relatively unproblematic today, and thus free of political difficulties. Similarly, white Australian reenactors tend to avoid reenacting their own colonial histories, which can be "fraught with contention when publicly performed, their 'authenticity' complicit with racism."[28]

But as in Australia and Britain, German reenactors have gravitated toward re-creation of the American Civil War in recent decades. Indianist role-play no longer serves the same interpretive functions (e.g., representing "freedom," or "ecologically natural" values) that many German reenactors now find most compelling. But for some, American Confederates and Union soldiers apparently do. Their "story," as Germans perceive it, can be reworked to express East and West Germans' current identities. Thus, German fans' historical reenactments continue, but with a different historical focus that is, nonetheless, American.

Many German fans who began in cowboy and Indianist clubs—and may still retain strong links to Western fandom, since Civil War reenactment overlap with cowboy and Indianist fans—today organize into either Confederate or Union units. Groups meet on the weekends to reenact the battles, and hold parties (Southern balls) in elaborate period-appropriate evening dress in the evenings. Across Germany, roles in Confederate units are apparently more popular than Union role reenactment, although this is particularly true in eastern Germany.[29]

Germans from former East Germany who began in Indianist hobbyist groups often take the roles of Confederates in these reenactments, since Southerners represent values that resonate with them. "The Southerners were rebels," one German Confederate reenactor from eastern Germany explained, and on the inside, he said, he and his friends had always been rebels in East Germany. Before 1990, wearing a Stetson had expressed rejection of the established order in East Germany, and now a Southern uniform served a similar function for him in reunified Germany. His wife, like many women in these groups, works as a battlefield "nurse" during reenacted battles, and dresses up as a Southern belle for the evening balls that follow the battles. When asked why eastern Germans in reenactment groups identified identify with the losers of the Civil War, she responded "Losers? Why do you call them the losers? Granted, they lost the war. But they were morally the winners. They fought for their values and kept their pride."[30]

Her response echoes the interpretation that many East Germans developed regarding their losses and role in Germany's reunification after 1990, in which East Germans were "conquered" by West Germany, and yet remain morally superior to the "Wessies." Since many of the Union side's reenactors come from Germany's western ("older") provinces, the battles allow both sides to pick and choose from a menu of symbols, artifacts, and values associated with each side in the American Civil War, and use them to express regional identities and tensions between former East and West Germany still present in German culture today. In Britain and Australia, American Civil War roles can also be vehicles for expressing reenactors' regional politics and identities.[31]

Robin Leipold, who grew up in East German Indianist circles, offered me a quite different explanation for why so many former East German Indians were now active in Confederate reenactment groups. A key part of Germans' attraction to Indianist groups had always been Western films, he explained, which originally inspired many Indianist hobbyists to become involved. In those films, he pointed out, the enemies of the Indian characters always wore Union military uniforms. Civil War Union roles were therefore associated for many East German viewers with the military actions undertaken against Indian characters by soldiers wearing the same uniform. Confederates, on the other hand, never seem to be shown in Western films acting against American Indian characters, he observed.[32] It is important to note that the interviews with and photos of former East Germans who had adopted Civil War reenactment, sometimes under a Confederate flag, were done before the changes in German politics that followed Angela Merkel's admission of hundreds of thousands of asylum seekers in 2015. Since that date, far right-wing nationalist German organizations have begun to use the Confederate flag, as well, but the German Indianists who adopted the hobby soon after German reunification seem largely to have had the motives discussed above.

Robin Leipold also showed me photographs of older fans he knew, formerly active in East German Indianist clubs, dressed in elaborate, authentic-looking Confederate uniforms, including the colorful uniforms of Zouave units, and other Confederate regional uniforms, with weapons and sometimes sashes. In one photo, a Confederate Zouave reenactment group posed in front of their "Longhorn Saloon," built as a club house by these German reenactors back when their club focused solely on cowboys and Indians. The Longhorn Saloon was modeled on buildings that we generally associate with trans-Mississippi

West, decades after the Civil War. For these German hobbyists, the setting and costumes reflected their personal trajectories as fans. From my point of view (as an American historian) the photo was disconcerting: a chronologically and geographically disorienting juxtaposition. Today, one sees a similar mélange of historical reenactors who assemble at the annual "Karl May Days" in Radebeul each May or at the Western-themed Pullman City in Bavaria, historical and geographical potpourris drawn from American history.

Many German cowboys and Indianist hobbyists have thus crossed over into reenactment of other historical cultures during the last twenty years as their Western club meetings and public performances have slowly ebbed, particularly in eastern Germany, apart from the still well-attended but private annual summer "the Week" gatherings of cowboy and Indianist hobbyists. In private gatherings of German Indianists that are now in some cases organized by people whose families have practiced Indianist hobbyism for two or three generations, however, their outfits, artifacts, and performances continue to be influenced by "authenticity," modeled as closely as possible on a past culture. But their gatherings are also reminiscent of the historical touristic practices studied by anthropologist Edward Bruner.

Around the world, Indigenous groups often perform "traditional" dances or songs for tourists, wearing "traditional" clothing, just as German Indianists previously offered public performances to entertain and educate other Germans. "Heritage" cultural performances for tourists are often dismissed by cultural critics as "inauthentic" and derivative productions, created for commercial purposes and tailored to suit the tastes of the tourist audiences. But Bruner argues that Indigenous performances for tourists have developed into social performances in their own right, and not as merely imitations of something more "authentic."[33]

German Indianist hobbyists certainly worked to produce the most "authentic" artifacts and performances possible: it was central to their goal of preserving what they originally saw as a "vanishing" culture. But over generations, their activities developed as social practices in their own right. In West Germany, their performances drew from a bricolage of Western genre tropes, including "Mexicans," cantinas, fur trappers, buffalo hunters, along with representations of a variety of Indigenous cultures. In East Germany before 1990 and continuing today, Indianist hobbyists developed their own traditions, including particular ceremonies done at summer gatherings, along with a unique style of storytelling. Tales of things that happened at eastern German Indianist gatherings are often handed down or collected. One respected Indianist hobbyist from eastern Germany no longer wears Indianist outfits, but instead has published a series of stories that were originally developed and told among East German Indianist hobbyists.[34] These are social practices in their own right, and are not merely an "imitation" of something else. Their activities and attitudes toward their hobbies tell us even more about these hobbyists' current beliefs and lives, than they do about the Indigenous cultures that hobbyists originally took as their models.

Some eastern German Indianist hobbyists continue to tell these stories and practice their social performances privately; others have gone into other fields of reenactment or different hobbies based on Indigenous cultures, like the modern German powwow scene.[35] The shift in hobbyist activities is reflected in the current inventory of the Red Fox Indian and Westernstore in Leipzig, founded by people who originally came out of the East German Indianist fandom. The store now sells outfits and artifacts for a variety of American historical reenactment roles, including the American Civil War.[36]

Karl May fans, by comparison, continue to celebrate a story world with "Indian" and white settler characters and cultures that they have long-since embraced as completely fictional, and indeed quintessentially German. May's original stories continue to be revived and reworked according to current tastes, and what audiences and fans are interested in. In 2016, the German television network RTL produced a remake miniseries based on the Winnetou novels, whose gritty, high-end production values and reinterpretation of the stories' ending provoked lively discussion among May fans. Each summer brings new productions of the stories, and new fan gatherings, at both large commercial open-air theaters and smaller amateur productions. The largest summer productions, at Bad Segeburg, in 2019 had broken each year's attendance record for the last seven years in a row.[37]

Fan groups that are organized around the May movies also continue to meet and mount fan pilgrimages to film locations, and the more literary Karl May Society recently elected a leadership board that included new and younger members. For these fans, historical authenticity in terms of the past "as it really was" is no longer an issue. What is up for debate is the "authenticity" or quality of newer productions compared to the original May novels, or in the case of the recent television series remake, the original 1960s May movies. May fans are conscious of their fandom's long history, and regularly discuss and commemorate the histories and anniversaries of their organizations and those of notable May-related productions.[38]

By contrast, the development of the *Little House* homesites and the novel-focused fan gatherings—although rooted in a fictional series—were strongly influenced by trends in public history during the late twentieth century. Several of the homesites are now open-air museums, and more than one employs costumed interpreters.[39] Several homesites have become resources for regional history, as well, receiving visits from school field trip groups and people from the region who come not only because of the association with Laura Ingalls Wilder but because the sites convey a sense of their regions' past cultures and lifestyles.

At LauraPalooza conferences and in online discussion groups and forums, *Little House* fans discuss genealogical research, nineteenth-century crafts and skills, the results of their own research, and over meals, more informally, the collections that some have developed of historical artifacts associated with Laura Ingalls Wilder's life and times. They resemble the many historical memorabilia collectors, genealogists, and other forms of serious history hobbyists interviewed in the 1994 survey. Some Laura fans have acquired so much expertise in her life and knowledge of interpretation skills that they have developed sidelines as costumed Laura Ingalls Wilder historical interpreters, offering popular, informative presentations at regional schools, libraries, and community centers. For all of the "bonnet heads," these activities reflect not only the pursuit of public history but also the celebration of a beloved story world and characters. For more conservative fans, *Little House* homesites and activities can also function as counter-narratives to more recent, revisionist histories of white settlement, and focus on aspects of the American national historical narrative that they prefer.

As many fans have observed, open-ended canons offer their own charms. A novel series like *Harry Potter*, where the books are published over many years, or a long-running television series like *Game of Thrones*, offer fans the opportunity to debate, speculate, draw, write, make videos, and explore many alternative endings and future paths for the characters for years, before the canon is "closed" and the story's ending—at least, the ending intended by the author—is known. Even when the story is completed, fans may continue to offer alternative versions for decades, each person cherry-picking what appeals out of the story world and reworking it in personal creative work, to suit their own tastes and needs.

Academic history is open-ended in a parallel sense. What actually happened (whether it is known or not, documented or not) will not change. But each generation's understanding of what happened in the past alters nonetheless.

As Becker observed, these new interpretations and histories mean that each generation "must inevitably play on the dead whatever tricks it finds necessary for its own peace of mind."[40]

Historically focused fandoms and other historical hobbies like reenactment have cross-hatching, overlapping connections to both academic history and media fandoms. Most members of historically focused fandoms eagerly consume historical fiction along with popular and academic histories in pursuit of their hobbies. At the same time, fans of historical fiction experience strong connections not only to a historical culture but also to a story and characters set in that time and place. They care greatly about the "authentic" re-creation of a particular historical place and time, about fashioning as perfectly as possible a specific artifact or piece of clothing. Their work is often an attempt to pin down the past "as it really was" like a butterfly in a glass display case. The intensive research done by Laura Ingalls Wilder's fans to determine exactly where her family's cabin had stood on the Osage Reserve or where the long gone schoolhouse where she first taught had stood; to track down the smallest details regarding the author's cousins or the dishes she cooked; the years-long scavenging for raw materials and labor put into an "authentic" Indigenous baby carrier by an East German hobbyist; the weeks of practice undertaken by German cowboys, to train themselves to use lassoes and perform other rodeo skills as faithfully to the originals (*Stilecht*) as possible; the impressive labor done and collections developed by Karl May fans so that they could better understand how the 1960s films were created and where they were filmed: these are efforts to recapture a past historical moment or culture, as it actually occurred. Their eyes are fixed on the past.

But in practice, like academic history, the pursuits of historical hobbyists are open-ended, not closed. As this book has argued, historically focused fandoms and other historical hobbies are embedded in cultures that themselves find it necessary (as Becker observed) "to play tricks on the dead" for "their own peace of mind," as each generation redefines its own interpretations of the past and as social conditions and values change around fans. Historically focused fandoms are thus subject to what might seem to them to be the whims of historiographical revision and outsiders, which can result in struggles over who has the right to represent particular histories and voices. And as we have seen, many members of historically focused fandoms choose not to leave behind events, people, or places in the past, even if the facts shift in how many people in their cultures now see those histories.

Even apart from outside social or political pressures, historical fandoms change their own internal practices over time. Civil War reenactment has always had many functions and meanings for participants; one of those functions was that the hobby for some was originally an all-male refuge from second-wave feminism. Changes in attitudes about how acceptable it was to treat women unequally, and the attraction of women to the hobby, led reenactors to increasingly include women whose hobby persona was based on the historical reality of women who passed as men and fought in the Civil War, a now widely accepted part of our understanding of the Civil War. Reenactors in Australia, Britain, and Germany cherry-picked *personas* and roles that aligned with their own personal or regional identities and values, and those needs changed over time. In the *Little House* fandom, fans who were interested in nonwhite histories researched the African American doctor mentioned in *Little House on the Prairie* or added displays on the histories of local Indigenous cultures to their homesites.

Historically focused fandoms and reenactment are by their nature performative, which means that they are open-ended, and always subject to reevaluation and revision. They are, one reenactor noted, "ephemeral site(s) of history, always ready to be constituted anew at the next reenactment."[41] New developments in the practice of their hobbies are inevitable, since changes in how we see the past are inevitable in both scholarly and popular history. As we have seen, this quality can make historically focused fans uncomfortable; after all, the concept of a traditional, unchanging, simpler past was part of the initial attraction for some of them. But ultimately the changing nature of the past makes these hobbies both fruitful as well as uncomfortable, offering new attractions to succeeding generations of hobbyists. The ever-changing past will continue to be an inviting foreign country to spend time in, but for its long-term fan visitors, it can be disconcertingly unstable terrain.

# NOTES

## Introduction. Living in Someone Else's Past

1. I am grateful for the interviews and assistance that I received from dozens of people active in the Wilder, German cowboy and Indianist, and Karl May fandoms (and in other historically focused fandoms) during my research for this book. Where I have quoted or used someone's information, I have used their names in the endnotes only if the interview partner agreed to this use. In cases where someone asked me not to attribute their names to particular quotations or information, I have not done so and have described the person in ways that preserve his/her anonymity. Please see endnote 3 of this section for a discussion of the methods I used in these interviews.

2. From a report in *Die Rheinpfaltz*, May 14, 1962. Here, and throughout this book, all translations from the German are my own, unless otherwise noted.

3. Except where noted otherwise, the descriptions of the homesites in this book are based on my own visits to the various Laura Ingalls Wilder homesites during the summer of 2019. See also William Anderson, *Laura Ingalls Wilder Country: The People and Places in Laura Ingalls Wilder's Life and Books* (New York: Harper Paperbacks, 1990). My research relies largely on archival research and other historical sources and uses traditional attribution for those sources, but the parts of this book that touch on current fan communities shade into ethnology. When researching and speaking with current Western fans, I was influenced by the approaches outlined in Kristina Busse's "The Ethics of Studying Online Fandom," in *The Routledge Companion to Media Studies*, ed. Melissa Click and Suzanne Stott (New York: Routledge, 2017), 9–17. In discussions with the current generation of fans in these communities, I always identified myself as a researcher who was working on a study that included their community, requested an interview as part of my research, and did not use their names if they asked me not to. I shared excerpts from drafts of my chapters to people

who are quoted, allowing them the opportunity to correct any statements by them that I had perhaps misunderstood. I do not use photos of living persons in this study without their permission. This book does not discuss private blogs or personal posts without that blog owner's permission, although I do link to organizations' public or individuals' professional or business webpages.

4. Not all of the people discussed in this book would have used the term "fan" in refer-ence to themselves. The term is a loaded one in some contexts, and some members of the Karl May Society, for example, might feel that "fans" were those whose activities were less scholarly than their own hobby, and instead call themselves "friends" of Karl May. German Indianist enthusiasts often refer to themselves as "friends of the Indians," "Indianists," or "hobbyists."

5. Foundational works in fan studies that introduced the concepts discussed here, which I drew on in understanding historical fandoms, include Henry Jenkins, *Textual Poachers: Television Fans and Participatory Culture*, 2nd ed. (New York: Routledge, 2012); Henry Jenkins, *Convergence Culture: Where Old and New Media Collide* (New York: New York University Press, 2006); Camille Bacon-Smith, *Enterprising Women: Television Fandom and the Creation of Popular Myth* (Philadelphia: University of Pennsylvania Press, 1992); Lisa Lewis, *The Adoring Audience: Fan Culture and Popular Media* (New York: Routledge, 1992); Matt Hills, *Fan Cultures* (New York: Routledge, 2002); Cornel Sandvoss, *Fans: The Mirror of Consumption* (Malden: Polity Press, 2005); Karen Hellekson and Kristina Busse, eds., *Fan Fiction and Fan Communities in the Age of the Internet: New Essays* (Jefferson, NC: McFarland, 2006), and within that collection, I particularly relied on Francesca Coppa, "A Brief History of Media Fandom," 41–60. See also Daniel Cavicchi, "Foundational Discourses of Fandom," in *A Companion to Media Fandom and Fan Studies*, ed. Paul Booth (Oxford: John Wiley and Sons, 2018), 27–46. Recent publications with useful summaries of foundational fan studies works and key concepts are also offered in Brigid Cherry, *Cult Media, Fan-dom, and Textiles: Handicrafting as Fan Art* (London: Bloomsbury, 2016) and Nicolle Lamerichs, *Productive Fandom: Intermediality and Affective Reception in Fan Cultures* (Amsterdam: University of Amsterdam Press, 2018).

6. See Cherry, *Cult Media* and Lamerichs, *Productive Fandom*. Examples of other recent fan studies works that focus on some of the specific productive and transformative fan activities discussed here include Rebecca Williams, *Theme Park Fandom: Spatial Transmedia, Materiality, and Participatory Cultures* (Amsterdam: University of Am-sterdam Press, 2020), whose discussion of cosplay I found useful, and E. Charlotte Stevens, *Fanvids: Television, Women, and Home Media Re-Use* (Amsterdam: Universi-ty of Amsterdam Press, 2020). For an important study that examines race and racism within and across modern fandoms, see Rukmini Pande, *Squee From the Margins:*

*Fandom and Race* (Iowa City: University of Iowa Press, 2018).

7. See the history of the Cologne Horde of Huns at http://www
.erstekölnerhunnenhorde.de/1.html, accessed August 1, 2019.

8. Stephen Gapps, "Performing the Past: A Cultural History of Historical Reenactment," (PhD diss., Sydney University of Technology, 2002), 244.

9. Mid-twentieth-century Sherlock Holmes films featured the hero battling Nazis
during World War II, and the 2010 BBC remake of this canon, *Sherlock*, sets the
story in today's London. But for decades, exploring Victorian London was part of
the charm for most Sherlock Holmes fans. See Michael Saler, "'Clap If You Believe
in Sherlock Homes': Mass Culture and the Re-Enchantment of Modernity, c.
1890–1940," *The Historical Journal* 46, no. 3 (2003): 599–622; Michael Saler, *As If:
Modern Enchantment and the Literary Prehistory of Virtual Reality* (New York: Oxford
University Press, 2012); Jon Lellenberg, ed., *Irregular Memories of the 'Thirties: An Archival History of the Baker Street Irregulars' First Decade: 1930–1940* (New York: Ford-
ham University Press, 1990) and the same author's subsequent volumes published in
this series; Roberta Pearson, "'It's Always 1895': Sherlock Holmes in Cyberspace," in
*Trash Aesthetics: Popular Culture and Its Audience*, ed. Deborah Cartmell, Heidi Kaye,
I. Q. Hunter, and Imelda Whelehan (London: Pluto Press, 1997), 143–61; Roberta
Pearson, "Bachies, Bardies, Trekkies, and Sherlockians," in *Fandom: Identities and
Communities in a Mediated World*, ed. Jonathan Gray, Cornel Sandvoss, C. Lee Har-
rington (New York: New York University Press, 2007), 98–109. For an analysis of the
BBC Sherlock series' connections to earlier versions of the story world, see Ariana
Scott-Zechlin, "'But It's the Solar System!': Reconciling Science and Faith through
Astronomy," and Anne Kustritz and Melanie Kohnen, "Decoding the Industrial and
Digital City: Visions of Security in Holmes' and Sherlock's London," both in *Sherlock
and Transmedia Fandom: Essays on the BBC Series*, ed. Louisa Ellen Stein and Kristina
Busse (Jefferson, NC: MacFarland, 2012). See also Betsy Rosenblatt and Roberta
Pearson, eds., "Sherlock Holmes, Fandom, Sherlockiana, and the Great Game," spe-
cial issue, *Transformative Works and Cultures* 23 (March 2017), accessed July 21, 2019,
https://journal.transformativeworks.org/index.php/twc/issue/view/27.

10. For discussions of the early transmedial nature of the *Wizard of Oz* fandom, see Matthew Freeman, "The Yellow Brick Road: Historicizing the Industrial Emergence of
Transmedia Storytelling," *International Journal of Communication* 8 (2014): 2362–81;
and Matthew Freeman, "*The Wonderful Game of Oz* and Tarzan Jigsaws: Commodifying Transmedia in Early Twentieth-Century Consumer Culture," *Intensities: The
Journal of Cult Media*, 7 (2014): 44–54.

11. Fan studies scholar Kristina Busse offered several plausible reasons for why the field
tends to overlook historically focused fandoms: the *Star Trek* fandom was among the

first fan communities studied in foundational works in the field; fan studies' original emphasis was on the ways that active fans fought back against copyright in their production of transformative fan works; and most fan scholars were initially based in film, media, and communications departments. Private communication from Kristina Busse, May 15, 2020.

12. The term often used for this hobby by participants after 1945 was *Indianistik*, or sometimes "friends of Indians." I have chosen to translate the term (when speaking of hobbyists) as "Indianists," in order to avoid conflation with actual Indigenous peoples. For discussions of German Indianist hobbyists, see Yolanda Broyles-Gonzalez, "Cheyennes in the Black Forest: A Social Drama," *The Americanization of the Global Village: Essays in Comparative Popular Culture*, ed. Roger Rollins (Bowling Green: Ohio University Press, 1989) 70–86; Suzanne Zantop, "Close Encounters: Deutsche and Indianer," in *Germans and Indians: Fantasies, Encounters, Projections*, ed. Colin Calloway, Gerd Gemunden, and Suzanne Zantop (Lincoln: University of Nebraska Press, 2002), 3–14; Suzanne Zantop, *Colonial Fantasies. Conquest, Family and Nation in Precolonial Germany, 1770–1870* (Durham, NC: Duke University Press, 1997); Hartmut Lutz, "German Indianthusiasm: A Socially Constructed German Nationalist Myth," in *Germans and Indians*, ed. Colin Calloway, Gerd Gemunden, and Suzanne Zantop, 167–84; Christian Feest, ed., *Indians and Europe: An Interdisciplinary Collection of Essays* (Lincoln: University of Nebraska Press, 1989 [A second, revised edition was published in 1999]) and Feest, "Europe's Indians," in *The Invented Indian: Cultural Fictions and Government Policies*, ed. James Clifton (New Brunswick: Transaction Publishers, 1994); Alina Weber, "'Indians' on German Stages: The History and Meaning of Karl May Festivals," (PhD diss., Indiana University, 2010); Katrin Sieg, "Indian Impersonation as Historical Surrogation," in *Germans and Indians*, ed. Colin Calloway, Gerd Gemunden, and Suzanne Zantop, 217–42; Sieg, *Ethnic Drag: Performing Race, Nation, and Sexuality in West Germany* (Ann Arbor: University of Michigan Press, 2009); H. Glenn Penny, "Elusive Authenticity: The Quest for the Authentic Indian in German Public Culture," *Comparative Studies in Society and History* 48, no. 4 (October 1, 2006): 798–819; Penny, *Kindred By Choice: Germans and American Indians Since 1800* (Chapel Hill: University of North Carolina Press, 2013); Petra Tjitske Kalshoven, *Crafting "The Indian": Knowledge, Desire, and Play in Indianist Reenactment* (New York: Berghahn Books, 2012).

13. See Sieg, *Ethnic Drag*, and also Lutz, "German Indianthusiasm." Some of the earliest work on this group argued that German hobbyists were motivated (whether they were aware of it or not) by a desire to work through complex feelings about Germans' responsibility for the Holocaust, escaping from feelings of complicity by identifying with peoples who had been targets of different genocidal policies, or the work argued

that they were motivated by other grievances. Kalshoven's and Penny's studies demonstrate that Germans' affinity for Indigenous cultures goes back to the early nineteenth century—thus long predating the Holocaust—and that Indianist groups were founded in several European nations and not only in Germany. See Penny, *Kindred By Choice* and Kalshoven, *Crafting "The Indian."* Above all, Penny argues persuasively that Germans' sense of affinity for Indigenous North American peoples is a *longue durée* phenomenon, and one that shows surprising continuities across political regimes and epochs.

14. Quoted in Katherine Johnson, "Rethinking (Re)doing: Historical Re-enactment and/as Historiography," *Rethinking History* 19 (2015): 196. For a global survey of Austen fandom, see Holly Luetkenhaus and Zoe Weinstein, *Austentatious: The Evolving World of Jane Austen Fans* (Iowa City: University of Iowa Press, 2019). Austen fans who seek to re-create the times of Regency England are parodied in the 2013 film *Austenland.*

15. Anne Brædder, Kim Esmark, Tove Kruse, Carsten Tage Nielsen, and Anette Warring, "Doing Pasts: Authenticity from the Reenactors' Perspective," *Rethinking History* 21, no. 2 (2017): 186. See also Johnson, "Rethinking (Re)doing," for a discussion of how the constrictions of women's period clothing teaches the wearers about the constraints on women's posture and movements in Regency period clothing. For the bodily experience of Civil War reenactors, see Stephen Gapps, "Mobile Monuments: A View of Historical Reenactment and Authenticity from inside the Costume Cupboard of History," *Rethinking History* 13, no. 3 (2009): 400–402.

16. See Anita Fellman's study of how the *Little House* series was received and interpreted by generations of readers, *Little House, Long Shadow: Laura Ingalls Wilder's Impact on American Culture* (Columbia: University of Missouri Press, 2008); Fellman discusses how readers' strong sense of identification with Laura Ingalls Wilder, combined with their ability to visit the homesites and reenact many of the activities described in the books, strengthens their conviction that the books are reliable guides to American history, and that the stories are true. H. Glenn Penny's research on German Indians also underscores their enormous concern for getting the details right in mimetic reproductions, in order to achieve historical "authenticity." See Penny, "Elusive Authenticity," and *Kindred By Choice.* One of the nineteenth-century "founding fathers" of academic historical research, Leopold von Ranke, pursued the goal of establishing "how things actually were." He would probably have understood these amateur historians' concerns, if not their methods.

17. Brædder et al., "Doing Pasts," 187.

18. Vanessa Agnew, "History's Affective Turn: Historical Reenactment and Its Work in the Present," *Rethinking History* 11, no. 3 (2007): 302. See also Johnson, "Rethink-

ing (Re)doing"; and Jerome de Groot, "Affect and Empathy: Re-enactment and Performance as/in History," *Rethinking History* 15, no. 4 (2011): 587–99. These articles discuss the phenomenon of reenactment, but it is important to note that the scholarship on this phenomenon uses a broader definition of the concept than is common in fan studies or colloquial English. The scholarly literature cited here is concerned not only with reenactment in the sense discussed in this book and in fan studies but also with the "re-creation" of history for the public in museum exhibits, television reality shows, monuments, performance art, "living history" farms or Colonial Williamsburg, and other public forms of depicting and performing the past.

19. See Tony Horwitz, *Confederates in the Attic: Dispatches from the Unfinished Civil War* (New York: Vintage Press, 1999). For living history interpreters and practitioners of public history, questions of how to represent chattel slavery have been difficult to resolve. See James Walvin, "What Should We Do about Slavery? Slavery, Abolition and Public History" in *Historical Reenactment: From Realism to the Affective Turn*, ed. Iain McCalman and Paul A. Pickering (Basingstoke: Palgrave Macmillan, 2010), 63–78, and Gapps, "Mobile Monuments," 404. See also Michael Brown, *Who Owns Native Culture?* (Cambridge, MA: Harvard University Press, 2003).

20. For the consistent framing of Indigenous North American peoples as "vanishing," or "doomed," see Warren Lewis, *Buffalo Bill's America: William Cody and the Wild West Show* (New York: Knopf, 2005), 93ff; Robert V. Hine and John Mack Faragher, *Frontiers: A Short History of the American West* (New Haven: Yale University Press, 2007), 100. This framing of Indigenous cultures as "vanishing" cultures forms the backdrop for James Fenimore Cooper's stories, and also for Karl May's Westerns. The most famous of May's Winnetou novels opens with the eulogy: "Yes, the red race is dying! From Tierra Del Fuego far north beyond the Great Lakes, the diseased giant lies stretched, overcome and defeated by an inexorable fate that knows no mercy," in Karl May, *Winnetou. Erster Band: Reiseerzählung, Band 7 der Gesammelten Werke* (Bamberg: Karl-May-Verlag, 1992), Introduction. For long-standing German popular understandings of Indigenous Americans as a doomed race, see Julia Stetler, "Buffalo Bill's Wild West in Germany: A Transnational History," (PhD diss., University of Nevada, Las Vegas, 2012), 96–116.

21. These changes in American historiography and popular understandings of American history are explored in depth in Chapter 5. Some of the best known works of the "new" Western historiography include: Richard White, *"It's Your Misfortune and None of My Own": A New History of the American West*, reprint ed. (Norman: University of Oklahoma Press, 1993); and Patricia Nelson Limerick, *The Legacy of Conquest: The Unbroken Past of the American West*, reprint ed. (New York: Norton, 1987); much of the late twentieth century historiography of the American West is summarized in

Robert V. Hine, John Mack Faragher, and Jon T. Coleman, *The American West: A New Interpretive History*, 2nd ed. (New Haven: Yale University Press, 2017).

22. Indigenous responses to and interactions with both the Karl May and *Little House* fan communities will be discussed in Chapter 5.

23. See Saler, "'Clap If You Believe in Sherlock Holmes'" and *As If: Modern Enchantment*. I agree with Saler's argument that immersion in imaginary worlds took a place in participants' lives that in some respects was analogous to the roles played by religious practice or magic in Early Modern European imaginations. Indeed, the deep immersion of a fan in an imaginary world (and the insertion of oneself in the story's narrative, in some fan fiction) bore a strong family resemblance to medieval affective piety, where devout Christians inserted themselves, in imagination, into a holy scene originally depicted in the Bible.

## Chapter 1. Who Owns the West?

1. For an up-to-date survey that synthesizes an enormous amount of research on the history of the American West, see Hine, Faragher, and Coleman, *The American West*.

2. For the shift from a policy of "Indian removal" to confinement in reservations, see Hine, Faragher, and Coleman, *The American West*, 179–84 and 283–88; see also the broader overview given in Roger Nichols, *American Indians in US History*, 2nd ed. (Norman: University of Oklahoma Press, 2014).

3. The literature on the Turner thesis is extensive. See Frederick Jackson Turner, "The Significance of the Frontier in American History," accessed August 29, 2019, http://xroads.virginia.edu/~hyper/turner/; Hine, Faragher, and Coleman, *The American West*, 339–42; Allan Bogue, "Frederick Jackson Turner Reconsidered," *The History Teacher* 27, no. 2 (1997): 195–221; Stephen McVeigh, *The American Western* (Edinburgh: Edinburgh University Press, 2007), 13–26; Richard Etulain, *Re-Imagining the Modern American West: A Century of Fiction, History, and Art* (Tucson: University of Arizona Press, 1996), 31–42.

4. Turner, "The Significance of the Frontier in American History," accessed August 29, 2019, http://xroads.virginia.edu/~hyper/turner/.

5. For the connections between Turner's narrative and Wilder's understanding of American history, see John E. Miller, *Laura Ingalls Wilder and Rose Wilder Lane: Authorship, Place, Time, and Culture* (Columbia: University of Missouri Press, 2016), 94–109.

6. McVeigh, *The American Western*, 23.

7. Bogue, "Frederick Jackson Turner Reconsidered," 195. For a discussion of what Anita Fellman calls "the bewitched historiographical space" occupied by the Turner thesis,

see Karen Jones and John Wills, *The American West: Competing Visions* (Edinburgh: Edinburgh University Press, 2009), 39–59.

8. See Sacvan Bercovitch, *The Puritan Origins of the American Self* (New Haven: Yale University Press, 2011). For the ways in which Laura Ingalls Wilder's novels tied into her contemporaries' national biography, see Caroline Fraser, "Laura Ingalls Wilder: The Making of an American Icon," *Missouri Historical Review* 113, no. 2 (2019): 94–104.

9. The substantial body of literature discussing the development of "Germanness" across disparate territories is summarized in Nancy Reagin, *Sweeping the German Nation: Domesticity and National Identity in Germany, 1870–1945* (New York: Cambridge University Press, 2007), 2–4.

10. Mario Carretero and Floor Van Alphen, "History, Collective Memories, or National Memories?" in *Handbook of Culture and Memory*, ed. Brady Wagoner (New York: Oxford University Press, 2018), 283.

11. For an overview of the history of "whiteness" in American culture, see Nell Irvin Painter, *The History of White People* (New York: Norton, 2010); see also David Roediger, *The Wages of Whiteness: Race and the Making of the American Working Class*, rev. ed. (New York: Verso, 2007). The Homestead Act of 1862 allowed any adult American citizen (except those who had born arms against the government) and any immigrant who was in the process of naturalization to file a homestead claim. Once the Fourteenth Amendment was ratified, this included Black Americans, and after 1870, Black immigrants. Before 1924, however, Indigenous individuals were generally excluded from citizenship, unless they had acquired it through a specific treaty concluded with their tribe, or through marriage. Asian immigrants could not acquire citizenship until 1954.

12. For the ways in which American theories of land ownership were interwoven with European patterns of land management, see Cheryl Harris, "Whiteness as Property," *Harvard Law Review* 106, no. 8 (1993): 1707–91; see also Natsu Taylor Saito, "Race and Decolonization: Whiteness as Property in the American Settler Colonial Project," *Harvard Journal on Racial & Ethnic Justice* 31 (Spring 2015): 1–42.

13. Etulain, *Re-Imagining the Modern American West*, 5–10 and 53–60.

14. Boyd Cothran, *Remembering the Modoc War: Redemptive Violence and the Making of American Innocence* (Chapel Hill: University of North Carolina Press, 2014), 21.

15. Hine and Faragher, *Frontiers*, 192.

16. See Cothran, *Remembering the Modoc War*, 18 and Hine, Faragher, and Coleman, *The American West*, 249–51. See also Benjamin Madley, *An American Genocide: The United States and the California Indian Catastrophe, 1846–1873* (New Haven: Yale University Press, 2016).

17. Cothran, *Remembering the Modoc War*, 19. See also Alissa Macoun, "Colonising White Innocence: Complicity and Critical Encounters," in *The Limits of Settler Colonial Reconciliation*, ed. Sarah Maddison, Tom Clark, and Ravi de Costa (Singapore: Springer, 2016), 85–102.

18. Hine, Faragher, and Coleman, *The American West*, 152.

19. Hine, Faragher, and Coleman, 153. See also Etulain, *Re-Imagining the Modern American West*, xxvi; and Julia Stetler, "Buffalo Bill's Wild West," 94–98. For the early circulation of such images in German-speaking Europe, see Penny, *Kindred By Choice*, 45–48.

20. Hine, Faragher, and Coleman, *The American West*, 351–53; see also Etulain, *Re-Imagining the Modern American West*, xxvii–xxviii. For the training and/or popularity of Bingham, Leutze, and Bierstadt in Germany, see Penny, *Kindred By Choice*, 48–51.

21. For the popularity of Cooper's novels in Germany, see Stetler, "Buffalo Bill's Wild West," 100–102 and Penny, *Kindred By Choice*, 35.

22. Hine, Faragher, and Coleman, *The American West*, 159–60; see also Etulain, *Re-Imagining the Modern American West*, xx–xxi; Louis Warren, *Buffalo Bill's America: William Cody and the Wild West Show* (New York: Alfred A. Knopf, 2005), 113; for women in Western genre fiction, see Victoria Lamont, *Westerns: A Women's History* (Lincoln: University of Nebraska Press, 2016).

23. Buffalo Bill and the *Wild West Show* were international entertainment juggernauts and have been the subjects of a number of studies; see Warren, *Buffalo Bill's America*; Robert W. Rydell and Rob Kroes, *Buffalo Bill in Bologna: The Americanization of the World, 1869–1922* (Chicago: University of Chicago Press, 2005); Joy S. Kasson, *Buffalo Bill's Wild West: Celebrity, Memory, and Popular History* (New York: Hill and Wang, 2000); Stetler, "Buffalo Bill's Wild West." See also Hine, Faragher, and Coleman, *The American West*, 342–44 ; and McVeigh, *The American Western*, 27–37.

24. Warren, *Buffalo Bill's America*, x–xi.

25. Stetler, "Buffalo Bill's Wild West," 32.

26. McVeigh, *The American Western*, 26. See also Peter Rollins and John O'Connor, *Hollywood's West: The American Frontier in Film, Television, and History* (Lexington: University Press of Kentucky, 2009), 1–34.

27. "Transmedial" refers to a story world that is developed across and consumed by audiences across a variety of media platforms, e.g., a single story world developed across novels, films, video games, and television shows.

28. Hine, Faragher, and Coleman, *The American West*, 443. What is counted as a "Western" varies, since the genre's boundaries are fluid; for early Western films, see also McVeigh, *The American Western*, 60–68, Jones and Wills, *The American West: Competing Visions*; and Rollins and O'Connor *Hollywood's West*. For a discussion of how the

genre has been repeatedly redefined and revived over the last seventy-five years, see Lee Clark Mitchell, *Late Westerns: The Persistence of a Genre* (Lincoln: University of Nebraska Press, 2018).

29. Hine, Faragher, and Coleman, *The American West*, 442 and Etulain, *Re-Imagining the Modern American West*, 27–28.

30. The scholarly literature on Germans' fascination with the historical West and Indigenous peoples is substantial. In addition to the literature on Indianist hobbyists noted in endnote 12 of the Introduction, see also Katinka Kocks, *Indianer im Kaiserreich: Völkerschauen und Wild West Shows Zwischen 1880 und 1914* (Gerolzhofen: Öttermann, 2004); D. L. Ashliman, "The American West in Twentieth-Century Germany," *The Journal of Popular Culture* II, no. 1 (1968): 81–90; Anne Dreesbach, *Gezähmte Wilde: Die Zurschaustellung "Exotischer" Menschen in Deutschland 1870–1940* (Frankfurt: Campus, 2005); Richard Cracroft, "World Westerns: The European Writer and the American West," in *A Literary History of the American West*, ed. J. Golden Taylor and Thomas Lyon (Fort Worth: Texas Christian University Press, 1998), 159–79; Lutz P. Koepnick, "Unsettling America: German Westerns and Modernity," *Modernism/Modernity* 2, no. 3 (1995): 1–22; Gerald D. Nash, "European Image of America: The West in Historical Perspective," *Montana: The Magazine of Western History* 42, no. 2 (1992): 2–16; Pamela Kort and Max Hollein, eds., *I Like America: Fictions of the Wild West* (Munich: Prestel, 2006); Jeffrey L. Sammons, "Nineteenth-Century German Representations of Indians from Experience," in *Germans and Indians: Fantasies, Encounters, Projections*, ed. Colin Calloway, Gerd Gemunden, and Suzanne Zantop (Lincoln: University of Nebraska Press, 2002), 185–94. Of particular note is H. Glenn Penny's impressively researched *Kindred By Choice*.

31. Stetler, "Buffalo Bill's Wild West," 102 and Penny, *Kindred By Choice*, 35.

32. "The German Coopers" is an apt term coined for these authors by Penny, *Kindred By Choice*, 40.

33. Penny, *Kindred By Choice*, 43–44.

34. This novel is considered by some to be the first Western novel in any language. See Penny, *Kindred By Choice*, 40–41 and Stetler, "Buffalo Bill's Wild West," 102–3; see also Ashliman, "The American West in Twentieth-Century Germany," 87; and Sammons, "Nineteenth-Century German Representations of Indians." The Austrian-American author whose *nom de plume* was Charles Sealsfield published fifty-seven German language Western novels during the second half of the nineteenth century. B. Traven, a pseudonym for a later German Western author whose works were first published between 1925 and 1940, is best known in the United States as the author of the *Treasure of the Sierra Madre*, later filmed by John Huston.

35. Penny, *Kindred By Choice*, 53–95.

36. Penny, 43–45; see also Sammons, "Nineteenth-Century German Representations of Indians," 185.

37. Tacitus's contribution to eighteenth- and nineteenth-century Germans' "creation myth" of their own nationality was substantial. See James Sheehan, *German History, 1770–1866*, reprint ed. (New York: Clarendon Press, 1991), 4; Stetler, "Buffalo Bill's Wild West," 55–79 and Penny, *Kindred By Choice*, 30–31. See also Kalshoven, *Crafting "The Indian,"* 66.

38 Zantrop, "Close Encounters: Deutsche and Indianer," 4.

39. Penny, *Kindred By Choice*, 96–115. Quotation is from page 110.

40. Penny, 112–18. See also Feest, "Europe's Indians," 317, for the widely shared German assumption that their nation would have been the better colonial power for Indigenous North Americans, compared to Anglo-Americans.

41. Kocks, *Indianer im Kaiserreich*.

42. Stetler, "Buffalo Bill's Wild West," 66.

43. Stetler, "Buffalo Bill's Wild West," 73–87; Dreesbach, *Gezähmte Wilde*, and Kocks, *Indianer im Kaiserreich*. For a discussion of how Germans saw themselves as disinterested and more accurate observers of exotic peoples during the nineteenth century (Germany's attempts to acquire colonies came much later than those of rival powers), see Susanne Zantop, *Colonial Fantasies*, 38–39.

44. For the exploitative treatment of African performers in such shows, see for example Rachel Holmes, *African Queen: The Real Life of the Hottentot Venus* (New York: Random House, 2009); for an overview of such exhibitions in nineteenth-century Britain, see Sadiah Qureshi, *Peoples on Parade: Exhibitions, Empire, and Anthropology in Nineteenth-Century Britain* (Chicago: University of Chicago Press, 2011).

45. For the salaries and treatment of these performers, see George Moses, *Wild West Shows and the Image of American Indians, 1883–1933* (Albuquerque: University of New Mexico Press, 1996).

46. Penny, *Kindred By Choice*, 260.

47. Edward Two-Two's decision to be buried in Dresden is the subject of a documentary: Betina Renner (dir.) *Bury My Heart in Dresden*, 2013 Deckert Distribution. See also John Koehler, "German 'Indians' Guard Grave," *The Saginaw News*, June 23, 1968.

48. For motives of Indigenous show performers, and why some welcomed the opportunity, see Moses, *Wild West Shows*; Warren, *Buffalo Bill's America*; Stetler, "Buffalo Bill's Wild West," 176; Penny, *Kindred By Choice*, 132–34. For the impact of the "exotic peoples shows" and the Sarrasani Circus Indigenous performers on the German public, see Rudolf Conrad, "Mutual Fascination: Indians in Dresden and Leipzig," in *Indians and Europe: An Interdisciplinary Collection of Essays*, 2nd ed., ed. Christian Feest (Lincoln: University of Nebraska Press, 1999), 455–74.

49. For the career of one entrepreneurial artist, whose show name was "Princess White Deer," see Ruth Phillips, "'From Wigwam to White Lights': Popular Culture, Politics, and the Performance of Native North American Identity in the Era of Assimilationism," in *Historical Reenactment: From Realism to the Affective Turn*, ed. Iain McCalman (London: Palgrave Macmillan, 2010), 159–69.

50. Penny, *Kindred By Choice*, 218–20.

51. Stetler, "Buffalo Bill's Wild West," 3, 208–25.

52. Stetler, 3.

53. From an interview given by Cody to the *Berliner Tageblatt* on July 27, 1890, quoted in Stetler, "Buffalo Bill's Wild West," 131.

54. Stetler, 214–15.

55. Mitchell, *Late Westerns*, 149–78. See also McVeigh, *The American Western*, 58–75 and 213–20; Hine, Faragher, and Coleman, *The American West*, 443–45.

56. Hine, Faragher, and Coleman, 446.

57. Irmela Schneider, *Amerikanische Einstellung: Deutsches Fernsehen und US-amerikanische Produktionen* (Heidelberg: Winter, 1992), 100–109; see also Nash, "European Image of America," 13.

58. See Knut Hickethier and Peter Hoff, *Geschichte des deutschen Fernsehens* (Stuttgart: Metzler, J B, 1998), 360.

59. For the propensity of fans outside the US to read their own emphases and interpretations into entertainments, see Nancy Reagin and Anne Rubenstein, "'I'm Buffy and You're History': Putting Fan Studies Back into History," *Transformative Works and Cultures* 6 (March 2011); see also Henry Jenkins, *Textual Poachers*.

60. See the list of German titles for *Bonanza* episodes at the *Bonanza* Wikia at http://bonanza.wikia.com/wiki/Bonanza_Wiki, accessed May 18, 2014. As discussed in Chapter 3, Western genre films made in East Germany often presented Indian characters as the films' protagonists and unambiguously as the heroes of their Westerns, who triumphed over the evil represented by American corporations and state authorities. West German films also took Indian characters as their protagonists and heroes but sometimes contrasted the relationships of Indians with a handful of rapacious white Americans (English-speaking "Yankees"), with Indians' positive encounters with well-meaning whites. See Henning Engelke and Simon Kopp, "Der Western im Osten. Genre, Zeitlichkeit und Authentizität im DEFA- und im Hollywood-Western," *Zeithistorische Forschungen* 2, no. 1 (2004), accessed July 5, 2013, http://www.zeithistorische-forschungen.de/site/40208210/default.aspx; see also Gerd Gemunden, "Between Karl May and Karl Marx: The DEFA Indianerfilme (1965–1983)," *New German Critique* no. 82 (2001): 25–38; and Holger Briel, "Native Americans in the Films of the GDR and Czechoslovakia," *European Journal of Ameri-*

can Culture 31, no. 3 (2012): 231–47.

61. Hine, Faragher, and Coleman, *The American West*, 447–49.

62. Foundational works in the New Western historiography include Limerick, *The Legacy of Conquest*; White, *"It's Your Misfortune and None of My Own"*; Donald Worster, *Rivers of Empire: Water, Aridity, and the Growth of the American West*, reprint ed. (New York: Oxford University Press, 1992). For a summary of this historiographical school's concerns see Patricia Nelson Limerick, Clyde Milner, and Charles Rankin, eds., *Trails: Toward a New Western History* (Lawrence: University Press of Kansas, 1991); for the sometimes critical response to this scholarship, see Gene Gressley, ed., *Old West/New West* (Norman: University of Oklahoma Press, 1994). For a discussion of the ways that historiography created by both white and Indigenous scholars has developed over time see Philip Deloria, "Historiography," in *A Companion to American Indian History*, ed. Philip Deloria and Neil Salisbury (Malden: Blackwell, 2002), 6–24.

63. Limerick, Milner, and Rankin, *Trails*, 85–86.

64. Limerick, Milner, and Rankin, 32.

65. Limerick, Milner, and Rankin, 87.

66. Quoted in Hine, Faragher, and Coleman, *The American West*, 403.

67. Anita Clair Fellman, *Little House, Long Shadow*, 163.

## Chapter 2. Buffalo Bill and Karl May

1. See the clubs' websites here: http://www.cowboyclub.de/ and https://www.old-texas-town.de/, both accessed October 3, 2019. See also Cindy Drexl, *Sehnsucht nach dem Wilden Westen: 100 Jahre Münchner Cowboy Club* (Munich: Volk Verlag München, 2013).

2. See the club's website at www.wild-west-girls.de; the club offered thirty-eight public performances at various country western and Western folk festivals and other events in 2018 alone. A video of the flag parade is posted at https://www.youtube.com/watch?v=LB7CuOyMPPg, accessed September 25, 2019.

3. For a list of cowboy and Indianist hobbyist clubs (largely from regions contained in former West Germany) that hold a summer gathering and collections of photos of previous summer meetups, see https://www.westernbund.de/galerien/, accessed October 3, 2019. Indianist hobbyists from regions formerly in East Germany still hold their own summer gatherings; see Penny, *Kindred By Choice*, 1–2. I am also indebted to staff of the Karl May Museum for sharing information about the former East German Indianist community that they belonged to, and for sharing photos of their gatherings.

4. See the Bad Segeberg show website at https://www.karl-may-spiele.de/indian -village-mehr/indian-village, accessed October 2, 2019.

5. For Karl May shows across Germany, see Weber, "'Indians' on German Stages." See also the large collection of Karl May summer show programs from across Germany, in the archive of the Karl May Museum.

6. See the theme park's website at https://www.pullmancity.de/en-US/, accessed October 3, 2019.

7. Conversation with Robin Leipold, Content Director of the Karl May Museum, April 1, 2019.

8. For a discussion of this phenomenon among later generations of television and literary fans of many series, see Jenkins, *Textual Poachers.*

9. Birgit Turski, "Indianistikgruppen der DDR—gegenwärtige Situation, Entwick-lung, Probleme" (Vordiplom Thesis, Karl Marx University of Leipzig, 1990), 18. See also Turski, *Die Indianistikgruppen der DDR: Entwicklung—Probleme—Aussichten* (Idstein/Taunus: Baum Publications, 1994). For the ways in which May's novels and particularly the character of Winnetou attracted hobbyists to Indianist clubs, see also Kalshoven, *Crafting "The Indian,"* 13.

10. Conrad, "Mutual Fascination."

11. See Gerhard Klussmeier, *Karl May: Biographie in Dokumenten und Bildern,* 2nd ed. (Hildesheim: Olms, 1992); see also Gert Üding, ed., *Karl-May Handbuch,* 3rd ed. (Wurzburg: Königshausen & Neumann, 2001); Colleen Cook, "Germany's Wild West: A Researcher's Guide to Karl May," *German Studies Review* 5, no. 1 (1982): 67–86; Reinhold Frigge, *Das Erwartbare Abenteuer: Massenrezeption und literarisches interesse am Beispiel der Reiseerzahlungen von Karl May* (Bonn: Bouvier, 1984). For May's status as the first pop cultural phenomenon, see also Vera Cuntz-Leng and Jacqueline Meintzinger, "A Brief History of Fan Fiction in Germany," *Transformative Works and Cultures* 19 (2015), https://doi.org/10.3983/twc.2015.0630. The Karl May Press alone sold over eighty million copies by 2013, and the Press estimates that over one hundred million copies of his works were sold in total during the twentieth century. See Bernhard Schmid and Juergen Seul, *100 Jahre: Verlagsarbeit fuer Karl May und sein Werk, 1913–2013* (Bamberg: Karl-May-Verlag, 2013), 177 and 182. For discussions of May's sales and surveys of his audiences, see Jochen Schulte-Sasse, "Karl Mays Amerika-Exotik und deutsche Wirklichkeit" in *Karl May: Studien zu Leben, Werk u. Wirkung e. Erfolgsschriftellers,* ed. Helmut Schmiedt (Königstein/Ts.: Hain, 1979), 101–29; see also Penny, *Kindred By Choice,* 65–68 and Stetler, "Buffalo Bill's Wild West," 108–10.

12. See Edward Said, *Orientalism* (New York: Vintage, 1979).

13. Schmid and Seul, *100 Jahre,* 26 and 182; the count of foreign language translations was

accurate as of 2013.

14. A "Mary Sue" is a fandom term for a story character who seems unrealistically perfect, displaying amazing and unexpected talents.

15. See Karl Markus Kreis, "German Wild West: Karl May's Invention of the Definitive Indian," in *I Like America: Fictions of the Wild West*, ed. Pamela Kort and Max Hollein (Munich: Prestel, 2006), 253–54.

16. See Peter Thompson, "From Karl May to Karl Marx: Ernst Bloch and the Native American Tribe as Concrete Utopia," in *Tribal Fantasies: Native Americans in the European Imaginary*, ed. James Mackay and David Stirrup (New York: Palgrave Macmillan, 2013), 95.

17. Warren, *Buffalo Bill's America*, 104–5.

18. Cook, "Germany's Wild West," 72. See also Klussmeier, *Karl May*, 37ff; see also Üding, *Karl-May Handbuch*, 67–111.

19. Author and May fan Heinrich Spörl, quoted at https://www.karl-may.de/Stimmen-zu-Karl-May, accessed October 27, 2020.

20. For one fan's attempt to nonetheless exonerate May of any conscious intent to deceive, see Reinhold Eichacker, "Was Karl May mir war. Ein Zeugnis unter vielen," *Karl-May-Jahrbuch* 2 (1919): 110–25; see also Adolf Wagner, "Wir Jungens und Karl May," *Karl-May-Jahrbuch* 2 (1919): 349–56; Wilhelm Hane, Franz Ernst, and Lisbeth Barchewitz, "Karl Mays Einfluss auf Unser Leben," *Karl-May-Jahrbuch* 3 (1920): 297–317.

21. See the correspondence between Nazi authorities and Wilhelm Fronemann in BA Berlin-Lichterfelde NS 12/83; see also Christian Heermann, *Old Shatterhand ritt nicht im Auftrage der Arbeiterklasse: Warum War Karl May in SBZ Und DDR "Verboten"?* (Dessau: Anhaltische Verlagsgesellschaft, 1995), 5; and Erich Heinemann, *Dreissig Jahre Karl-May-Gesellschaft: 1969–1999: Erinnerungen und Betrachtungen* (Hamburg: Hansa, 2000), 18ff.

22. For the complex relationship between the Karl May Press and the author's most devoted readers, see Heinemann, *Dreissig Jahre Karl-May-Gesellschaft*.

23. Ellery Quinn, a mid-twentieth-century Sherlockian, opened his first Holmes story "with no realization that I stood—rather, I sat—on the brink of my fate. I had no inkling, no premonition that in another minute, my life's work, such as it is, would be [determined] . . . I was lost! Ecstatically, everlastingly lost!" See Phillip Schreffler, *Sherlock Holmes by Gas-Lamp: Highlights from the First Four Decades of the Baker Street Journal* (New York: Fordham University Press, 1989), 19–23. For a discussion of these "first time" accounts see Matt Hills, "Returning to Becoming-a-Fan Stories: Theorizing Transformational Objects and the Emergence/Extension of Fandom," in *The Ashgate Research Companion to Fan Culture*, ed. Linda Duits, Koos Zwaan, and

Stijn Reijnders (Surrey, UK: Ashgate Press, 2014), 9–22.

24. Hane, Ernst, and Barchewitz, "Karl Mays Einfluss auf unser Leben," 310–11.

25. Cracroft, "World Westerns," 159–79; Sammons, "Nineteenth-Century German Representations of Indians," 185; D. L. Ashliman, "The American West in Twentieth-Century Germany," 81–92.

26. The relationship between the two lead characters can easily be read by fans as homo-romantic or even homoerotic, although such readings were vehemently rejected by earlier leading Karl May fans and by the Karl May Society founders. Slash stories or readings generally played only a marginal role in Karl May fandom before the late twentieth century, however, although by the early twenty-first century, fan fiction that pairs the two characters was not difficult to locate on the internet, and the pairing is now enthusiastically championed by some fans.

27. Both men became leading members of the Karl May Society, which published an enormous body of work on May and his stories in its newsletter, yearbook, and special editions of May's work. See Heinemann, *Dreissig Jahre Karl-May-Gesellschaft*, 149.

28. See Weber, "'Indians' on German Stages."

29. One early example was the Karl-May-Vereinigung, which sponsored occasional meetings and a newsletter. It was founded in Berlin in 1912 but apparently dissolved by 1915. See this group's newsletter in the *Archiv der Karl-May-Gesellschaft*. See also Üding, *Karl-May Handbuch*, 559.

30. Üding, *Karl-May Handbuch*, 554–58; even though the original editions of the stories entered the public domain after 1962, the owner of the Karl May Press zealously continues to defend the Press's trademark rights over "Winnetou" and other intellectual properties associated with May's stories. See Irmgard Elhachoumi, "Showdown zum Aktenzeichen Winnetou," *Karl May & Co* 19 (2019): 90–92. See also Cuntz-Leng and Meintzinger, "A Brief History of Fan Fiction in Germany."

31. Philip DeLoria, *Indians in Unexpected Places* (Lawrence: University Press of Kansas, 2004), 11. Indian hobbyism similar to German Indianist hobbyism was beginning to emerge in the United States during the 1930s, but it did not become a widespread pastime in the US before the 1960s, as we shall see in Chapter 3.

32. Frank's birth name was Ernst Tobis; he adopted "Patty Frank" during his years as an acrobat and gymnast. See "Patty (Eigentl. Ernst Tobis) Frank | Sächsische Biografie | ISGV"at http://saebi.isgv.de/biografie/Patty_Frank_(1876–1959), accessed May 6, 2008; see also Frank's autobiographical essay, *Ein Leben im Banne Karl May's. Erlebnisse und Kleine Erzaehlungen* (Radebeul: Kupky & Dietze, 1940) and Wolfgang Seifert, *Patty Frank: Der Zirkus, die Indianer, das Karl-May-Museum* (Bamberg: Karl-May-Verlag, 1998).

33. See the many reports on club gatherings in the newspaper clippings section of the

*Archiv der Karl-May-Gesellschaft*, e.g., "Karlsruher Indianer feierten Geburtstag"; see also Penny, *Kindred By Choice*, 145–46; and the links to the home pages of (primarily West German) cowboy and Indian clubs on https://www.westernbund.de /%C3%BCber-uns/mitgliedsvereine/, accessed October 3, 2019; many of these clubs' public websites contain short historical essays about their origins and history.

34. For a list of the Manitou Club members' professions, see "Belege und Rechnungen 'Manitou Club'" in the Karl May Museum archive. Sommer referred to himself as "Fremont Fred" in some letters, but his usual club name appears to have been "Fred Black"; see Drexl, *Sehnsucht nach dem Wilden Westen*, 29. The Dresden club began to meet during the 1920s and formally registered as an association in 1931. See also a short memoir by one educated German who called himself a *Sonderlinge* (an "odd one") among his academic circle because of his engagement with Indianist hobbyists, since Westerns were seen as "pulp fiction" literature and not "good" literature: Hermann Dengler, "Wie ich Indianer wurde," *Karl-May-Jahrbuch* 16 (1933): 450–63. For the working-class roots of one group of Indian hobbyists after 1945, see Broyles-Gonzalez, "Cheyennes in the Black Forest."

35. Gary Fine, *Shared Fantasy: Role-Playing Games as Social Worlds* (Chicago: University of Chicago Press, 2002), 236–37.

36. Taken from the exchange of letters between the "chiefs" of the Dresden and Munich clubs, who had a frequent and cordial correspondence in the archive of the Karl May Museum, folder labeled "Documents of the Manitou Club"; see particularly the letters dated June 23, 1934 and April 10, 1933, which contain descriptions of each club's current membership and activities. See also Siefert, *Patty Frank*, 156 and 170. For the Munich club's early history, see also Drexl, *Sehnsucht nach dem Wilden Westen* and Penny, *Kindred By Choice*, 145–49. See also Peter Bolz, "Life Among the 'Hunkpapas': A Case Study in German Indian Folk Lore," in *Indians and Europe: An Interdisciplinary Collection of Essays*, 2nd ed., ed. Christian Feest (Lincoln: University of Nebraska Press, 1999), 484, for the ways in which the Munich Club members, like other hobbyist clubs of this period, included members who researched and specialized in both cowboys and Indian role-play.

37. See the motion submitted at the club's 1934 annual meeting in "85 Belege und Rechnungen 'Manitou Club,'" in the Karl May Museum Archive, "Documents of the Manitou Club" folder.

38. For discussions of club members' purchase of beads, moccasins, and other materials, see Karl May Museum Archive folder "Documents of the Manitou Club" folder, "85 Belege und Rechnungen 'Manitou Club.'" The Munich club had a lively exchange of eagle feathers for years with the Lakota of the Pine Ridge Reservation in South Dakota, who sent them leggings, moccasins, and other articles of clothing in exchange.

See Drexl, *Sehnsucht Nach Dem Wilden Westen*, 28.

39. See correspondence between Manitou club and the Munich club, esp. letter from Fremont Fred Sommer dated July 6, 1933 in Karl May Museum Archive, "Documents of the Manitou Club" folder.

40. See the description of the "Munich Cowboy Club 25th anniversary," http://www .in-der-helle.de/kmg/scan2.php?litNr=2031, accessed July 18, 2008; Heermann, *Old Shatterhand*, 84–85; see also Birgit Turski, "The Indianist Groups in the GDR: Development—Problems—Prospects," *European Review of Native American Studies* 7, no. 1 (1993): 43.

41. Saler, "'Clap If You Believe in Sherlock Holmes.'" The Sherlockian "Great Game" is a shared, tongue-in-cheek pretense among fans that Sherlock Holmes and Watson truly existed, and that Arthur Conan Doyle was simply Watson's literary agent.

42. See "Das ist 'Wild-West' wie's im Buch steht! 25 Jahre Münchner Cowboy-Club" in the *Münchner Zeitung*, April 4, 1938. It seems likely that the film shown at the anniversary party was the same as a fan film made that year by the club members; the script was written and the film directed by club member Kurt Ulrich, alias the "Pecos Kid," with the acting done by the club members. See Drexl, *Sehnsucht Nach Dem Wilden Westen*, 31.

43. See Penny, *Kindred By Choice*, 221–28, for a discussion of how Germans attributed an essentialized masculinity to Indigenous men, in particular. This was an interesting exception to the tendency of Europeans to feminize colonial subjects.

44. See account of museum's foundation in Seifert, *Patty Frank*, 117ff.

45. Friedrich von Borries, *Sozialistische Cowboys: Der Wilde Westen Ostdeutschlands*, 1. Aufl., Originalausg, Edition Suhrkamp 2528 (Frankfurt: Suhrkamp, 2008), 17.

46. E. A. Schmid, "Die Indianerhuldigung in Radebeul," *Karl-May-Jahrbuch* 12 (1929): 33. Although this account described all the visitors as Lakota, Robin Leipold noted to me that only the lead performer was Lakota; the others were Acoma Pueblo. The Sarrasani show performers returned for a second visit to May's grave during the Nazi period, as well. See Penny, *Kindred By Choice*, 163–66.

47. See Penny, *Kindred By Choice*, 163–98, for a thoughtful discussion of continuities in the political instrumentalization of Indigenous peoples in twentieth-century Germany.

48. See the correspondence of the National Socialist Teacher's League leadership with both Fronemann and the Karl May Press in BA NS 12/83.

49. For Roxin's recollection of his experiences in a Nazi organization for children, see Heinemann, *Dreissig Jahre Karl-May-Gesellschaft*, 104.

50. Correspondence with Fronemann and May Verlag in BA NS 12/83; see also the discussions of Karl May's compatibility with Nazi values in BA 12/153. These admonitions regarding invoking the Party in private company's advertising were not unusual.

Nazi authorities often took a dim view of private businesses profiting from any claimed endorsements by Hitler or other Nazi leaders. In the case of the Karl May Press, however, the National Socialist Teacher's League's repeated rebukes for using Hitler's name or the League's own endorsement (expressed in their approval of the books for their catalog of "good literature") were generally ignored by the Press.

51. See the report on the Saxon Nazi Party leaders' visit to the museum in the December 22, 1933 issue of *Der Freiheitskampf* (the Nazi provincial paper for Sachsen). See also Juliane Hanzig, "'—nicht zu vergessen—ein Trunk "Feuerwasser"' Ein Bild und seine Geschichte. Ein persönlicher Werkstattbericht," *Magazin des Karl-May-Museums* no. 1 (2020): 60–65.

52. See the article by Klara May published in the *Freiheitskampf* (the regional Nazi newspaper for Saxony) on February 18, 1934, "Unter dem Hakenkreuz um die Erde" ("Under the Swastika Around the World"). The National Socialist Teacher's League leadership was aware of this connection, and in internal correspondence commented that Klara May was even greeted by Hitler personally at a public performance. See the correspondence in BA Berlin-Lichterfelde NS 12/83, and a private communication from Robin Leipold (February 27, 2021) regarding May's later membership in the NSDAP.

53. See Barbara Haible, *Indianer im Dienste der NS-Ideologie: Untersuchungen zur Funktion von Jugendbüchern über nordamerikanische Indianer im Nationalsozialismus* (Hamburg: Kovac, 1998); and Penny, *Kindred By Choice*, 164–72.

54. For examples of press reports on Frank and the tours he gave of his museum (including to Nazi youth groups) see "Pimpfe bei Karl May" in *Hilf' mit!*, n.d., 1938; "Wer war uns Old Shatterhand?" in *Schwarze Korps* (the SS official newspaper), April 1, 1937; "Auf Winnetous Spuren Großzügiger Ausbau des Karl-May-Museums in Radebeul" in *Freiheitskampf*, February 21, 1937; and "Aus dem Reiche Old Shatterhands" in *Hannoverscher Anzeiger*, October 1, 1933; see also the magazine clipping "Hitlerjugend auf dem Spuren Karl Mays," n.d.; all clippings found in the the newspaper clippings section of the *Archiv der Karl-May-Gesellschaft*.

55. None of the cowboy and Indian clubs I found information on were dissolved after 1933, since they were evidently (and unsurprisingly) seen as completely "unpolitical." They must have been *gleichgeschaltet* (forced to purge Jewish members and accept Nazi oversight); however, since this requirement was imposed on all voluntary associations in Germany, presumably any Jewish members were asked to resign, or dropped out under pressure. For a discussion of this process of social isolation of German Jews in civil society and voluntary organizations, see Marion Kaplan, *Between Dignity and Despair: Jewish Life in Nazi Germany* (New York: Oxford University Press, 1999). See also Penny, *Kindred By Choice*, 164–72.

56. Heinemann, *Dreissig Jahre Karl-May-Gesellschaft*, 18ff. See also Üding, *Karl-May Handbuch*, 559.

57. Heinemann, *Dreissig Jahre Karl-May-Gesellschaft*, 152.

58. See the advertising flyers for the 1938, 1939, 1940, and 1941 Karl May *Freilichtspiele* in the archive of the Karl May Museum; the quotation from one production's prologue comes from the 1940 Berlin Werder production program in the museum's archive, but this speech was apparently included in other Karl May productions during the war as well; see Ulrich Neumann, "Zirkusflair und Kriegsgeschrei: Karl-May-Spiele Rathen 1940," *Karl May & Co* no. 155 (Feb. 2019): 76. See also the many press reports on diverse theatrical and other derivative productions of May stories in the press clippings files of the Archiv der Karl-May-Gesellschaft, Part II (1913–1969), at http://www.in-der-helle.de/kmg/, accessed May 8, 2008. See also Weber, "'Indians' on German Stages," 214.

59. Borries, *Sozialistische Cowboys*, 17.

## Chapter 3. A Wall Runs through It

1. For the internal discussion about Karl May's social value within the East German Ministry of Culture see BA Berlin-Lichterfelde DR 1/8660, "Einschaetzung der Werke Karl May im DDR Kultusministerium 1964–1965" and DR 1/6242, "Minsterium fuer Kultur, HA Schöne Literatur, Abt. Belletristik, Kunst, und Musikliteratur— letters and memos re Karl May"; for the reevaluation of Karl May by East German leaders during the 1980s see the Politbuero correspondence in BA Berlin-Lichterfelde DY 30/18570. See also Heermann, *Old Shatterhand*, 10.

2. See letters sent by fans protesting the confiscation of May books purchased abroad by East German border guards in BA Berlin-Lichterfelde, DR 1/6241, "Minsterium für Kultur, HA Schöne Literatur, Abt. Belletristik, Kunst, und Musikliteratur."

3. BA Berlin-Lichterfelde, DR 1/6241.

4. Heermann, *Old Shatterhand*, 110.

5. Heermann, 36–46, 82; Borries, *Sozialistische Cowboys*, 19.

6. This exchange is recounted in Heermann, *Old Shatterhand*, 84. See also the history of the Manitou Club in the *Stetson City Tribune* 3, June 24, 1996, "Festausgabe Anlässlich des 50-jährigen Jubiläums des Indian und Westernclub Old Manitou 1956 e.V.," 8–9. See also Robin Leipold and Volkmar Göschka, "Indianer im Wilden Osten." *Magazin des Karl-May-Museums* no. 1 (2020): 34–41.

7. Quoted in Borries, *Sozialistische Cowboys*, 32.

8. Borries, 32. See also the account of the Stasi raid of the club and the confiscation of their "Colts" in the *Stetson City Tribune* 3, June 24, 1996, "Dunkle Wolken ueber Man-

itous Kindern," 6–7. In a sense, fans who insisted on dressing and posing as cowboys were an East German variant on the *Halbstarken* (young toughs) so criticized by both East and West German authorities and educators during the 1950s and 1960s.

9. See Turski, "The Indianist Groups in the GDR," 43–48, which describes some of the internal debates over giving up white Western *personas* as long-running and sometimes "grim." In photos of DDR hobbyist summer gatherings in the Karl May Museum archive, a 1956 photo shows a few club members dressed as cowboys, but those costumes disappeared in photos taken during the mid-1960s.

10. Borries, *Sozialistische Cowboys*, 110.

11. See photos of the Dresden Zoo performances by the Manitou Club in Karl May Museum Archive, *Stetson City Tribune* June 24, 1996, "Festausgabe anlässlich des 50-jährigen Jubiläums des Indian und Westernclub Old Manitou 1956 e.V.," 11; see also Leipold and Göschka, "Indianer im Wilden Osten," 34–41.

12. See Karl May Museum Archive, *Stetson City Tribune* 3, June 24, 1996, "Festausgabe anlässlich des 50-jährigen Jubiläums des Indian und Westernclub Old Manitou 1956 e.V.," and *Stetson City Tribune* 2, Aug. 31, 1996, "Festausgabe anlässlich des 40-jährigen Jubiläums des Indian und Westernclub Old Manitou 1956 e.V.," reprint ed. See also Borries, *Sozialistische Cowboys*, 25–29.

13. See the Karl May Museum's holdings of the 1979–88 issues of a newsletter created by an East German Indianist hobbyist club, *Wampum*, which reported on the activities of several clubs, and also many sympathetic, detailed reports on the treatment and position of Indigenous Americans.

14. Turski, "The Indianist Groups in the GDR," 44. See also Penny, "Elusive Authenticity."

15. Fortieth-anniversary issue of *Stetson City Tribune*, 9, and a private communication from Robin Leipold, February 27, 2021.

16. See the regular instructions and drawings given in *Wampum*, and in the *Informationsblatt f. Indianistik*, two East German hobbyist newsletters, and in their West German counterpart, the *Dakota Scout*. See also Penny, "Elusive Authenticity." Philip Deloria discusses a parallel movement and focus on authenticity among white American "Indian" hobbyists during the 1950s and 1960s. See Philip Deloria, *Playing Indian*, rev. ed. (New Haven: Yale University Press, 1999), 127–52.

17. Kalshoven, *Crafting "The Indian,"* 234–35. See also Bolz, "Life Among the 'Hunkpapas.'"

18. See Gapps, "Mobile Monuments" and Gapps, "Performing the Past." For a discussion of authenticity in fan handicrafts in fandoms that are organized around *Downton Abbey* and other historical television series and movies, see Cherry, *Cult Media*, 152ff; Kalshoven, *Crafting "The Indian,"* 181; Penny, "Elusive Authenticity." For a discussion of how Indigenous North Americans understand authenticity within living history

presentations and their own craft traditions, see Laura Peers, *Playing Ourselves: Interpreting Native Histories at Historic Reconstructions* (Lanham: Alta Mira Press, 2007), xviii ff; and Peers, "The Great Box Project," https://www.prm.ox.ac.uk/haidabox, accessed February 24, 2020; for discussions of authenticity in cultural tourism, see Edward Bruner, *Culture on Tour: Ethnographies of Travel* (Chicago: University of Chicago Press, 2005).

19. Gapps, "Mobile Monuments," 398.

20. "Die Lagerfeuer am Däbersee sind verglommen," in the *Sächsiches Tageblatt*, September 15, 1957.

21. Kalshoven, *Crafting "The Indian,"* 182.

22. These disputes would be characterized as "fan wank," in today's fandoms.

23. See Kalshoven, *Crafting "The Indian,"* 104 and 253, and Bolz "Life Among the 'Hunkpapas,'" 486.

24. The wrangling over rules will seem familiar to anyone who has been exposed to bitter disputes among modern historical reenactors, or to fans of literary or media canons.

25. For disputes over anachronisms in modern historical reenactor performances, clothing, and artifacts, see Gapps, "Mobile Monuments," 399 and Gapps, "Performing the Past," 244 ff; for similar disputes and terminology used among American twentieth-century military reenactors, see Jenny Thompson, *War Games: Inside the World of Twentieth-Century Reenactors* (Washington DC: Smithsonian Books, 2004), xviii. For media fan negotiations of authenticity and resulting disputes, see Kristina Busse, "May the Force Be With You: Fan Negotiations of Authority," in *Framing Fan Fiction: Literary and Social Practices in Fan Fiction Communities*, ed. Kristina Busse (Iowa City: University of Iowa Press, 2017), 99–120.

26. Turski, "The Indianist Groups in the GDR," 44.

27. Interview with Robin Leipold, Content Director of the Karl May Museum, April 1, 2019. For long-standing connections between some Lakota communities and German Indian hobbyists, see Penny, *Kindred By Choice*, 252–55, 260–63.

28. Penny, *Kindred By Choice*, 188–91.

29. Penny, 188–98; see also Feest, "Europe's Indians," 321, for a discussion of the AIM's monopoly during the 1970s among white Europeans as the representative of all Indigenous peoples in Europe.

30. See the discussion of the challenges in creating Stetson City in *Stetson City Tribune* 2, August 31, 1996, "Festausgabe anlässlich des 40-jährigen Jubiläums des Indian und Westernclub Old Manitou 1956 e.V.," reprint ed., 20.

31. "Festausgabe anlässlich," 17. For the continuing popularity of The Week among Eastern German hobbyists after the collapse of the DDR, see Kalshoven, *Crafting "The Indian,"* 75, and Penny, *Kindred By Choice*, 1–2. See also Leipold and Göschka,

"Indianer im Wilden Osten," 34–41.

32. Turski, *Die Indianistikgruppen der DDR*, 18.

33. Turski, 15–16.

34. Heermann, *Old Shatterhand*, 84–85.

35. Heermann, 158–59. This reward to the Stasi fan informer would be analogous to giving a die-hard Harry Potter fan an apartment with a view of Hogwarts Castle. The anecdote also underscores the continuing overlap between Indianist hobbyists and Karl May fans in East Germany.

36. Briel, "Native Americans in the Films of the GDR," 239.

37. For a conservative American view of Reed, see "Who is Dean Reed?" *Time Magazine*, November 27, 1978.

38. Borries, *Sozialistische Cowboys*, 57.

39. For examples, see two Indianist newsletters, *Wampum* (East German) and *Die Fährte* (West German), which regularly published articles with instructions on how to create replica clothing and artifacts. See also Borries, *Sozialistische Cowboys*, 57–61.

40. Conrad, "Mutual Fascination," 455–56; see also Birgit Turski, *Die Indianistikgruppen der DDR*, 29–30 and 40–41. During the 1970s and later, smaller Indianist clubs emerged across Eastern Europe as well, and some had regular contacts with East German hobbyists. See Kalshoven, *Crafting "The Indian,"* 73 and Turski, "The Indianist Groups in the GDR."

41. See the interview with Felbers, who looked back on years of *Indianistik* activism in East Germany, in Jan Sternberg, "Wilder Osten," in the *Frankfurter Rundschau*, March 23, 2005.

42. Sternberg, "Wilder Osten."

43. Drexl, *Sehnsucht nach dem Wilden Westen*, 38–44 and Penny, *Kindred By Choice*, 204–8.

44. Drexl, *Sehnsucht nach dem Wilden Westen*, 38.

45. Bolz, "Life Among the 'Hunkpapas,'" 485.

46. Penny, *Kindred By Choice*, 157–59. See also Feest, "Europe's Indians"; Drexl, *Sehnsucht nach dem Wilden Westen*; and the website of the Western League at https://www.westernbund.de/%C3%BCber-uns/mitgliedsvereine/, accessed October 31, 2019. Note that estimates as to the membership totals of German hobbyist organizations vary; see also Nash, "European Image of America," 14–15.

47. See the Hudson Bay Indian Trading Post website here: https://www.hudsons-bay.de/, accessed November 5, 2020.

48. Drexl, *Sehnsucht nach dem Wilden Westen*, 48–60, 68.

49. Kalshoven, *Crafting "The Indian,"* 30–31.

50. Nash, "European Image of America," 15.

51. An impressive array of May spin-off products in many product categories was displayed in an exhibit organized in the Osnabrück Cultural Historical Museum in 2019, "Blutsbrüder. Der Mythos Karl May in Dioramen."

52. For an overview of the range of commercial products and entertainments that became available in West Germany during this period, see Michael Petzel, *Das Grosse Karl May-Lexikon: [Von der Wueste Zum Silbersee: Der Grosse Deutsche Abenteuer-Mythos: Alles Uber die Winnetou-Welt]* (Berlin: Lexikon Imprint, 2000).

53. Ute Poiger, "A New, 'Western' Hero? Reconstructing German Masculinity in the 1950s," in *The Miracle Years: A Cultural History of West Germany, 1949–1968*, ed. Hannah Schissler (Princeton: Princeton University Press, 2001), 413.

54. Ashliman, "The American West in Twentieth-Century Germany," 84.

55. Petzel, *Das Grosse Karl May-Lexikon*, 33–34; see also "Besucherrekord in Segeberg" in *Schleswig-Holsteinische Volkszeitung*, August 22, 1961; and a year-by-year tally of visitors to Bad Segeberg given in the Karl-May-Wiki at http://igbserver.wiwi .tu-dresden.de/~thomas/wiki/index.php/Bad_Segeberg, accessed July 18, 2008. See also Reinhard Marheinecke and Nicolas Finke, *Karl May Am Kalkberg. Geschichte und Geschichten der Karl-May-Spiele Bad Sageberg Seit 1952* (Bamberg: Karl-May-Verlag, 1999); see also Weber, "'Indians' on German Stages."

56. Peter Zastrow and Hans-Werner Baurycza, *Eine Stadt Spielt Indianer. Aust den Anfangsjahren der Karl-May-Festspiele in Bad Segeberg* (Duderstadt: EPV, 2011), 102–4 and Weber, "'Indians' on German Stages," 241.

57. Weber, 203.

58. See Jochen Bludau and Fred Aurich, *Elspe: Deutschlands Wilder Westen* (Heilbronn: Hohenloher Druck- und Verlagshaus Gerabronn, 1981); and Weber, "'Indians' on German Stages," 252–54.

59. See the annual programs of the Pluwig theatricals in the archive of the Karl May Museum; see also Bludau and Aurich, *Elspe*, and Weber, "'Indians' on German Stages."

60. See the annual programs of the Karl May Treffen meetups in the Karl May Museum archive; see also the announcements of annual gatherings at summer theatrical sites in the *Karl May Rundbrief* (later renamed *Karl May & Co*), a popular fandom magazine since the 1980s. See also Weber, "'Indians' on German Stages," 300.

61. Petzel, *Das Grosse Karl May-Lexikon*; Christian Unucka, *Karl May im Film: Eine Bilddokumentation* (Dachau: Vereinigte Verlagsgesellschaften Franke, 1980); see also Jürgen Wehnert, *Karl-May-Welten* (Bamberg: Karl-May-Verlag, 2005).

62. See the newsletters of fan clubs devoted to Brice and the Karl May films at the Karl May Archive, Binder 2.3.1.1ff.6, Film, "Fans und Fanclubs—'Rauchzeichen' (Hennicke)" and Binder 2.3.2.2ff.6. FILM.

63. In fact, the spin-off products do fill an archive: the Karl May Archive, in Göttingen,

which contains a superbly well-organized archive of the material culture surrounding Karl May films and stage productions. Tours of Croatia and other film locations remain popular today; see the Karl May Archive, Binder FILM Folgewirtschaft, Tourismus, Diverse.

64. See the *Mitteilungen der Arbeitsgemeinschaft Karl-May-Biographie*, 1963–1968 in the Karl May Gesellschaft Archive.

65. See the account of the KMG's foundation in Erich Heinemann, *Dreissig Jahre Karl-May-Gesellschaft*; membership information is given on 230–31.

66. Heinemann, *Dreissig Jahre Karl-May-Gesellschaft*, 45.

67. Ashliman, "The American West in Twentieth-Century Germany."

68. Heinemann, *Dreissig Jahre Karl-May-Gesellschaft*, 150.

69. Heinemann, 235.

70. Jenkins, *Textual Poachers*, 51.

71. Michael Petzel, "Der letzte Drehort," in *Karl-May-Welten*, ed. Jürgen Wehnert (Bamberg: Karl-May-Verlag), 198.

72. Fan tourism overall is a growing field in fan studies. See Will Brooker, "Everywhere and Nowhere: Vancouver, Fan Pilgrimage and the Urban Imaginary," *International Journal of Cultural Studies* 10 (2007): 423–44; Roger C. Aden, *Popular Stories and Promised Lands: Fan Cultures and Symbolic Pilgrimages* (Tuscaloosa: University of Alabama Press, 1999); Henrik Linden and Sara Linden, *Fans and Fan Culture: Tourism, Consumerism, and Social Media* (New York: Palgrave MacMillan, 2017), 105–30. See also Abby Waysdorf and Stijn Reijnders, "The Role of Imagination in the Film Tourist Experience: The Case of *Game of Thrones*," *Participations: Journal of Audience and Reception Studies* 14 (2017): 170–91; and Waysdorf and Reijnders, "Fan Homecoming: Analyzing the Role of Place in Long-Term Fandom of *The Prisoner*," *Popular Communication* 17 (2019): 50–65.

73. Heinemann, *Dreissig Jahre Karl-May-Gesellschaft*, 43–44.

74. See Karl May Museum press clippings reporting on the ride, and the program published to advertise it in the archive's holdings; see also Erwin Muller, "Die Karl-May-Szene in Deutschland: Ein Überblick," *Karl-May-Gesellschaft-Nachtrichten* no. 108 (June 1996). For hundreds of photos of costumed role-play at "Karl May Festivals" in recent years, see the photo gallery hosted by the fan magazine *Karl May & Co* at http://www.karl-may-magazin.de/galerie/pixlie.php, accessed April 12, 2008 and also https://www.karl-may-magazin.de/aktuell/galerie/, accessed October 31, 2019.

75. Saler, "'Clap If You Believe in Sherlock Holmes,'" 606. Saler argues that starting with Holmes fans and continuing throughout the twentieth century, "the double-consciousness of the ironic imagination enabled adults to immerse themselves in these worlds while simultaneously remaining grounded in the real."

76. See the Karl May Day festival programs in the Karl May Museum archive, Kulturamt der Stadt Radebeul and Karl-May-Museum Radebeul, "Program der Karl-May-Festtage 1998," Radebeul: n.p., 1998 and Kulturamt der Stadt Radebeul and Karl-May-Museum Radebeul, *Die Radebeuler Karl-May-Festtage*. Radebeul: n.p., 2000. See also Weber, "'Indians' on German Stages," 286–300; the replacement of Indianist hobbyists with Indigenous performers is discussed in chapter 5.
77. Weber, "'Indians' on German Stages," 291.

## Chapter 4. Little Houses on the Prairie

1. Laura Ingalls Wilder, *Little House in the Big Woods* (New York: Harper Collins, 1971), 1.
2. The series offers considerable detail about the design and building process for each of the houses that Wilder lived in with her family. These descriptions, along with the information on his house that Charles Ingalls included on his homestead claim paperwork and contemporary documentation and photographs, underlie homesite restorations and replica buildings. In some cases the original buildings themselves are still standing.
3. Wendy McClure, *The Wilder Life: My Adventures in the Lost World of "Little House on the Prairie"* (New York: Riverhead Books, 2011), 1 and 7.
4. Interview with Kitty Latane, November 26, 2019.
5. For a discussion of how gender functions in the stories, see Ann Romines, "Putting Things in Order: The Domestic Aesthetic of Laura Ingalls Wilder's Little House Books" in *The Material Culture of Gender and the Gender of Material Culture*, ed. Katherine Martinez and Kenneth Ames (Hanover: University Press of New England, 1997), 181–95; see also Romines, *Constructing the Little House: Gender, Culture, and Laura Ingalls Wilder* (Amherst: University of Massachusetts Press, 1997).
6. Interview with Vicki Johnston on June 20, 2019. Discussions with other homesites' staff members confirmed that outside of groups of schoolchildren brought for field trips, visitors to the sites were also largely female, either groups of adult female friends, or family groups where the mother and/or daughter had brought the family to tour the houses. This matched my own observations of visitors to the homesites that I visited; most of the men I saw at homesites appeared to be "trailing spouses" of adult female fans.
7. The four novels set in and around De Smet are *By the Shores of Silver Lake*, *The Long Winter*, *Little Town on the Prairie*, and *These Happy Golden Years*. I am not including *The First Four Years* in this tally, since this rough draft manuscript was first published after Wilder's death, and was not part of her original series.
8. See Gapps, "Performing the Past," 245 ff.

9. J. Caroline Toy, "Constructing the Fannish Place: Ritual and Sacred Space in a Sherlock Fan Pilgrimage," *Journal of Fandom Studies* 5 (2017): 253. See also Will Brooker, "'It Is Love': The Lewis Carroll Society as a Fan Community." *American Behavioral Scientist* 48, no. 7 (2005): 859–80; and Brooker, "Everywhere and Nowhere," 423–44. See also Aden, *Popular Stories and Promised Lands.*

10. Peers, *Playing Ourselves,* xxx and 89–90.

11. Interview with Kitty Latane, November 26, 2019.

12. Caroline Fraser, *Prairie Fires: The American Dreams of Laura Ingalls Wilder* (New York: Metropolitan Books, 2017), 396.

13. See Fellman, *Little House, Long Shadow,* 80–82. Rose (who edited her mother's books) sought to present the family as even more self-sufficient than they actually were, omitting ways in which they were helped by state and federal governments.

14. Christine Woodside, *Libertarians on the Prairie: Laura Ingalls Wilder, Rose Wilder Lane, and the Making of the Little House* (New York: Arcade Publishing, 2016), 9–15 and Fellman, *Little House, Long Shadow.*

15. Fellman, *Little House, Long Shadow,* 163–64, 221, 247.

16. The literature on Wilder's life and that of her daughter, and on the influence of the book series in American culture, is considerable. The secondary literature I draw on in this chapter includes Donald Zochert, *Laura: The Life of Laura Ingalls Wilder* (New York: Avon, 1976); William Anderson, *Laura Ingalls Wilder: A Biography* (New York: Harper Collins, 1992); Miller, *Laura Ingalls Wilder and Rose Wilder Lane,* and Miller, *Becoming Laura Ingalls Wilder: The Woman Behind the Legend* (Columbia: University of Missouri Press, 1998); and Pamela Smith Hill, *Laura Ingalls Wilder: A Writer's Life* (Pierre: South Dakota State Historical Society, 2007). See here especially Fraser, *Prairie Fires;* see also Fellman, *Little House, Long Shadow,* and Fellman, "Everybody's 'Little Houses': Reviewers and Critics Read Laura Ingalls Wilder," *Publishing Research Quarterly* 12, no. 1 (Spring 1996): 3–20; Phillip Heldrich, "'Going to Indian Territory': Attitudes Towards Native Americans in *Little House on the Prairie,*" *Great Plains Quarterly* 20, no. 2 (2000): 99–109; Donna Campbell, "'Wild Men' and Dissenting Voices: Narrative Disruption in *Little House on the Prairie,*" *Great Plains Quarterly* 20, no. 2 (2000): 111–22; Frances Kaye, "Little Squatter on the Osage Diminished Reserve: Reading Laura Ingalls Wilder's Kansas Indians," *Great Plains Quarterly* 23, no. 2 (May 2000): 123–40.

17. Miller, *Laura Ingalls Wilder and Rose Lane Wilder,* 94–95. For the influence of the frontier thesis, see also Fellman, *Little House, Long Shadow,* 74–75.

18. Miller, *Laura Ingalls Wilder and Rose Lane Wilder,* 93–108; and Romines, "Putting Things in Order."

19. Brian Cannon, "Homesteading Remembered: a Sesquicentennial Perspective," *Ag-*

*ricultural History* 87, no. 1 (2017): 25; and Hine and Faragher, *Frontiers*, 147 ff; see also Fraser, *Prairie Fires*, 95–99.

20. Fraser, *Prairie Fires*, 166.

21. Fraser, 135.

22. See Anderson, *Laura Ingalls Wilder*, 138 and Fraser, *Prairie Fires*, 135–53.

23. Anderson, *Laura Ingalls Wilder*, 161–219 and Fraser, *Prairie Fires*, 472.

24. Fellman, *Little House, Long Shadow*, 120ff and 162.

25. Fellman, *Little House, Long Shadow*, 162–63.

26. Fraser, *Prairie Fires*, 479.

27. Anderson, *Laura Ingalls Wilder*, 210, and Fraser, *Prairie Fires*, 458–60. Many fan letters to Wilder are preserved in the DeSmet homesite archive.

28. "The Story of the Laura Ingalls Wilder Home Association," *Rocky Ridge Review* (Summer 2007): 2.

29. Aubrey Sherwood letter to Mrs. Addison Wilson, dated July 17, 1965, in "Sherwood" folder, De Smet Archive; and "Society Celebrates 50 Years," *Lore* 33, no. 2 (Fall 2007): 1. See also William Anderson, "In the Beginning," *Lore* 36, no. 1 (Spring 2010): 1.

30. The estimates regarding current and recent homesite annual attendance at Mansfield and De Smet were given to me by homesite staff at the DeSmet, Mansfield, and Malone homesites; I am particularly indebted to Vicki Johnston, who assembled a great deal of visitor data for me. Unfortunately, no historical attendance data for the homesites was available. The population figures for the homesite towns were taken from the 2010 census or from later estimates, if those were available from the Census Bureau.

31. The Walnut Grove production was originally staged as a play and moved to an out-door amphitheater for summer performances; see the history of the pageant in the 2007 production program, "Laura Ingalls Wilder Pageant, 'Fragments of A Dream.'" I am indebted to the staff of the Laura Ingalls Wilder Museum and Tourist Center in Walnut Grove, for the attendance figures for the pageant and other information about its production. In Pepin, staff at the Laura Ingalls Wilder Museum and Gift Shop offered me information about their annual "Laura Days" festival and atten-dance.

32. During my own visits to the homesites in 2019, I spoke with many fans who were completing this homesite circuit. For the organized group tours of homesites, see the *Little House Site Tours* offerings at http://lhsitetours.homestead.com/, accessed December 2, 2019.

33. Interview with Walnut Grove homesite staff member, June 12, 2019.

34. For the uses of heritage tourism and reenactment to boost regional economies and reify local community identities, see Elizabeth Carnegie and Scott McCabe, "Re-

in *Tourism* 11, no. 4 (2008): 349–68.

35. The work put into the pageants by local residents in the three homesite towns that offer them is clearly enormous. Four of the homesites (Malone, Burr Oak, Mansfield, and De Smet) have the original buildings where the Ingalls or Wilders lived, and the expense and labor involved in preserving sometimes fragile, very old buildings is substantial.

36. "Laura Ingalls Wilder Pageant: 'Fragments of a Dream,'" 2003 pageant program. This text was repeated in subsequent pageant programs.

37. For the Japanese fans of Wilder and the animated Japanese television series based on the books, see Hisayo Ogushi, "The Little House in the Far East: The American Frontier Spirit and Japanese Girls' Comics," *The Japanese Journal of American Studies* 27 (2016): 21–44. See also the articles on *Little House* exhibits and publications in Japan in the *Lore,* 14 no. 2 (Fall 1988).

38. Melody Miyamoto, "From the Little House to the School House and Beyond. Experiential Learning through the World of Laura Ingalls Wilder," *Journal of the West* 49, no. 3 (2010): 34.

39. My impression was confirmed in interviews with a homesite staff member (November 14, 2019) and Sarah Uthoff (August 5, 2019), Barbara Walker (November 22, 2019) and Kitty Latane (November 26, 2019), where I asked about the racial demographics of the fan community.

40. Bruner, *Culture on Tour,* 136.

41. Barbara Walker interview, November 22, 2019. Walker's *The Little House Cookbook* (New York: Harper Collins, 1979) has gone through three editions as of this writing.

42. Interview with Kitty Latane, November 26, 2019. Latane, a traditional craftswoman, organizes the crafts area of the Pepin "Laura Days" each year.

43. Fellman, *Little House, Long Shadow,* 146.

44. Cherry, *Cult Media,* 152.

45. Interview with Julie Frances Miller, November 19, 2019.

46. Interview with Sarah Uthoff, August 5, 2019.

47. Fellman, *Little House, Long Shadow,* 144–50.

48. Interview with Miller. A video of her playing the pump organ at the Ingalls home for other fans can be seen here: https://www.youtube.com/watch?v=f4GGTTUk8kQ&feature=youtu.be.

49. See the programs and other information about LauraPalooza conferences at the Laura Ingalls Wilder Legacy and Research Association website: http://www.liwlra.org/, accessed February 24, 2021.

50. Laura McLemore interview, December 19, 2019.

51. Interview with Kitty Latane, November 26, 2019.

52. Interview with Laura McLemore, December 19, 2019.

53. Zochert, *Laura*, 32–33.

54. Fanfiction.net hosts 442 *Little House* stories by fans, compared to over 616,000 stories about the *Harry Potter* series. *Anne of Green Gables* had 862 stories posted on Archive of Our Own, and 985 on Fanfiction.net. These sites were searched on November 22, 2019.

55. Quoted in Fellman, "Everybody's 'Little Houses,'" 16.

56. Fellman, "Everybody's 'Little Houses.'"

57. Quoted in Fraser, *Prairie Fires*, 395.

58. Warren, *Buffalo Bill's America*, xv–xvi.

59. I saw the plaque when I visited the homesite on June 12, 2019. For the *Little House* books' substantial impact on American public school curricula before the late twentieth century, and their alignment with popular understandings of American history, see Fellman, *Little House, Long Shadow*. See also Fraser, "Laura Ingalls Wilder: The Making of an American Icon."

60. Fellman, "Everybody's 'Little Houses.'"

61. Miller, *Laura Ingalls Wilder and Rose Wilder Lane*, 85.

62. Romines, *Constructing the Little House* and "Putting Things in Order."

63. Andrew Hartman, *A War For the Soul of America: A History of the Culture Wars* (Chicago: University of Chicago Press, 2016), 214. In recent decades, the ranks of homeschoolers have broadened considerably, as families concerned about their children's IEPs, bullying, or what they see as other shortcomings of public schools have turned to homeschooling as well.

64. Fellman, *Little House, Long Shadow*, 178–80. See examples of homeschooling conventions and publishers' websites at https://www.myjoyfilledlife.com/homeschool -conventions-by-state/ and https://teachthemdiligently.net/homeschool -conventions/atlanta-ga/?idev_id=215, accessed December 2, 2019. While many homeschooling organizations are secular, others are explicitly conservative and Christian, as reflected in the biographical profile of Phil Robertson, star of *Duck Dynasty* and a speaker at one of the largest homeschool convention circuits, who claims that, "based on my observation of the last 60 years of no God, no morals in the school system, I highly recommend taking responsibility for your child's education. The Department of Education has become the department of indoctrination." See https://greathome schoolconventions.com/speakers/phil-robertson, accessed December 2, 2019.

65. Fellman, *Little House, Long Shadow*, 246.

66. I surveyed a broad variety of homeschooling literature and social studies curriculum available online (including websites of publishers who cater to homeschoolers and

homeschooling conventions) during the summer of 2019, and *Little House* readings
or hands-on activities were frequently included, being particularly prominent in
"westward expansion" and "pioneer" curricular units. Pinterest, for example, attracts
many homeschooling parents and features numerous homeschooling boards that
include *Little House* materials, as well.

67. Fellman, *Little House, Long Shadow*, 255; interview with Sarah Uthoff, August 5, 2019,
and with Bill Anderson, November 14, 2019; and interview with Cathy Sorensen, December 3, 2019. I am indebted to Sorensen for her expertise regarding homeschooling
trends, and the use of *Little House* books in such curricula. Sorensen surveyed a large
Iowa Facebook group of homeschoolers regarding their use of Wilder's books, and
over half of those who responded said that they had incorporated the books into
their homeschooling curricula; most of the rest planned to do so in the future. About
25 percent had taken their children to visit a homesite.

68. Interviews with Sarah Uthoff, August 5, 2019; Bill Anderson, November 14, 2019. The
same assumption is implicit in the displays at all the homesites that I visited.

69. Brædder et al., "Doing Pasts."

## Chapter 5. "And Then the American Indians Came Over"

1. Hine, Faragher, and Coleman, *The American West*, 409–11. See also Feest, "Europe's
Indians," 329; Penny, *Kindred By Choice*, 183–88; and Turski, "The Indianist Groups in
the GDR," 45.

2. See Chapter 3 for a discussion of Banks's visit to and endorsement of East German
hobbyists; see also Penny, *Kindred By Choice*, 183–84 and 189–94.

3. For a discussion of the origins of "survivance," see Gerald Vizenor, "Aesthetics of
Survivance: Literary Theory and Practice," in *Survivance: Narratives of Native Presence*, ed. Gerald Vizenor (Lincoln: University of Nebraska Press, 2008), 1ff; see also
Vizenor, *Manifest Manners: Narratives on Postindian Survivance* (Lincoln: University
of Nebraska Press, 1999).

4. Hine, Faragher, and Coleman, *The American West*, 412–13. Of course, census
self-identification is not identical to tribal membership or the legal categories used
by the federal authorities. For one example of a tribal culture that was devastated by
termination of its federal recognition and rights in 1954, and its political and cultural
resurgence (which led to the tribe's re-recognition by the federal government in
1986), see Cothran, *Remembering the Modoc War*, 190–92.

5. For discussions of a variety of national master narratives, see James Wertsch, "National Memory and Where to Find It," in *The Handbook of Culture and Memory*, ed.
Brady Wagoner (New York: Oxford University Press, 2018); and Carretero and Van

Alphen, "History, Collective Memories, or National Memories?"

6. Carrereto and Van Alphen, "History, Collective Memories, or National Memories?," 290.

7. See David Thelen, "Reliving History and Rethinking the Past," in *Over (T)Here : Transatlantic Essays in Honor of Rob Kroes*, ed. Kate Delaney and Ruud Janssens (Amsterdam: VU University Press, 2005), 174–84.

8. For Indigenous perspectives on public history and living history sites, see Peers, *Playing Ourselves*; for discussions of Indigenous historians' challenges to previous historiography, see Deloria, "Historiography," and Haunani-Kay Trask, *From a Native Daughter: Colonialism and Sovereignty in Hawaii* (Honolulu: University of Hawaii Press), 115ff. For Indigenous critiques of children's literature classics, see the blog *American Indians in Children's Literature* maintained by Nambé Pueblo librarian and educator Dr. Debbie Reese here: https://americanindiansinchildrensliterature.blogspot.com/, accessed December 20, 2019. For the ways in which the new historiography was reflected at the Homestead National Monument, see Cannon, "Homesteading Remembered." This "fracturing" and re-centering of historiography was not unique to the history of the American West and was happening at the same time to the historiography of the British Empire, for example.

9. See Hartman, *A War for the Soul of America*, 261–66. The quotation is from page 266.

10. Hartman, 263.

11. Hartman, 265. Cheney is the wife of Dick Cheney, who served as vice president from 2001 to 2009.

12. For a discussion of how American history textbooks can be influenced by local partisan political cultures, see the comparison of US history textbooks prepared for Texas and California in Dana Goldstein, "Two States. Eight Textbooks. Two American Stories," *The New York Times*, January 12, 2020, https://www.nytimes.com/interactive/2020/01/12/us/texas-vs-california-history-textbooks.html, accessed March 3, 2020. Overall, however, both represent a considerable change compared to textbooks from the 1950s and 1960s.

13. Hartman, *A War for the Soul of America*, 265. Although the number of homeschooled children in the United States has grown steadily since the 1960s, Christian conservatives make up only one (nonetheless substantial) segment of this movement. For President Trump's revival of this critique during his 2020 reelection campaign, see Michael Crowley, "Trump Calls for 'Patriotic Education' to Defend American History From the Left," *New York Times* September 17, 2020, https://www.nytimes.com/2020/09/17/us/politics/trump-patriotic-education.html. Conservatives' rejection of changes in American historiography also drove their critical reaction to the New York Times *1619 Project*.

14. McVeigh, *The American Western*, 151–52.

15. Hine, Faragher, and Coleman, *The American West*, 448–49. Western films largely ceased production during the 1980s, perhaps due to the epic financial disaster of *Heaven's Gate*; see Alexandra Keller, "Historical Discourse and American Identity in Westerns Since the Reagan Era," in *Hollywood's West: The American Frontier in Film, Television, and History*, ed. Peter Rollins and John O'Connor (Lexington: University Press of Kentucky, 2005), 240. *Dances with Wolves* still recycled earlier tropes of a white man as the champion of Indigenous cultures, but still marked a definite shift from earlier presentations of white settlement. The revival of the genre in Hollywood films after 1990, with movies like *Unforgiven*, was in a different mode that was usually less affirmative of Western white settlement, as discussed by Keller, "Historical Discourse and American Identity."

16. David Pierson, "Turner Network Television's Made for TV Western Films," in *Hollywood's West: The American Frontier in Film, Television, and History*, ed. Peter Rollins and John O'Connor (Lexington: University Press of Kentucky, 2005), 289–90.

17. Jones and Wills, *The American West: Competing Visions*, 260–83. For the repeated reinvention of the genre, see Mitchell, *Late Westerns*.

18. Keller, "Historical Discourse and American Identity," 242.

19. Indeed, the encounters with Indian characters in the one book that discusses them extensively (*Little House on the Prairie*) seems rather free-floating, in terms of time and location: the incidents in the book could have taken place anywhere on the Plains. This was perhaps because Wilder was simply too young at the time to have clear memories herself.

20. Wilder, *Little House in the Big Woods*, 1–2. When a reader pointed this out in 1952, Wilder asked her editor to change the phrasing to "there were no settlers," commenting that "It was a stupid blunder of mine. Of course Indians are people and I did not mean to imply that they were not"; see Fraser, *Prairie Fires*, 476–77. Wilder's editor corrected the phrasing in the 1953 edition of the book, but the original text can still be found in later editions.

21. For the reaction of one Indigenous scholar and parent to the erasure of Indigenous cultures in *Little House in the Big Woods*, see Michael Dorris, "Twisting the Words" in *Paper Trail: Essays* (New York: Harper Collins, 1994). See also the account by one Indigenous mother and scholar, Waziyatawin (formerly known as Angela Cavender Wilson), who challenged the use of Wilder's books in her children's school: Waziyatawin Angela Cavender Wilson, "Burning Down the House: Laura Ingalls Wilder and American Colonialism," in *Unlearning the Language of Conquest: Scholars Expose Anti-Indianism in America*, ed. Four Arrows (Don Trent Jacobs) (Austin: University of Texas Press, 2006), 66–80.

22. Fraser, *Prairie Fires*, 16–24. The quotation from the Minnesota governor is from page 22. See also Penny, *Kindred By Choice*, 69–95.

23. Laura Ingalls Wilder, *Little House on the Prairie* (New York: Harper Collins, 1971), 134–43. For a discussion of the historical context of Wilder's book and how the Osage might have seen the Ingalls family, see Kaye "Little Squatter on the Osage Diminished Reserve"; see also John E. Miller, "American Indians in the Fiction of Laura Ingalls Wilder," *South Dakota History* 30, no. 3 (2000): 303–20; Sharon Smulders, "'The Only Good Indian': History, Race, and Representation in Laura Ingalls Wilder's *Little House on the Prairie*," *Children's Literature Association Quarterly* 27, no. 4 (2003): 191–202; Waziyatawin, "Burning Down the House"; Heldrich, "'Going to Indian Territory'"; and Campbell, "'Wild Men' and Dissenting Voices."

24. Wilder, *Little House on the Prairie*, 134–39.

25. For the removal of the Osage from their Diminished Reserve, see Zochert, *Laura*, 45 and Fraser, *Prairie Fires*, 50–59.

26. Wilder's characters echo here the arguments advanced by early nineteenth-century American legal theorists, who argued that property rights only accrued to individual owners who "improved" and used their lands as white settlers did. Indigenous stewardship of their lands was not seen as such by white writers, who could only perceive such lands as "wilderness." By this theory, only whites could have property rights protected by law. See Harris, "Whiteness as Property," 1721–24.

27. Wilder, *Little House on the Prairie*, 284. Laura Ingalls Wilder almost certainly did not know all the details of treaty disputes between the Osage and the federal government, which formed the backdrop of Osage responses to white settlers on their lands. She did, however, know that her parents had chosen to squat lands that belonged to Indigenous people; see Fraser, *Prairie Fires*, 531.

28. Wilder, *Little House on the Prairie*, 236.

29. Fraser, *Prairie Fires*, 59.

30. Zochert, *Laura*, 43.

31. Anderson, *Laura Ingalls Wilder*, 39; see also Fraser, *Prairie Fires*, 52–53; and Miller, *Becoming Laura Ingalls Wilder*, 23–24.

32. *Lore*, Spring/Summer 1994 issue, "Laura Ingalls Wilder and the Native American."

33. Waziyatawin (formerly Angela Cavender Wilson) went on to make a successful career as an Indigenous historian and activist; her daughter Autumn became a midwife and doula, and Indigenous activist as well; Autumn Cavender Wilson's biographical information is here: https://robinainstitute.umn.edu/people/autumn-cavender-wilson, accessed December 1, 2019.

34. See *The Plainsman* December 16, 1998 report on the Yellow Medicine East school board meeting held a few days previously.

35. See De Smet archive, folder with title "Racism," which contains a copy of Cavender Wilson's original complaint.

36. See the account of her presentation and the school board discussion in Waziyatawin, "Burning Down the House," 69–70. Her daughter's teacher was such an engaged Little House fan, Waziyatawin noted, that she attended the Wilder pageant held each summer in Walnut Grove, MN.

37. Waziyatawin, "Burning Down the House," which contains Tellefson's response; both the complaint and the teacher's response were sent to the Memorial Society by an employee of the Yellow Medicine East school district and are now in the Society's archive.

38. See the newspaper clippings with reports on the debate over the book's use in Minnesota schools in the De Smet archive, "Racism" folder, particularly the Willmar *West Central Tribune* editorial on December 8, 1998; the Minneapolis *Star Tribune* editorial on December 12, 1998; and the Granite Falls *Advocate Tribune* editorial advocating for the book's removal from school curricula (n.d.). Even the Upper Sioux Community was apparently divided, as reflected in the letter sent by other parents, including those in the Upper Sioux Community, to the Willmar *West Central Tribune* on December 17, 1998.

39. See the De Smet Archive, "Racism" folder, which contains the Granite Falls *Advocate Tribune* report on the YME School Board meeting in its December 17, 1998 issue; see also Munger's subsequent email to De Smet Memorial Society, which describes how the school and teachers responded to the controversy (dated March 18, 1999) in the De Smet Archive, "Racism" folder. See also Waziyatawin, "Burning Down the House."

40. Interview with Sarah Uthoff, August 5, 2019; for the impact of the No Child Left Behind Act on reading instruction, see also Fellman, *Little House, Long Shadow*, 255. I am indebted to Dr. Laura McLemore, who has many years of teaching experience both at the college and elementary school levels in Kansas, and who discussed changes in basal readers and the popularity of the *Birchbark House* series with me.

41. Interview with a staff member at the Pepin Wilder museum, June 9, 2019. The description of the museum's exhibits is based on my own visit to the Laura Ingalls Wilder Museum in Pepin in June 2019.

42. See the description of the design and planning meetings in the Summer 2003 edition of the *Rocky Ridge Review*, and the description of the final Master Plan in the Winter 2009 issue of the *Rocky Ridge Review*, from which the quotation is taken. When I visited the site in 2019, only part of the Master Plan had been funded and put into effect. At the time that I visited the Walnut Grove Museum and the De Smet homestead living history farm, neither had yet incorporated information about local Indigenous

cultures and their histories, and instead focused tightly on celebrating history of the settler communities around the time that the Ingalls lived in each area.

43. See the memo from Nina Lindsay to the ALSC Board of Directors (n.d.), "ALSC Awards Program in Context of Strategic Plan," ALSC Board MW 2018 DOC #29, located here: http://www.ala.org/alsc/sites/ala.org.alsc/files/content/awardsgrants/bookmedia/wildermedal/DOC%2029%20ALSC%20Awards%20Program%20in%20Context%20of%20Strategic%20Plan.pdf, accessed December 1, 2019.

44. See the ALSC Awards Program Review Task Force's report (dated May 15, 2018) to the Board, ALSC Board AC 2018 DOC #25 here: http://www.ala.org/alsc/sites/ala.org.alsc/files/content/awardsgrants/bookmedia/wildermedal/DOC%2025%20Award%20Program%20Review%20Task%20Force%20Wilder%20Award%20Recommendation.pdf, accessed December 5, 2019.

45. ALSC Board AC 2018 DOC #25.

46. See the report on the reactions of ALA members in Kara Yurio, "ALSC Changes Wilder Award to Children's Literature Legacy Award," *School Library Journal*, June 24, 2018, https://www.slj.com/?detailStory=alsc-changes-name-wilder-award-childrens-literature-legacy-award, accessed December 20, 2019.

47. See the discussion among school librarians in the post on the name change here: https://www.slj.com/?detailStory=alsc-changes-name-wilder-award-childrens-literature-legacy-award, accessed December 10, 2019.

48. See the LIWLRA's statement here: http://beyondlittlehouse.com/2018/06/25/liwlra-response-to-the-renaming-of-the-ala-laura-ingalls-wilder-award/, accessed December 20, 2019.

49. Interview with Pamela Smith Hill, December 20, 2019.

50. For the discussions within the Politbüro which led to the decision to allow publication of May's novels in East Germany, see the BA Berlin-Lichterfelde, DY 30/18570.

51. See Mary Fulbrook, *A History of Germany, 1914–2014*, 4th ed. (New York: Wiley-Blackwell, 2014), 259ff; see also Fulbrook, *The People's State: East German Society from Hitler to Honecker* (New Haven: Yale University Press, 2005).

52. Fulbrook, *A History of Germany*, 292ff.

53. Turski, *Die Indianistikgrupen der DDR*, 63ff.

54. The increase in visits by Indigenous North American artists and entrepreneurs to Germany is discussed in the interviews with such Indigenous visitors in Harmut Lutz, Florentine Strelczyk, and Renae Watchman, eds. *Indianthusiasm: Indigenous Responses* (Waterloo: Wilfred Laurier University Press, 2020).

55. Turski, *Die Indianistikgrupen der DDR*, 63.

56. Borries, *Sozialistische Cowboys*, 15.

57. See the interview with Drew Hayden Taylor in Lutz, Strelczyk, and Watchman, *Indi-*

*anthusiasm*, 181–82. For other criticisms of modern Indigenous people by Germans, see the interviews in *Indianthusiasm* on 36, 60, 99–100, 103, 128–29.

58. Renae Watchman, "Powwow Overseas: The German Experience." In *Powwow*, edited by Clyde Ellis, Luke Eric Lassiter, and Gary H. Dunham (Lincoln: University of Nebraska Press, 2005), 242. For other positive responses by Indigenous artists and performers to fans and other Germans interested in Indigenous cultures, see Lutz, Strelczyk, and Watchman, *Indianthusiasm*, 150, 176–77, 188–89.

59. Penny, "Elusive Authenticity," 815–17.

60. See the NAAoG's statement regarding the participation of non-Indigenous people in their powwows, and the use of Indigenous regalia by hobbyists here: http://www .naaog.de/dancing-and-singing.html, accessed March 1, 2020.

61. Interview with Robin Leipold, Content Director of the Karl May Museum, April 2, 2019.

62. Leipold and *Göschka*, "Indianer im Wilden Osten," 41. See also Kalshoven, *Crafting "The Indian,"* 149.

63. Quoted in Penny, "Elusive Authenticity," 817. See also Bolz, "Life Among the 'Hunk-papas,'" which quotes the leader of a Frankfurt Indianist hobbyist club as claiming that their membership was declining already by 1970s, from 120 to 54.

64. See Kalshoven, *Crafting "The Indian"*; Penny, *Kindred By Choice*, 1–2; and photos and descriptions of the annual summer gatherings of the predominantly western German provincial *Westernbund* at https://www.westernbund.de/aktuelles/, accessed December 3, 2019. Eastern province hobbyists continue to hold their own restricted annual summer gatherings, which primarily feature Indianist activities, while hobbyists in the western provinces feature a wide variety of role-play at their summer campus. German clubs in the western provinces still include members playing Indian *personas* on their websites and publicity materials aimed at the general public, but images of club members dressed as cowboys or performing other white frontier roles predominate.

65. Several documentaries about German Indianist hobbyists were made by Indigenous artists during the last twenty years, sometimes critical. See for example John Black-bird, dir. 2007, *Indianer*, First Nation Films; Drew Hayden Taylor, dir. 2018, *Searching for Winnetou*, CBC Documentary; Red Haircrow, dir. 2018, *Forget Winnetou! Loving in the Wrong Way*, Vtape.

66. Penny, *Kindred By Choice*, 272.

67. Penny, 277–85.

68. Marta Carlson, "Germans Playing Indian," in *Germans and Indians: Fantasies, Encounters, Projections*, ed. Colin Calloway, Gerd Gemunden, and Suzanne Zantop (Lincoln: University of Nebraska Press, 2002), 215–16.

69. Ward Churchill, *Fantasies of the Master Race* (Monroe: Common Courage, 1992), 224, quoted in Sieg, "Indian Impersonation," 217.

70. For a critique of the ways in which the Karl May Museum displays are organized and more on the Chippewa scalp conflict, see Lisa Michelle King, "Revisiting Winnetou: The Karl May Museum, Cultural Appropriation, and Indigenous Self-Representation," *Studies in Native American Literatures* 28, no. 2 (Summer 2016): 25–55. When I visited the museum in 2019, no scalps were on display and the section of the museum featuring Indigenous artifacts had been somewhat updated. In 2020, the Museum agreed to turn over the scalps to representatives of the US government for ethical reasons although their provenance was still unclear; the US government was expected to give the scalps to the Sault Ste. Marie Tribe (private communication from Robin Leipold, February 27, 2020).

71. Quoted in Gerald McMaster, "The Double Entendre of Re-Enactment," found at www.vtape.org/wp-content/uploads/2014/01/Vtape-Double-Entendre-of-Re-Enactment-imagineNATIVE-2007.pdf, 17, accessed July 11, 2019.

72. See the NAAoG's statement on non-Natives participating in powwows here: http://www.naaog.de/dancing-and-singing.html, accessed March 1, 2019.

73. See the current calendar of powwow gatherings in and near Germany here: https://www.powwow-kalender.de/, accessed March 2, 2020. My conclusions about the participants of powwows are drawn from conversations with hobbyists, and also the photos posted afterward from such gatherings. For example, see here: https://www.powwow-kalender.de/report/winter-powwow20.html, accessed March 2, 2020. See also Watchman, "Powwow Overseas," for her account of a 2005 visit to a German-run powwow.

74. Roy Rosenzweig and David Thelen, *The Presence of the Past: Popular Uses of History in American Life* (New York: Columbia University Press, 1998), 272–74.

75. See Kalshoven, *Crafting "The Indian,"* 226 and also 29, 194–99, and 209.

76. Penny, *Kindred By Choice*, 275–76.

77. Kalshoven, *Crafting "The Indian,"* 195–209.

78. See Drexl, *Sehnsucht nach dem Wilden Westen*, 55ff; see also the photos of costumed hobbyists dressed as historical celebrities from *Westernbund* gatherings here: https://www.westernbund.de/galerien/, accessed December 10, 2019.

79. Interview with Robin Leipold, then the Curator of the Karl May Museum, April 2, 2019. The "Old Manitou" club's public website is no longer maintained, but some of the club's activities from the early 2000s, as shown on their public website, are still available on the Wayback Internet archive here: https://web.archive.org/web/20021118161313/http://www.planet-interkom.de/home/annett.scheibel/, accessed December 3, 2019. For the withdrawal of East German hobbyists from

the public sphere, and the decision of some to participate in other types of hobbies related to historical cultures, see Kalshoven, *Crafting "The Indian."*

80. See Kathleen Loock, "Remaking Winnetou, Reconfiguring German Fantasies of Indianer and the Wild West in the Post-Reunification Era," *Communications: The European Journal of Communication Research* 44, no. 3 (2019): 323–41.

81. See the interview with Director Philipp Stölzl here: https://spirit-fanzine.de /interviews/texte/Winnetou_2016_i.html, accessed October 15, 2020.

82. See the announcement regarding the new Bad Segeberg record here: https://www .karl-may-spiele.de/nav-top/abschluss-in-2019-1756, accessed February 20, 2020.

## Conclusion. Indians into Confederates

1. Interview with Pamela Smith Hill, December 20, 2019; see also the 2018 statement of the LIWLRA about the depiction of Indian characters in Wilder's books, which reflects the fandom's understanding of racist stereotypes in earlier literature: http: //beyondlittlehouse.com/2018/06/25/liwlra-response-to-the-renaming-of-the -ala-laura-ingalls-wilder-award/, accessed March 6, 2020.

2. Interview with Cathy Sorensen, December 3, 2019.

3. See the LIWLRA's announcement at http://www.liwlra.org/about-us/, accessed March 1, 2021.

4. Interview with Pamela Smith Hill, December 20, 2019.

5. Laura Ingalls Wilder, *Little Town on the Prairie*, (New York: Harper Collins), 277.

6. Interview with Pamela Smith Hill, December 20, 2019.

7. See Arngrim's readings and the hundreds of fan comments they inspired at https: //www.facebook.com/alison.arngrim, accessed October 22, 2020. Arngrim generally uses her site as a professional promotion page.

8. For a history of "official" historical reenactment in pageants and parades, and the emergence of amateur historical reenactment, see Gapps, "Performing the Past"; see also Thompson, *War Games*.

9. Gapps, "Performing the Past," 242.

10. Gapps, 314ff.

11. Gapps, 269–71.

12. Agnew, "History's Affective Turn," 302.

13. Gapps, "Performing the Past," 245. See also the definition of living history offered by the Association for Living History, Farm, and Agricultural Museums here: https: //exarc.net/issue-2019-3/mm/book-review-anthology. Plimouth Plantations, a well-known open-air museum, introduced costumed interpreters in 1969 and thus developed the site into an early living history museum; the site became influential in

the world of historical museums as a result. See Gapps, "Performing the Past," 251.

14. The literature on "reenactment" (defined broadly) and living history is substantial. I have drawn in this chapter on Agnew, "History's Affective Turn"; Larry Beck and Ted Cable, *The Gifts of Interpretation: Fifteen Guiding Principles for Interpreting Nature and Culture*, 3rd ed. (Urbana: Sagamore Publishing, 2011); Brædder et al., "Doing Pasts"; Carnegie and McCabe, "Re-Enactment Events and Tourism"; Michael A. Cramer, *Medieval Fantasy as Performance: The Society for Creative Anachronism and the Current Middle Ages* (Lanham: The Scarecrow Press, Inc., 2010); De Groot, "Affect and Empathy"; Fine, *Shared Fantasy*; Deb Fuller, "How to Run a Reenactment—Introduction to Reenactment and Reenactors, Part 1," *EXARC* no. 1 (2019). https://exarc.net/issue-2019-1/mm/how-run-reenactment-part-1, accessed January 20, 2020; Gapps, "Mobile Monuments," "Performing the Past, " and "Museums of the Living Dead: Performance, Body, and Memory at Living History Museums," *Journal of Curatorial Studies* 7, no. 2 (2018): 248–70; Horwitz, *Confederates in the Attic*; Kalshoven, *Crafting "The Indian"*; Iain McCalman and Paul Pickering, *Historical Reenactment: From Realism to the Affective Turn* (Basingstoke: Palgrave Macmillan, 2010); Patrick McCarthy, "'Living History' as the 'Real Thing': A Comparative Analysis of the Modern Mountain Man Rendezvous, Renaissance Fairs, and Civil War Reenactments," *ETC: A Review of General Semantics* 71, no. 2 (2014): 106–23; Gerald McMaster, "The Double Entendre of Re-Enactment," www.vtape.org/wp-content/uploads/2014/01/Vtape-Double-Entendre-of-Re-Enactment-imagineNATIVE-2007.pdf, accessed July 11, 2019; Maja Mikula, "Historical Re-Enactment: Narrativity, Affect and the Sublime," *Rethinking History* 19, no. 4 (2015): 583–601: Peers, *Playing Ourselves*; Lucy Worsley, "An Intimate History of Your Home," *The Historian*, Autumn (2011): 6–9; James Graham, "Breathing Life Back Into The Past," *British Heritage Travel* 38, no. July/August (2017): 64–67: David Vanderstel, "'And I Thought Historians Only Taught': Doing History beyond the Classroom," *OAH Magazine of History* 16, no. 2 (2002): 5–7; Johnson, "Rethinking (Re)doing"; David Thelen, "Learning from the Past: Individual Experience and Re-Enactment," *Indiana Magazine of History* 99 (2003): 155–71, and "Reliving History and Rethinking the Past."

15. Agnew, "History's Affective Turn."

16. Stephen Gapps, "Performing the Past," 248, notes that paralleling the growth in public history and costumed interpretation after 1960, schoolchildren in the English-speaking world also began to be exposed to "role-playing" techniques in scenarios used to teach history; Gapps offers the intriguing speculation that people who grew up in this system began to create medieval fantasy role-playing games, e.g., D&D, once they were young adults during the 1970s.

17. Rosenzweig and Thelen, *The Presence of the Past*, 34.

18. Rosenzweig and Thelen, 109.

19. Rosenzweig and Thelen, 91.

20. Rosenzweig and Thelen, 35.

21. Rosenzweig and Thelen, 36.

22. Gapps, "Museums of the Living Dead."

23. Fuller, "How to Run a Reenactment," 3.

24. Fuller, 3.

25. Kalshoven, Crafting "The Indian," 226–27.

26. Gapps, "Mobile Monuments," 398–99.

27. Many "Hun Horde" role-playing clubs have websites with photos of their gatherings. See, for example, the club website of the "First Hun Horde of Herdorf" at http://www.herdorfer-hunnenhorde.de/, accessed October 15, 2008.

28. Gapps, "Performing the Past," 244. On the other hand, in North America some of the costumed interpreters at living history museums are themselves Indigenous, and use their performances as a way to challenge or correct white visitors' perceptions of their colonial pasts and Indigenous cultures. See Laura Peers, Playing Ourselves.

29. For profiles of German Civil War reenactors, see Phillip Schmitt and Cara Koehler, "A Field Trip Back in Time: American Civil War Reenactment in Walldürn, Germany" at https://www.uni-bamberg.de/amerikanistik/exkursionen/a-field-trip-back-in-time-american-civil-war-reenactment-in-wallduern-germany/, accessed January 24, 2020; Yoni Appelbaum, "Confederates on the Rhine," The Atlantic, June 2, 2011, https://www.theatlantic.com/international/archive/2011/06/confederates-on-the-rhine/239724/; Caitlan Carroll, "The South Rises Again—in Eastern Germany," The Local.De, July 1, 2011, https://www.thelocal.de/20110701/36013; and Borries, Sozialistische Cowboys, 192ff.

30. See Borries, Sozialistische Cowboys, 193–94. This woman's interpretation of the South parallels the view of East Germans after the Wall's collapse offered in nostalgic stories about East Germans and "the change" given in films like Goodbye, Lenin!, for example.

31. Gapps, "Performing the Past," 302.

32. Interview with Robin Leipold, the Karl May Museum Content Director, April 2, 2019. I found the Museum's collection of photographs of German cowboys, Indians, and Civil War reenactors fascinating; I could not reproduce them here, since I could not locate and obtain consent from the people depicted in the photos.

33. Bruner, Culture on Tour.

34. See for example Harald Guendel's 2009 Von Moccasins Getrampelte Pfade. "Indianism remained alive, [Guendel] felt, when people told stories about their adventures in the hobby—not when they sat at home making authentic replicas. He was no longer,

as he put it, an 'outfit-Indianist'"; see Kalshoven, *Crafting "The Indian,"* 25.

35. The "powwow scene," which some Indianists have become active in, is popular in Germany; the gatherings often involve Indigenous guests, as discussed in Chapter 5. See the central German calendar for powwow gatherings here: https://www .powwow-kalender.de, accessed January 24, 2020.

36. See the description of the store here: https://web2.cylex.de/firma-home/red -fox—indian—_-westernstore-2289630.html, accessed January 15, 2020.

37. See the announcement "Siebter Zuschauer-Rekord in Folge: 402.110 Besucher sahen „Unter Geiern" at https://www.karl-may-spiele.de/nav-top/abschluss-in-2019-1756, accessed January 24, 2020.

38. The fan community magazine *Karl May & Co* regularly features articles commemorating anniversaries of May productions or groups, along with articles that discuss the history of the fandom. The community also organizes events to commemorate important fandom anniversaries.

39. The homesites in Malone, NY and Walnut Grove, MN are open-air museums, and so is the De Smet Ingalls farm homestead site, located on the outskirts of De Smet. The De Smet Memorial Society within the town of De Smet, which maintains the Ingalls's homes and other historic buildings, employs costumed interpreters, and its sites are perhaps better described as living history. The Mansfield site offers tours of the Wilders' property and a museum dedicated to the Ingalls's and Wilders' lives and times. All of these properties thus reflect recent trends in museum and public history education.

40. Carl Becker, "Every Man His Own Historian," *American Historical Review* 37, no. 2 (1932): 235.

41. Gapps, "Mobile Monuments," 398.

# BIBLIOGRAPHY

## Archival Sources—Germany

Berlin, Bundesarchiv Lichterfelde
Göttingen, Karl-May-Archiv
Munich, Stadtarchiv München
Radebeul, Karl-May-Museum and Archiv der Karl-May-Gesellschaft

## Archival Sources—United States

De Smet, South Dakota, Laura Ingalls Wilder Memorial Society
Malone, New York, Almanzo and Laura Ingalls Wilder Association and Homestead
Mansfield, Missouri, Laura Ingalls Wilder Home & Museum
Pepin, Wisconsin, Laura Ingalls Wilder Museum
Walnut Grove, Minnesota, Laura Ingalls Wilder Museum

## Selected Periodicals

*The Advocate Tribune*, Granite Falls, Minnesota
*The Central Tribune*, Willmar, Minnesota
*Dakota Scout*
*Die Fährte: Interessengemeinschaft Deutschsprechender Indianerfreunde*
*Dresdner Anzeiger*
*Informationsblatt f. Indianistik*
*Karl-May-Bote*
*Karl May & Co*

*Karl-May-Jahrbuch*

*Karl May in Leipzig*

*Karl May Rundbrief*

*Karl-May-Star-Clubzentrale Journal*

*Karl-May-Treff*

*Laura Ingalls Wilder Lore*, newsletter of the De Smet Laura Ingalls Wilder Memorial
Society

*The Mansfield Mirror*, Mansfield, Missouri

*Meinolf-Pape-Club Nachrichten*

*Minneapolis Star Tribune*

*Pierre-Brice-Club-Kurier*

*The Plainsman*, Huron, South Dakota

*Rauchzeichen*

*The Rocky Ridge Review*, newsletter of the Mansfield Wilder Home Association

*Sächsisches Tageblatt*

*Sächsische Zeitung*

*Wampum*

## Published Primary Sources

"1. Kölner Hunnen Horde - 50 Jahre und Kein Bißchen Leise!" Accessed
November 8, 2008. http://www.erstekölnerhunnenhorde.mynetcologne.de
/13.html?*session*id*key*=*session*id*val*.

"2008 Wilder Festival at Hoover Library Report." Accessed January 29, 2011.
http://nl.newsbank.com/nl-search/we/Archives?p_action=doc&p_
docid=122EA3C5B1F1D7C8&p_docnum=1.

"About the Laura Ingalls Wilder Award," December 16, 2015. https://wayback.archive-it
.org/6087/20151216102442/http://www.ala.org/alsc/awardsgrants/bookmedia
/wildermedal/wilderabout.

"Ansprachen zu der Feier 70 Jahre Karl-May-Museum." Accessed May 6, 2008.
http://www.karl-may-stiftung.de/kultus.html.

Appelbaum, Yoni. "Confederates on the Rhine." *The Atlantic*, June 2, 2011. https://www
.theatlantic.com/international/archive/2011/06/confederates-on-the-rhine/239724/.

Bannick, Betty, and Ronald Kelsey. *On the Stage by Plum Creek: The First Twenty-five Years
of the Laura Ingalls Wilder Pageant "Fragments of a Dream."* 2002. Booklet.

Carroll, Caitlan. "The South Rises Again—in Eastern Germany." *The Local.De*, July 1, 2011.
https://www.thelocal.de/20110701/36013.

*Dear Laura: Letters from Children to Laura Ingalls Wilder*. New York: Harper Collins, 1996.

Dengler, Hermann. *Führer durch das Karl May-Museum*. Radebeul bei Dresden: Karl-May-Verlag, 1928.

———. "Wie Ich Indianer Wurde." *Karl-May-Jahrbuch* 16 (1933): 450–63.

Eichacker, Reinhold. "Was Karl May Mir War. Ein Zeugnis Unter Vielen." *Karl-May-Jahrbuch* 2 (1919): 110–25.

"First Western Reenactors homepage." Accessed March 17, 2009. http://www.first-western-reenactors.com/index.htm.

Frank, Patty. *Ein Leben im Banne Karl May's. Erlebnisse und Kleine Erzählungen*. Radebeul: Kupky & Dietze, 1940.

Hane, Wilhelm, Franz Ernst, and Lisbeth Barchewitz. "Karl Mays Einfluss auf Unser Leben." *Karl-May-Jahrbuch* 3 (1920): 297–317.

Heermann, Christian. "Die Erbe des Yotanka." *Wochenpost*, February 25, 1972.

Heinemann, Erich. *Dreissig Jahre Karl-May-Gesellschaft: 1969–1999: Erinnerungen und Betrachtungen*. Hamburg: Hansa, 2000.

———. *Silberstern. Nr. 112, Gut Gemacht, Winnetou*. Stuttgart: Oncken, 1964.

Karl-May-(Film)-Fan-Gruppe. "KMFF-Treffen-Berlin Program." Berlin: n.p., 2013.

Karl-May-Freunde-Pluwig, e.V. "Der Geist des Llano Estabado, Jubiläumsausgabe Programheft." Pluwig: n.p., 2011.

———. "Der Schwarze Mustang Programheft." Pluwig: n.p., 2007.

———. "Im Tal des Todes. Programheft." Pluwig: n.p., 2013.

———. "Winnetou I Programheft." Pluwig: n.p., 2003.

———. "Winnetou II Programheft." Pluwig: n.p., 2005.

"Karl-May-Treffen '93 Bad Segeberg." 1993. Conference booklet.

Karl May Verlag. *25 Jahre Karl-May-Verlags 1913–1938*. Radebeul bei Dresden: Karl-May-Verlag, 1938.

Koehler, John. "German 'Indians' Guard Grave." *The Saginaw News*, June 23, 1968.

Kulturamt der Stadt Radebeul and Karl-May-Museum Radebeul. *Die Radebeuler Karl-May-Festtage*. Radebeul: n.p., 2000.

———. "Program der Karl-May-Festtage 1998." Radebeul: n.p., 1998.

Laroche, Jutta, and Reinhard Marheinecke. *Winnetous Testament Band 1: Winnetous Kindheit*. Darmstadt: CBK-Productions, 1999.

May, Karl. *Winnetou. Erster Band: Reiseerzählung, Band 7 der Gesammelten Werke*. Bamberg: Karl-May-Verlag, 1992.

———. *Gesammelte Werke: Über 300 Titel*. 3rd ed. Prague: e-artnow, 2015.

"Mescalero-Apachen Freiburg Homepage." Accessed July 19, 2013. http://www.mescalero-apachen.de/index1.htm.

Neun, Herbert. "Harry und Herr De." *Berliner Tagesblatt*, August 21, 1938.

Old Manitou Indian- und Westernclub 1956 e.V. *Stetson City Tribune Festausgabe Anlässlich des 50jährigen Jubiläums des Indian- und Westernclub Old Manitou 1956 e.V.* Dresden: n.p., 2006.

———. *Stetson-City-Tribune*. Special Issue for the 30th Anniversary of the Old Manitou Club. Dresden: n.p., July 1986.

"Patty (Eigentl. Ernst Tobis) Frank | Sächsische Biografie | ISGV." Accessed May 6, 2008. http://isgv.serveftp.org/SAEBI/artikel.php?SNR=1484#.

Rebhuhn, Wilhelm. *Karl May Lebt. Unsterbliche Gestalten—Spannende Abenteuer. Eine Bilderfolge Aus Den Karl-May-Spielen in Bad Segeberg*. Bamberg: Karl-May-Verlag, 1962.

Red Haircrow, dir. *Forget Winnetou! Loving in the Wrong Way*. Vtape, 2018.

Schmid, E. A. "Die Indianerhuldigung in Radebeul." *Karl-May-Jahrbuch* 12 (1929): 7–33.

"Sternritt zum 150. Geburtstag von Karl May Program." 1992. Booklet.

Stolte, Heinz Hermann. *Der Volksschriftsteller Karl May: Beitrag Zur Literarischen Volkskunde*. Repr. d. Erstausg. von 1936. Bamberg: Karl-May-Verlag, 1979.

Sutton, Roger. "Editorial: The Right to Read By Yourself." *The Horn Book*, September 4, 2018. https://www.hbook.com/?detailStory=editorial-right-read.

Wagner, Adolf. "Wir Jungens und Karl May." *Karl-May-Jahrbuch* 2 (1919): 349–56.

Walker, Barbara. *The Little House Cookbook*. New York: Harper Collins, 1979.

Wehnert, Jürgen. *Karl-May-Welten*. Bamberg: Karl-May-Verlag, 2005.

"Wie Ein Terrier. Der Karl-May-Verlag Kämpft um Seinen Einzigen Autor." *Der Spiegel*, May 1, 1995.

Wilder, Laura Ingalls. *Little House in the Big Woods*. New York: Harper Collins, [1932] 1971.

———. *Farmer Boy*. New York: Harper Collins, [1933] 1971.

———. *Little House on the Prairie*. New York: Harper Collins, [1935] 1971.

———. *On the Banks of Plum Creek*. New York: Harper Collins, [1937] 1971.

———. *By the Shores of Silver Lake*. New York: Harper Collins, [1939] 1971.

———. *The Long Winter*. New York: Harper Collins, [1940] 1971.

———. *Little Town on the Prairie*. New York: Harper Collins, [1935] 1971.

———. *These Happy Golden Years*. New York: Harper Collins, [1943] 1971.

———. *The First Four Years*. New York: Harper Collins, 1972.

———. *Pioneer Girl: The Annotated Autobiography*. Edited by Pamela Smith Hill. Pierre: South Dakota Historical Society Press, 2014.

Wilder Pageant Committee. "Laura Ingalls Wilder Pageant: Fragments of a Dream." Walnut Grove: n.p., 1993.

———. "Laura Ingalls Wilder Pageant: Fragments of a Dream." Walnut Grove: n.p., 2003.

———. "Laura Ingalls Wilder Pageant: Fragments of a Dream." Walnut Grove: n.p., 2007.

Woodson, Jacqueline. "On Remembering Everything: Children's Literature Legacy Award Acceptance Speech." Accessed December 2, 2019. https://alair.ala.org/bitstream/handle/11213/9274/children-literature-legacy-2018-w.pdf?sequence=1&isAllowed=y.

Yorio, Kara. "ALSC Changes Wilder Award to Children's Literature Legacy Award." *School Library Journal.* Accessed December 2, 2019. https://www.slj.com/?detailStory=alsc -changes-name-wilder-award-childrens-literature-legacy-award.


## Secondary Literature

Adamson, Glenn. *Thinking through Craft.* New York: Berg, 2007.

Aden, Roger C. *Popular Stories and Promised Lands: Fan Cultures and Symbolic Pilgrimages.* Tuscaloosa: University of Alabama Press, 1999.

Agnew, Vanessa. "History's Affective Turn: Historical Reenactment and Its Work in the Present." *Rethinking History* 11, no. 3 (2007): 299–312.

Anderson, William. "In the Beginning." *Lore* 36, no. 1 (Spring 2010): 1.

———. *Laura Ingalls Wilder: A Biography.* New York: Harper Collins, 1992.

———. *Laura Ingalls Wilder Country: The People and Places in Laura Ingalls Wilder's Life and Books.* New York: Harper Paperbacks, 1990.

Ashliman, D. L. "The American West in Twentieth-Century Germany." *The Journal of Popular Culture* II, no. 1 (1968): 81–90.

Bacon-Smith, Camille. *Enterprising Women: Television Fandom and the Creation of Popular Myth.* Philadelphia: University of Pennsylvania Press, 1992.

———. *Science Fiction Culture.* Philadelphia: University of Pennsylvania Press, 2000.

Baym, Nancy K. *Tune In, Log On: Soaps, Fandom, and Online Community.* Thousand Oaks: Sage Publications, 1999.

Beck, Larry, and Ted Cable. *The Gifts of Interpretation: Fifteen Guiding Principles for Interpreting Nature and Culture.* 3rd ed. Urbana: Sagamore Publishing, 2011.

Becker, Carl. "Every Man His Own Historian." *American Historical Review* 37, no. 2 (1932): 221–36.

Bercovitch, Sacvan. *The Puritan Origins of the American Self.* New Haven: Yale University Press, 2011.

Berger, Dina, and Andrew Grant Wood. *Holiday in Mexico: Critical Reflections on Tourism and Tourist Encounters.* Durham, NC: Duke University Press, 2009.

Bludau, Jochen, and Fred Aurich. *Elspe: Deutschlands Wilder Westen.* Heilbronn: Hohenloher Druck- und Verlagshaus Gerabronn, 1981.

Böhme, Lothar, et al. *Wildwest Romantik auf Deutschen Freilichtbuhnen Catalog for Exhibition at the Friedrich Gerstäcker Museum Braunschweig 1995.* Brunswick: POFF Publik Offset, 2008. Exhibition catalog.

Bogue, Allan. "Frederick Jackson Turner Reconsidered." *The History Teacher* 27, no. 2 (1997): 195–221.

Bolz, Peter. "Life Among the 'Hunkpapas': A Case Study in German Indian Lore." In

*Indians and Europe: An Interdisciplinary Collection of Essays*, 2nd ed., edited by Christian Feest, 475–90. Lincoln: University of Nebraska Press, 1999.

Booth, Paul. "Framing Alterity: Reclaiming Fandom's Marginality." *Transformative Works and Cultures* 28 (2018). https://doi.org/10.3983/twc.2018.1420.

———, ed. *A Companion to Media Fandom and Fan Studies*. Oxford: John Wiley & Sons, 2018.

Borries, Friedrich von. *Sozialistische Cowboys: Der Wilde Westen Ostdeutschlands*. 1. Aufl., Originalausg. Edition Suhrkamp 2528. Frankfurt: Suhrkamp, 2008.

Brædder, Anne, Kim Esmark, Tove Kruse, Carsten Tage Nielsen, and Anette Warring. "Doing Pasts: Authenticity from the Reenactors' Perspective." *Rethinking History* 21, no. 2 (2017): 171–92.

Breitenborn, Uwe. "'Memphis Tennessee' in Borstendorf: Boundaries Set and Transcended in East German Television Entertainment." *Historical Journal of Film, Radio and Television* 24, no. 3 (2004): 391–402.

Briel, Holger. "Native Americans in the Films of the GDR and Czechoslovakia." *European Journal of American Culture* 31, no. 3 (2012): 231–47.

Brooker, Will. "Everywhere and Nowhere: Vancouver, Fan Pilgrimage and the Urban Imaginary." *International Journal of Cultural Studies* 10 (2007): 423–44.

———. "'It Is Love': The Lewis Carroll Society as a Fan Community." *American Behavioral Scientist* 48, no. 7 (2005): 859–80.

———. *Using the Force: Creativity, Community and Star Wars Fans*. New York: Continuum, 2002.

Brown, Michael. *Who Owns Native Culture?* Cambridge, MA: Harvard University Press, 2003.

Broyles-Gonzalez, Yolanda. "Cheyennes in the Black Forest: A Social Drama." In *The Americanization of the Global Village: Essays in Comparative Popular Culture*, edited by Roger Rollins, 70–86. Bowling Green: Bowling Green University Popular Press, 1989.

Bruner, Edward. *Culture on Tour: Ethnographies of Travel*. Chicago: University of Chicago Press, 2005.

Busse, Kristina. "The Ethics of Studying Online Fandom." In *The Routledge Companion to Media Studies*, edited by Melissa Click and Suzanne Stott, 9–17. New York: Routledge, 2017.

———. "Fandom-Is-a-Way-of-Life versus Watercooler Discussion; or, The Geek Hierarchy as Fannish Identity Politics." Flow TV, November 17, 2006. Accessed January 10, 2008. https://www.flowjournal.org/2006/11/taste-and-fandom/.

———. "May the Force Be With You: Fan Negotiations of Authority." In *Framing Fan Fiction: Literary and Social Practices in Fan Fiction Communities*, edited by Kristina Busse, 99–120. Iowa City: University of Iowa Press, 2017.

Campbell, Donna. "'Wild Men' and Dissenting Voices: Narrative Disruption in *Little House on the Prairie*." *Great Plains Quarterly* 20, no. 2 (2000): 111–22.

Campt, Tina Marie. *Other Germans: Black Germans and the Politics of Race, Gender, and Memory in the Third Reich*. Ann Arbor: University of Michigan Press, 2005.

Cannon, Brian. "Homesteading Remembered: a Sesquicentennial Perspective." *Agricultural History* 87, no. 1 (2017): 1–29.

Carlson, Marta. "Germans Playing Indian." In *Germans and Indians: Fantasies, Encounters, Projections*, edited by Colin Calloway, Gerd Gemunden, and Suzanne Zantop, 213–16. Lincoln: University of Nebraska Press, 2002.

Carnegie, Elizabeth, and Scott McCabe. "Re-Enactment Events and Tourism: Meaning, Authenticity and Identity." *Current Issues in Tourism* 11, no. 4 (2008): 349–68.

Carretero, Mario, and Floor Van Alphen. "History, Collective Memories, or National Memories?" In *Handbook of Culture and Memory*, edited by Brady Wagoner, 283–304. New York: Oxford University Press, 2018.

Cavicchi, Daniel. "Foundational Discourses of Fandom." In *A Companion to Media Fandom and Fan Studies*, edited by Paul Booth, 27–46. Oxford: John Wiley and Sons, 2018.

———. "Loving Music: Listeners, Entertainments, and the Origins of Music Fandom in Nineteenth-Century America." In *Fandom: Identities and Communities in a Mediated World*, edited by Jonathan Gray, Cornel Sandvoss, and C. Lee Harrington, 235–49. New York: New York University Press, 2007.

Cherry, Brigid. *Cult Media, Fandom, and Textiles: Handicrafting as Fan Art*. London: Bloomsbury, 2016.

Chin, Bertha, and Lori Hitchcock Morimoto. "Towards a Theory of Transcultural Fandom." *Participations* 10, no. 1 (2013): 92–108.

Clifton, James, ed. *The Invented Indian: Cultural Fictions and Government Policies*. New Brunswick: Transaction Publishers, 1994.

Conrad, Rudolf. "Mutual Fascination: Indians in Dresden and Leipzig." In *Indians and Europe: An Interdisciplinary Collection of Essays*, 2nd ed., edited by Christian Feest, 455–74. Lincoln: University of Nebraska Press, 1999.

Cook, Colleen. "Germany's Wild West: A Researcher's Guide to Karl May." *German Studies Review* 5, no. 1 (1982): 67–86.

Coppa, Francesca. "A Brief History of Media Fandom." In *Fan Fiction and Fan Communities in the Age of the Internet: New Essays*, edited by Karen Hellekson and Kristina Busse, 41–60. Jefferson, NC: McFarland, 2006.

Corrin, Chris. *Gender and Identity in Central and Eastern Europe*. New York: Routledge, 1999.

Cothran, Boyd. *Remembering the Modoc War: Redemptive Violence and the Making of American Innocence*. Chapel Hill: University of North Carolina Press, 2014.

Cracroft, Richard. "World Westerns: The European Writer and the American West." In *A Literary History of the American West*, edited by J. Golden Taylor and Thomas Lyon, 159–79. Fort Worth: Texas Christian University Press, 1998. http://www2.tcu.edu /depts/prs/amwest/html/wl0159.html.

Cramer, Michael A. *Medieval Fantasy as Performance: The Society for Creative Anachronism and the Current Middle Ages*. Lanham: The Scarecrow Press, Inc., 2010.

Cronon, William. *Nature's Metropolis: Chicago and the Great West*. Rev ed. New York: Norton, 1992.

Cuntz-Leng, Vera, and Jacqueline Meintzinger. "A Brief History of Fan Fiction in Germany." *Transformative Works and Cultures* 19 (2015). https://doi.org/10.3983 /twc.2015.0630.

De Groot, Jerome. "Affect and Empathy: Re-enactment and Performance as/in History." *Rethinking History* 15, no. 4 (2011): 587–99.

DeKosnik, Abigail. *Rogue Archives: Digital Culture Memory and Media Fandom*. Cambridge, MA: MIT Press, 2016.

Deloria, Philip. "Historiography." In *A Companion to American Indian History*, edited by Philip Deloria and Neil Salisbury, 6–24. Malden: Blackwell, 2002.

——— . *Indians in Unexpected Places*. Lawrence: University Press of Kansas, 2004.

——— . *Playing Indian*. Rev. ed. New Haven: Yale University Press, 1999.

Derecho, Abagail. "Archonic Literature: A Definition, a History, and Several Theories of Fan Fiction." In *Fan Fiction and Fan Communities in the Age of the Internet: New Essays*, edited by Karen Hellekson and Kristina Busse, 61–78. Jefferson, NC: McFarland, 2006.

Dittmar, Claudia. "GDR Television in Competition with West German Programming." *Historical Journal of Film, Radio, and Television* 24, no. 3 (2004): 327–43.

Dorris, Michael. "Twisting the Words." In his *Paper Trail: Essays*, 268–81. New York: Harper Collins, 1994.

Drägar, Lothar, Rolf Krusche, and Klaus Hoffmann. *Indianer Nordamerikas. Karl-May-Museum Radebeul/Dresden*. Munich: K.M. Lipp Verlag, 1992.

Dreesbach, Anne. *Gezähmte Wilde: Die Zurschaustellung "Exotischer" Menschen in Deutschland 1870–1940*. Frankfurt: Campus, 2005.

Drexl, Cindy. *Sehnsucht nach dem Wilden Westen: 100 Jahre Münchner Cowboy Club*. Munich: Volk Verlag München, 2013.

Duffett, Mark. *Understanding Fandom. An Introduction to the Study of Media Fan Culture*. London: Bloomsbury Academic, 2013.

Durica, Paul. "Past Imperfect, Or the Pleasures and Perils of the Reenactment." *Journal of American Studies* 52, no. 4 (2018): 929–42.

Edgerton, Gary. *The Columbia History of American Television*. New York: Columbia University Press, 2007.

Edwards, Alexandra. "Literature Fandom and Literary Fans." In *A Companion to Media Studies and Fan Studies*, edited by Paul Booth, 47–76. Oxford: John Wiley and Sons, 2018.

Elhachoumi, Irmgard. "Showdown zum Aktenzeichen Winnetou." *Karl May & Co* 19 (2019): 90–92.

Engelke, Henning, and Simon Kopp. "Der Western im Osten. Genre, Zeitlichkeit und Authentizität im DEFA- und im Hollywood-Western." *Zeithistorische Forschungen* 2, no. 1 (2004): online edition.

Etulain, Richard. *Re-Imagining the Modern American West: A Century of Fiction, History, and Art*. Tucson: University of Arizona Press, 1996.

Feest, Christian. "Europe's Indians." In *The Invented Indian: Cultural Fictions and Government Policies*, edited by James Clifton, 313–32. New Brunswick: Transaction Publishers, 1994.

———. "Germany's Indians in a European Perspective." In *Germans and Indians: Fantasies, Encounters, Projections*, edited by Colin Calloway, Gerd Gemunden, Suzanne Zantop, 25–46. Lincoln: University of Nebraska Press, 2002.

———. "Indians and Europe? Editor's Postscript." In *Indians and Europe: An Interdisciplinary Collection of Essays*, edited by Christian Feest, 609–28. Lincoln: University of Nebraska Press, 1989.

———, ed. *Indians and Europe: An Interdisciplinary Collection of Essays*. Lincoln: University of Nebraska Press, 1989. A second, revised edition was published in 1999.

Fehrenbach, Heide. *Cinema in Democratizing Germany : Reconstructing National Identity after Hitler*. Chapel Hill: University of North Carolina Press, 1995.

Fellman, Anita Clair. "Everybody's 'Little Houses': Reviewers and Critics Read Laura Ingalls Wilder." *Publishing Research Quarterly* 12, no. 1 (Spring 1996): 3–20.

———. *Little House, Long Shadow: Laura Ingalls Wilder's Impact on American Culture*. Columbia: University of Missouri Press, 2008.

Fenemore, Mark. *Sex, Thugs and Rock 'N' Roll: Teenage Rebels in Cold-War East Germany*. Illustrated ed. New York: Berghahn Books, 2007.

Fine, Gary. *Shared Fantasy: Role-Playing Games as Social Worlds*. Chicago: University of Chicago Press, 2002.

Flanery, Karen "K-nut." *Fandom Is for the Young, or, One Convention Too Many*. New York: Vantage Press, 1981.

Fransen, Lilli, Anna Norgard, and Else Ostergard. *Medieval Garments Reconstructed: Norse Clothing Patterns*. Aarhus: Aarhus University Press, 2010.

Fraser, Caroline. "Laura Ingalls Wilder: The Making of an American Icon." *Missouri Historical Review* 113, no. 2 (2019): 94–104.

———. *Prairie Fires: The American Dreams of Laura Ingalls Wilder*. New York:

Metropolitan Books, 2017.

Freeman, Matthew. "*The Wonderful Game of Oz* and Tarzan Jigsaws: Commodifying Transmedia in Early Twentieth-Century Consumer Culture." *Intensities: The Journal of Cult Media* 7 (2014): 44–54.

———. "The Yellow Brick Road: Historicizing the Industrial Emergence of Transmedia Storytelling." *International Journal of Communication* 8 (2014): 2362–81.

Frigge, Reinhold. *Das Erwartbare Abenteuer: Massenrezeption und Literarisches Interesse am Beispiel der Reiseerzahlungen von Karl May*. Bonn: Bouvier, 1984.

Fritzsche, Peter. *Stranded in the Present: Modern Time and the Melancholy of History*. Cambridge, MA: Harvard University Press, 2004.

Fulbrook, Mary. *A History of Germany, 1914–2014*. 4th ed. New York: Wiley-Blackwell, 2014.

———. *The People's State: East German Society from Hitler to Honecker*. New Haven: Yale University Press, 2005.

Fuller, Deb. "How to Run a Reenactment—Introduction to Reenactment and Reenactors, Part 1." *EXARC* no. 1 (2019). https://exarc.net/issue-2019-1/mm/how-run-reenactment-part-1.

Fuller, Kathryn H. *At the Picture Show: Small-Town Audiences and the Creation of Movie Fan Culture*. Washington, DC: Smithsonian Institution Press, 1996.

Gapps, Stephen. "Mobile Monuments: A View of Historical Reenactment and Authenticity from inside the Costume Cupboard of History." *Rethinking History* 13, no. 3 (2009): 395–409.

———. "Museums of the Living Dead: Performance, Body, and Memory at Living History Museums." *Journal of Curatorial Studies* 7, no. 2 (2018): 248–70.

———. "Performing the Past: A Cultural History of Historical Reenactments." PhD diss., Sydney University of Technology, 2002.

Gemunden, Gerd. "Between Karl May and Karl Marx: The DEFA Indianerfilme (1965–1983)." *New German Critique* no. 82 (2001): 25–38.

Graham, James. "Breathing Life Back Into the Past." *British Heritage Travel* 38, no. July/August (2017): 64–67.

Gray, Jonathan, Cornel Sandvoss, and C. Lee Harrington, eds. *Fandom: Identities and Communities in a Mediated World*. New York: New York University Press, 2007.

Gressley, Gene, ed. *Old West/New West*. Norman: University of Oklahoma Press, 1994.

Haible, Barbara. *Indianer im Dienste der NS-Ideologie: Untersuchungen Zur Funktion von Jugendbüchern über Nordamerikanische Indianer im Nationalsozialismus*. Hamburg: Kovac, 1998.

Hämäläinen, Pekka. "The Rise and Fall of Plains Indian Cultures." *The Journal of American History* 90, no. 3 (2003): 833–62.

Hanzig, Juliane. "'—nicht zu vergessen—ein Trunk "Feuerwasser"' Ein Bild und seine Geschichte. Ein persönlicher Werkstattbericht." *Magazin des Karl-May-Museums* no. 1 (2020): 60–65.

Harrington, C. Lee, and Denise D. Bielby. *Soap Fans: Pursuing Pleasure and Making Meaning in Everyday Life*. Philadelphia: Temple University Press, 1995.

Harris, Cheryl. "Whiteness as Property." *Harvard Law Review* 106, no. 8 (1993): 1707–91.

Hartman, Andrew. *A War For the Soul of America: A History of the Culture Wars*. Chicago: University of Chicago Press, 2016.

Hayward, Jennifer. *Consuming Pleasures: Active Audiences and Serial Fictions from Dickens to Soap Opera*. Lexington: University Press of Kentucky, 1997.

Heermann, Christian. *Old Shatterhand ritt nicht im Auftrag der Arbeiterklasse: Warum War Karl May in SBZ Und DDR "Verboten"?* Dessau: Anhaltische Verlagsgesellschaft, 1995.

Heldrich, Phillip. "'Going to Indian Territory': Attitudes Towards Native Americans in *Little House on the Prairie*." *Great Plains Quarterly* 20, no. 2 (2000): 99–109.

Hellekson, Karen, and Kristina Busse, eds. *Fan Fiction and Fan Communities in the Age of the Internet: New Essays*. Jefferson, NC: McFarland, 2006.

———, eds. *The Fan Fiction Studies Reader*. Iowa City: University of Iowa Press, 2014.

Herbert, Paul. *The Sincerest Form of Flattery: An Historical Survey of Parodies, Pastiches, and Other Imitative Writings of Sherlock Holmes, 1891–1980* [corrected galley]. Bloomington: Gaslight Publications, 1983.

Hickethier, Knut, and Peter Hoff. *Geschichte des deutschen Fernsehens*. Stuttgart: Metzler, J B, 1998.

Hill, Pamela Smith. *Laura Ingalls Wilder: A Writer's Life*. Pierre: South Dakota State Historical Society, 2007.

Hilliard, Christopher. *To Exercise Our Talents: The Democratization of Writing in Britain*. Cambridge, MA: Harvard University Press, 2006.

Hills, Matt. *Fan Cultures*. New York: Routledge, 2002.

———. "Fiske's 'Textual Productivity' and Digital Fandom: Web 2.0 Democratization vs. Fan Distinction?" *Participations: Journal of Audience and Reception Studies* 10, no. 1 (2013): 130–53.

———. "From Dalek Half Balls to Daft Punk Helmets: Mimetic Fandom and the Crafting of Replicas." *Transformative Works and Cultures* 16 (2014). Accessed January 5, 2018. https://doi.org/10.3983/twc.2014.0531.

———. "Returning to Becoming-a-Fan Stories: Theorizing Transformational Objects and the Emergence/Extension of Fandom." In *The Ashgate Research Companion to Fan Culture*, edited by Linda Duits, Koos Zwaan, and Stijn Reijnders, 9–22. Surrey, UK: Ashgate Press, 2014.

Hine, Robert V., and John Mack Faragher. *Frontiers: A Short History of the American West*.

New Haven: Yale University Press, 2007.

Hine, Robert V., John Mack Faragher, and Jon T. Coleman. *The American West: A New Interpretive History*. 2nd ed. New Haven: Yale University Press, 2017.

Hines, Stephen. *"I Remember Laura": America's Favorite Storyteller as Remembered by Her Family, Friends, and Neighbors*. Nashville: Thomas Nelson Publishers, 1994.

Hoff, Peter, and Wolfgang Mühl-Benninghaus. "Depictions of America in GDR Television Films and Plays, 1955–1965." *Historical Journal of Film, Radio and Television* 24, no. 3 (2004): 403–10. https://doi.org/10.1080/0143968042000277593.

Holmes, Rachel. *African Queen: The Real Life of the Hottentot Venus*. New York: Random House, 2009.

Horwitz, Tony. *Confederates in the Attic: Dispatches from the Unfinished Civil War*. New York: Vintage, 1999.

Hughes, Linda K., and Michael Lund. *The Victorian Serial*. Charlottesville: University of Virginia Press, 1991.

Imre, Aniko. "Eastern Westerns: Enlightened Edutainment and National Transvestism." *New Review of Film and Television Studies* 9, no. 2 (2011): 152–69.

Jenkins, Henry. *Convergence Culture: Where Old and New Media Collide*. New York: New York University Press, 2006.

———. *Textual Poachers: Television Fans and Participatory Culture*. 2nd ed. New York: Routledge, 2012.

Johnson, Jeffrey K. *Super-History: Comic Book Superheroes and American Society, 1938 to the Present*. Jefferson, NC: McFarland, 2012.

Johnson, Katherine. "Rethinking (Re)doing: Historical Re-enactment and/as Historiography." *Rethinking History* 19 (2015): 193–206.

Jones, Karen, and John Wills. *The American West: Competing Visions*. Edinburgh: Edinburgh University Press, 2009.

Kalshoven, Petra Tjitske. *Crafting "The Indian": Knowledge, Desire, and Play in Indianist Reenactment*. New York: Berghahn Books, 2012.

Kaplan, Deborah. "Construction of Fan Fiction Character through Narrative." In *Fan Fiction and Fan Communities in the Age of the Internet: New Essays*, edited by Karen Hellekson and Kristina Busse, 134–52. Jefferson, NC: McFarland, 2006.

Kaplan, Marion. *Between Dignity and Despair: Jewish Life in Nazi Germany*. New York: Oxford University Press, 1999.

Kasson, Joy S. *Buffalo Bill's Wild West: Celebrity, Memory, and Popular History*. New York: Hill and Wang, 2000.

Kaye, Frances. "Little Squatter on the Osage Diminished Reserve: Reading Laura Ingalls Wilder's Kansas Indians." *Great Plains Quarterly* 23, no. 2 (May 2000): 123–40.

Keller, Alexandra. "Historical Discourse and American Identity in Westerns Since the

Reagan Era." In *Hollywood's West: The American Frontier in Film, Television, and History*, edited by Peter Rollins and John O'Connor, 239–60. Lexington: University Press of Kentucky, 2009.

King, Lisa Michelle. "Revisiting Winnetou: The Karl May Museum, Cultural Appropriation, and Indigenous Self-Representation." *Studies in Native American Literatures* 28, no. 2 (Summer 2016): 25–55.

Kiracofe, Roderick, and Mary Elizabeth Johnson. *The American Quilt: A History of Cloth and Comfort 1750–1950*. New York: Clarkson Potter, 2004.

Kitchen, E. F., and Leo Braudy. *Suburban Knights: A Return to the Middle Ages*. New York: Powerhouse Books, 2010.

Klussmeier, Gerhard. *Karl May: Biographie in Dokumenten Und Bildern*. 2nd ed. Hildesheim: Olms, 1992.

Kocks, Katinka. *Indianer im Kaiserreich: Völkerschauen und Wild West Shows Zwischen 1880 und 1914*. Gerolzhofen: Öttermann, 2004.

Koepnick, Lutz P. "Unsettling America: German Westerns and Modernity." *Modernism/Modernity* 2, no. 3 (1995): 1–22.

Kort, Pamela, and Max Hollein, eds. *I Like America: Fictions of the Wild West*. Munich: Prestel, 2006.

Kosciuszko, Bernhard. *Die Alten Jahrbücher: Dokumente Früher Karl-May-Forschung, Eine Bestandsaufnahme*. Ubstadt: KMG-Press, 1984.

Kreis, Karl Markus. "German Wild West: Karl May's Invention of the Definitive Indian." In *I Like America: Fictions of the Wild West*, edited by Pamela Kort and Max Hollein, 249–73. Munich: Prestel, 2006.

Kuhn, Annette. *An Everyday Magic: Cinema and Cultural Memory*. New York: I. B. Tauris, 2002.

Kustritz, Anne, and Melanie Kohnen. "Decoding the Industrial and Digital City: Visions of Security in Holmes' and Sherlock's London." In *Sherlock and Transmedia Fandom: Essays on the BBC Series*, edited by Louisa Ellen Stein and Kristina Busse, 85–100. Jefferson, NC: MacFarland, 2012.

Lamb, Jonathan. "Historical Re-Enactment, Extremity, and Passion." *The Eighteenth Century* 49, no. 3 (2008): 239–50.

Lamerichs, Nicolle. *Productive Fandom: Intermediality and Affective Reception in Fan Cultures*. Amsterdam: University of Amsterdam Press, 2018.

Lamont, Victoria. *Westerns: A Women's History*. Lincoln: University of Nebraska Press, 2016.

Leipold, Robin, and Volkmar Göschka. "Indianer im Wilden Osten." *Magazin des Karl-May-Museums* no. 1 (2020): 34–41.

Lellenberg, Jon, ed. *Irregular Memories of the 'Thirties: An Archival History of the Baker*

*Street Irregulars' First Decade: 1930–1940*. New York: Fordham University Press, 1990.

Levine, Lawrence. *Highbrow/Lowbrow: The Emergence of Cultural Hierarchy in America*. Cambridge, MA: Harvard University Press, 1990.

Lewis, Lisa A. *The Adoring Audience: Fan Culture and Popular Media*. New York: Routledge, 1992.

Lewis, Warren. *Buffalo Bill's America: William Cody and the Wild West Show*. New York: Knopf, 2005.

Limerick, Patricia Nelson. *The Legacy of Conquest: The Unbroken Past of the American West*. Reprint ed. New York: Norton, 1987.

Limerick, Patricia Nelson, Clyde Milner, and Charles Rankin, eds. *Trails: Toward a New Western History*. Lawrence: University Press of Kansas, 1991.

Linden, Henrik, and Sara Linden. *Fans and Fan Culture: Tourism, Consumerism, and Social Media*. New York: Palgrave MacMillan, 2017.

Lipsitz, George. *The Possessive Investment in Whiteness*. Rev. ed. Philadelphia: Temple University Press, 2006.

Loock, Kathleen. "Remaking Winnetou, Reconfiguring German Fantasies of Indianer and the Wild West in the Post-Reunification Era." *Communications: The European Journal of Communication Research* 44, no. 3 (2019): 323–41.

Luetkenhaus, Holly, and Zoe Weinstein. *Austentatious. The Evolving World of Jane Austen Fans*. Iowa City: University of Iowa Press, 2019.

Lutz, Hartmut. "German Indianthusiasm: A Socially Constructed German Nationalist Myth." In *Germans and Indians: Fantasies, Encounters, Projections*, edited by Colin Calloway, Gerd Gemunden, and Suzanne Zantop, 167–84. Lincoln: University of Nebraska Press, 2002.

Lutz, Hartmut, Florentine Strelczyk, and Renae Watchman, eds. *Indianthusiasm: Indigenous Responses*. Waterloo: Wilfred Laurier University Press, 2020.

Maase, Kaspar. *BRAVO Amerika: Erkundungen Zur Jugendkultur der Bundesrepublik in Den Fünfziger Jahren*. Hamburg: Junius, 1992.

———. "Establishing Cultural Democracy: Youth, 'Americanization,' and the Irresistible Rise of Popular Culture." In *The Miracle Years: A Cultural History of West Germany, 1949–1968*, edited by Hannah Schissler, 428–50. Princeton: Princeton University Press, 2001.

Mackay, James, and David Stirrup, eds. *Tribal Fantasies: Native Americans in the European Imaginary, 1900–2010*. New York: Palgrave Macmillan, 2013.

Macoun, Alissa. "Colonising White Innocence: Complicity and Critical Encounters." In *The Limits of Settler Colonial Reconciliation*, edited by Sarah Maddison, Tom Clark, and Ravi de Costa, 85–102. Singapore: Springer, 2016.

Madley, Benjamin. *An American Genocide: The United States and the California Indian*

*Catastrophe, 1846–1873.* New Haven: Yale University Press, 2016.

Marheinecke, Reinhard, and Nicolas Finke. *Karl May Am Kalkberg. Geschichte und Geschichten der Karl-May-Spiele Bad Sageberg Seit 1952.* Bamberg: Karl-May-Verlag, 1999.

McCalman, Iain, and Paul Pickering. *Historical Reenactment: From Realism to the Affective Turn.* Basingstoke: Palgrave Macmillan, 2010.

McCarthy, Patrick. "'Living History' as the 'Real Thing': A Comparative Analysis of the Modern Mountain Man Rendezvous, Renaissance Fairs, and Civil War Reenactments." *ETC: A Review of General Semantics* 71, no. 2 (2014): 106–23.

McClure, Wendy. *The Wilder Life: "My Adventures in the Lost World of Little House on the Prairie."* New York: Riverhead Books, 2011.

McKay, Ian. *The Quest of the Folk: Antimodernism and Cultural Selection in Twentieth-Century Nova Scotia.* Montreal: McGill-Queen's University Press, 2009.

McMaster, Gerald. "The Double Entendre of Re-Enactment." Accessed July 11, 2019. www.vtape.org/wp-content/uploads/2014/01/Vtape-Double-Entendre-of-Re -Enactment-imagineNATIVE-2007.pdf.

McVeigh, Stephen. *The American Western.* Edinburgh: Edinburgh University Press, 2007.

Mikula, Maja. "Historical Re-Enactment: Narrativity, Affect and the Sublime." *Rethinking History* 19, no. 4 (2015): 583–601.

Miller, John E. "American Indians in the Fiction of Laura Ingalls Wilder." *South Dakota History* 30, no. 3 (2000): 303–20.

——. *Becoming Laura Ingalls Wilder: The Woman Behind the Legend.* Columbia: University of Missouri Press, 1998.

——. *Laura Ingalls Wilder and Rose Wilder Lane: Authorship, Place, Time, and Culture.* Columbia: University of Missouri Press, 2016.

Mitchell, Lee Clark. *Late Westerns: The Persistence of a Genre.* Lincoln: University of Nebraska Press, 2018.

Miyamoto, Melody. "From the Little House to the School House and Beyond: Experiential Learning through the World of Laura Ingalls Wilder." *Journal of the West* 49, no. 3 (2010): 34–40.

Mooney-Getoff, Mary J. *Laura Ingalls Wilder, a Bibliography: For Researchers, Writers, Teachers, Librarians, Students and Those Who Enjoy Reading about Laura.* Southold: Wise Owl Press, 1980.

Moses, George. *Wild West Shows and the Image of American Indians, 1883–1933.* Albuquerque: University of New Mexico Press, 1996.

Muller, Erwin. "Die Karl-May-Szene in Deutschland: Ein Überblick." *Karl-May-Gesellschaft-Nachtrichten* no. 108 (June 1996).

Nash, Gerald D. "European Image of America: The West in Historical Perspective."

*Montana: The Magazine of Western History* 42, no. 2 (1992): 2–16.

Neumann, Ulrich. "Zirkusflair und Kriegsgeschrei: Karl-May-Spiele Rathen 1940." *Karl May & Co* no. 155 (Feb. 2019): 74–80.

Nichols, Roger. *American Indians in US History*. 2nd ed. Norman: University of Oklahoma Press, 2014.

Novick, Peter. *That Noble Dream: The "Objectivity Question" and the American Historical Profession*. 4th ed. Ideas in Context. Cambridge, UK: Cambridge University Press, 1988.

Ode, Jeanne. "Historical Musings: Laura Ingalls Wilder and the Serendipity of Research: Blog Posts from the Pioneer Girl Project." *South Dakota History* 45, no. 1 (2015): 68–92.

O'Donnell, Patrick. *The Knights Next Door: Everyday People Living Middle Ages Dreams*. Lincoln: iUniverse, 2004.

Ogushi, Hisayo. "The Little House in the Far East: The American Frontier Spirit and Japanese Girls' Comics." *The Japanese Journal of American Studies* 27 (2016): 21–44.

Painter, Nell Irvin. *The History of White People*. New York: Norton, 2010.

Pande, Rukmini. *Squee From the Margins: Fandom and Race*. Iowa City: University of Iowa Press, 2018.

Pearson, Roberta. "Bachies, Bardies, Trekkies, and Sherlockians." In *Fandom: Identities and Communities in a Mediated World*, edited by Jonathan Gray, Cornel Sandvoss, and C. Lee Harrington, 98–109. New York: New York University Press, 2007.

———. "'It's Always 1895': Sherlock Holmes in Cyberspace." In *Trash Aesthetics: Popular Culture and Its Audience*, edited by Deborah Cartmell, Heidi Kaye, I. Q. Hunter, and Imelda Whelehan, 143–61. London: Pluto Press, 1997.

———. "Janeites and Sherlockians: Literary Societies, Cultural Legitimacy, and Gender." In *A Companion to Media Fandom and Fan Studies*, edited by Paul Booth, 495–508. Oxford: John Wiley and Sons, 2018.

Peers, Laura. *Playing Ourselves: Interpreting Native Histories at Historic Reconstructions*. Lanham: Alta Mira Press, 2007.

Penny, H. Glenn. "Elusive Authenticity: The Quest for the Authentic Indian in German Public Culture." *Comparative Studies in Society and History* 48, no. 4 (October 1, 2006): 798–819.

———. *Kindred By Choice: Germans and American Indians Since 1800*. Chapel Hill: University of North Carolina Press, 2013.

———. *Objects of Culture: Ethnology and Ethnographic Museums in Imperial Germany*. Chapel Hill: University of North Carolina Press, 2002.

Perry, Joe. "Healthy for Family Life: Television, Masculinity, and Domestic Modernity During West Germany's Miracle Years." *German History* 25, no. 4 (2007): 560–95.

Perry, Nicole. "Verwoben in 'Indianenthusiasm': A Uniquely German Entanglement."

*Journal of Indigenous Studies and First Nations and First Peoples' Cultures* 2, no. 2 (2018): 227–45.

Petzel, Michael. *Das Grosse Karl May-Lexikon: [Von der Wueste zum Silbersee: Der Grosse Deutsche Abenteuer-Mythos : Alles Uber die Winnetou-Welt]*. Berlin: Lexikon Imprint, 2000.

———. "Der letzte Drehort." In *Karl-May-Welten*, edited by Jürgen Wehnert, 198–214. Bamberg: Karl-May-Verlag, 2005.

Phillips, Ruth. "'From Wigwam to White Lights': Popular Culture, Politics, and the Performance of Native North American Identity in the Era of Assimilationism." In *Historical Reenactment: From Realism to the Affective Turn*, edited by Iain McCalman, 159–69. London: Palgrave Macmillan, 2010.

Pierson, David. "Turner Network Television's Made for TV Western Films." In *Hollywood's West: The American Frontier in Film, Television, and History*, edited by Peter Rollins and John O'Connor, 281–98. Lexington: University Press of Kentucky, 2009.

Poiger, Uta G. *Jazz, Rock, and Rebels: Cold War Politics and American Culture in a Divided Germany*. Berkeley: University of California Press, 2000.

———. "A New, 'Western' Hero? Reconstructing German Masculinity in the 1950s." In *The Miracle Years: A Cultural History of West Germany, 1949–1968*, edited by Hannah Schissler, 412–27. Princeton: Princeton University Press, 2001.

Pugh, Sheenagh. *The Democratic Genre: Fan Fiction in a Literary Context*. Glasgow: Seren, 2006.

Qureshi, Sadiah. *Peoples on Parade: Exhibitions, Empire, and Anthropology in Nineteenth-Century Britain*. Chicago: University of Chicago Press, 2011.

Ray, Karen. "Sugar Candy, Sage Dressing, and Seed Wheat: The Immediacy of Food in the Little House Books." *The Heritage of the Great Plains* 41, no. 2 (2009): 4–17.

Reagin, Nancy. "Dances With Worlds: Karl May, 'Indian' Hobbyists, and German Fans of the American West since 1912." *Participations: Journal of Audience & Reception Studies* 13 (May 2016): 553–83.

———. "Socialist Indians and Capitalist Cowboys: The Uses of Westerns in Both Germanies." In *The Cold War and Entertainment Television*, edited by Lori Maguire, 69–81. Cambridge, UK: Cambridge Scholars Publishing, 2016.

———. *Sweeping the German Nation: Domesticity and National Identity in Germany, 1870–1945*. New York: Cambridge University Press, 2007.

Reagin, Nancy, and Anne Rubenstein. "'I'm Buffy and You're History': Putting Fan Studies Back into History." *Transformative Works and Cultures* 6 (March 2011). Accessed June 1, 2011. https://doi.org/10.3983/twc.2011.0272.

Roediger, David. *The Wages of Whiteness: Race and the Making of the American Working Class*. Rev. ed. New York: Verso, 2007.

Rollins, Peter, and John O'Connor. *Hollywood's West: The American Frontier in Film, Television, and History*. Lexington: University Press of Kentucky, 2009.

Romines, Ann. *Constructing the Little House: Gender, Culture, and Laura Ingalls Wilder*. Amherst: University of Massachusetts Press, 1997.

———. "Putting Things in Order: The Domestic Aesthetic of Laura Ingalls Wilder's Little House Books." In *The Material Culture of Gender and the Gender of Material Culture*, edited by Katherine Martinez and Kenneth Ames, 181–95. Hanover: University Press of New England, 1997.

Rosenblatt, Betsy, and Roberta Pearson, eds. "Sherlock Holmes, Fandom, Sherlockiana, and the Great Game." Special issue, *Transformative Works and Cultures* 23 (March 2017). Accessed July 21, 2019. https://journal.transformativeworks.org/index.php/twc/issue/view/27.

Rosenzweig, Roy, and David Thelen. *The Presence of the Past: Popular Uses of History in American Life*. New York: Columbia University Press, 1998.

Rubenstein, Anne. *Bad Language, Naked Ladies, and Other Threats to the Nation: A Political History of Comic Books in Mexico*. Durham, NC: Duke University Press, 1998.

Rydell, Robert W., and Rob Kroes. *Buffalo Bill in Bologna: The Americanization of the World, 1869–1922*. Chicago: University of Chicago Press, 2005.

Said, Edward. *Orientalism*. New York: Vintage, 1979.

Saito, Natsu Taylor. "Race and Decolonization: Whiteness as Property in the American Settler Colonial Project." *Harvard Journal on Racial & Ethnic Justice* 31 (Spring 2015): 1–42. Accessed February 22, 2021. https://papers.ssrn.com/sol3/papers.cfm?abstract_id=2593121.

Saler, Michael. *As If: Modern Enchantment and the Literary Prehistory of Virtual Reality*. New York: Oxford University Press, 2012.

———. "'Clap If You Believe in Sherlock Holmes': Mass Culture and the Re-Enchantment of Modernity, c. 1890–1940." *The Historical Journal* 46, no. 3 (2003): 599–622.

Sammons, Jeffrey L. "Nineteenth-Century German Representations of Indians from Experience." In *Germans and Indians: Fantasies, Encounters, Projections*, edited by Colin Calloway, Gerd Gemunden, and Suzanne Zantop, 185–94. Lincoln: University of Nebraska Press, 2002.

Sandvoss, Cornel. *Fans: The Mirror of Consumption*. Malden: Polity Press, 2005.

Schissler, Hanna. *The Miracle Years*. Princeton: Princeton University Press, 2000.

Schmid, Bernhard, and Juergen Seul. *100 Jahre: Verlagsarbeit fuer Karl May und Sein Werk, 1913–2013*. Bamberg: Karl-May-Verlag, 2013.

Schmitt, Phillip, and Cara Koehler. "A Field Trip Back In Time: American Civil War Reenactment in Walldürn, Germany." Universität Bamberg website. Accessed October

27, 2016. https://www.uni-bamberg.de/amerikanistik/exkursionen/a-field-trip-back
-in-time-american-civil-war-reenactment-in-wallduern-germany/.

Schneider, Irmela. *Amerikanische Einstellung: Deutsches Fernsehen und US-amerikanische Produktionen*. Heidelberg: Winter, 1992.

Schreffler, Phillip. *Sherlock Holmes by Gas-Lamp: Highlights from the First Four Decades of the Baker Street Journal*. New York: Fordham University Press, 1989.

Schubert, Markus, and Hans-Joerg Stiehler. "A Program Structure Analysis of East German Television, 1968–1974." *Historical Journal of Film, Radio, and Television* 24, no. 3 (2004): 345–53.

Schulte-Sasse, Jochen. "Karl Mays Amerika-Exotik und deutsche Wirklichkeit." In *Karl May: Studien zu Leben, Werk u. Wirkung e. Erfolgsschriftellers*, edited by Helmut Schmiedt, 101–29. Königstein/Ts.: Hain, 1979.

Schwoch, James. *Global TV: New Media and the Cold War, 1946–69*. Champaign: University of Illinois Press, 2008.

Scott-Zechlin, Ariana. "'But It's the Solar System!': Reconciling Science and Faith through Astronomy." In *Sherlock and Transmedia Fandom: Essays on the BBC Series,* edited by Louisa Ellen Stein and Kristina Busse, 56–69. Jefferson, NC: MacFarland, 2012.

Seidman, Rachel. "This Little House of Mine." *The Interactive Journal of Early American Life* 3, no. 3 (2003). http://www.common-place-archives.org/vol-03/no-03/seidman /index.shtml.

Seifert, Wolfgang. *Patty Frank: Der Zirkus, die Indianer, das Karl-May-Museum*. Bamberg: Karl-May-Verlag, 1998.

Sheehan, James. *German History, 1770–1866*. Reprint ed. New York: Clarendon Press, 1991.

Sieg, Katrin. *Ethnic Drag: Performing Race, Nation, Sexuality in West Germany*. Ann Arbor: University of Michigan Press, 2009.

———. "'Indian Impersonation as Historical Surrogation." In *Germans and Indians: Fantasies, Encounters, Projections*, edited by Colin Calloway, Gerd Gemunden, and Susanne Zantrop, 217–42. Lincoln: University of Nebraska Press, 2002.

Smulders, Sharon. "'The Only Good Indian': History, Race, and Representation in Laura Ingalls Wilder's *Little House on the Prairie*." *Children's Literature Association Quarterly* 27, no. 4 (2003): 191–202.

Stephan, Alexander. *Americanization and Anti-Americanism: The German Encounter with American Culture after 1945*. New York: Berghahn Books, 2005.

Stetler, Julia. "Buffalo Bill's Wild West in Germany: A Transnational History." PhD diss., University of Nevada, Las Vegas, 2012.

Stevens, E. Charlotte. *Fanvids: Television, Women, and Home Media Re-Use*. Amsterdam: University of Amsterdam Press, 2020.

Stolte, Heinz. *Das Phänomen Karl May*. Bamberg: Karl-May-Verlag, 1969.

Subramanian, Jane M. *Laura Ingalls Wilder: An Annotated Bibliography of Critical, Biographical, and Teaching Studies.* Westport: Greenwood Press, 1997.

Sullivan, John. *Media Audiences: Effects, Users, Institutions, and Power.* London: Sage, 2013.

Thelen, David. "Learning from the Past: Individual Experience and Re-Enactment." *Indiana Magazine of History* 99 (2003): 155–71.

———. "Reliving History and Rethinking the Past." In *Over (T)Here : Transatlantic Essays in Honor of Rob Kroes,* edited by Kate Delaney and Ruud Janssens, 174–84. Amsterdam: VU University Press, 2005.

Thies, Frank. "Freizeitkultur – Die Lebenswelt der Deutschen Country & Western Szene." PhD diss., University of Hamburg, 2010.

Thompson, Jenny. *War Games: Inside the World of Twentieth-Century Reenactors.* Washington, DC: Smithsonian Books, 2004.

Thompson, Peter. "From Karl May to Karl Marx: Ernst Bloch and the Native American Tribe as Concrete Utopia." In *Tribal Fantasies: Native Americans in the European Imaginary,* edited by James Mackay and David Stirrup, 85–100. New York: Palgrave Macmillan, 2013.

Tompkins, Jane. *West of Everything: The Inner Life of Westerns.* New York: Oxford University Press, 1992.

Toy, J. Caroline. "Constructing the Fannish Place: Ritual and Sacred Space in a Sherlock fan Pilgrimage." *Journal of Fandom Studies* 5 (2017): 251–66.

Trask, Haunani-Kay. *From a Native Daughter: Colonialism and Sovereignty in Hawaii.* Honolulu: University of Hawaii Press, 1993.

Trigger, Bruce. *Natives and Newcomers: Canada's "Heroic Age" Reconsidered.* Montreal: McGill-Queen's University Press, 1986.

Turski, Birgit. *Die Indianistikgruppen der DDR: Entwicklung—Probleme—Aussichten.* Idstein/Taunus: Baum Publications, 1994.

———. "The Indianist Groups in the GDR: Development—Problems—Prospects." *European Review of Native American Studies* 7, no. 1 (1993): 43–48.

———. "Indianistikgruppen der DDR—gegenwärtige Situation, Entwicklung, Probleme." Vordiplom Thesis, Karl Marx University of Leipzig, 1990.

Üding, Gert, ed. *Karl-May Handbuch.* 3rd ed. Wurzburg: Königshausen & Neumann, 2001.

Unucka, Christian. *Karl May im Film: Eine Bilddokumentation.* Dachau: Vereinigte Verlagsgesellschaften Franke, 1980.

Vanderstel, David. "'And I Thought Historians Only Taught': Doing History beyond the Classroom." *OAH Magazine of History* 16, no. 2 (2002): 5–7.

Vizenor, Gerald. "Aesthetics of Survivance: Literary Theory and Practice." In *Survivance: Narratives of Native Presence,* edited by Gerald Vizenor, 1–24. Lincoln: University of Nebraska Press, 2008.

———. *Manifest Manners: Narratives on Postindian Survivance*. Lincoln: University of Nebraska Press, 1999.

Walvin, James. "What Should We Do about Slavery? Slavery, Abolition and Public History." In *Historical Reenactment: From Realism to the Affective Turn*, edited by Iain McCalman and Paul A. Pickering, 63–78. Basingstoke: Palgrave Macmillan, 2010.

Wanzo, Rebecca. "African American Acafandom and Other Strangers: New Genealogies of Fan Studies." *Transformative Works and Cultures*, no. 20 (2015). Accessed June 23, 2017. https://doi.org/10.3983/twc.2015.0699.

Warren, Louis. *Buffalo Bill's America: William Cody and the Wild West Show*. New York: Alfred A. Knopf, 2005.

Watchman, Renae. "Powwow Overseas: The German Experience." In *Powwow*, edited by Clyde Ellis, Luke Eric Lassiter, and Gary H. Dunham, 241–57. Lincoln: University of Nebraska Press, 2005.

Waysdorf, Abby, and Stijn Reijnders. "Fan Homecoming: Analyzing the Role of Place in Long-Term Fandom of *The Prisoner*." *Popular Communication* 17 (2019): 50–65.

———. "The Role of Imagination in the Film Tourist Experience: The Case of *Game of Thrones*." *Participations: Journal of Audience and Reception Studies* 14 (2017): 170–91.

Waziyatawin Angela Cavender Wilson. "Burning Down the House: Laura Ingalls Wilder and American Colonialism." In *Unlearning the Language of Conquest: Scholars Expose Anti-Indianism in America*, edited by Four Arrows (Don Trent Jacobs), 66–80. Austin: University of Texas Press, 2006.

Weber, Alina. "'Indians' on German Stages: The History and Meaning of Karl May Festivals." PhD diss., Indiana University, 2010.

Wertsch, James. "National Memory and Where to Find It." In *The Handbook of Culture and Memory*, edited by Brady Wagoner, 259–82. New York: Oxford University Press, 2018.

White, Richard. *"It's Your Misfortune and None of My Own": A New History of the American West*. Reprint ed. Norman: University of Oklahoma Press, 1993.

Wilhelm, Hermann. *München und der Wilde Westen*. Munich: Haidhauser Hefte, 2015.

Williams, Rebecca. *Theme Park Fandom: Spatial Transmedia, Materiality, and Participatory Cultures*. Amsterdam: University of Amsterdam Press, 2020.

Wolf, Mark J. P. *Building Imaginary Worlds: The Theory and History of Subcreation*. New York: Routledge, 2014.

Wolf, Virginia. "Laura Ingalls Wilder's Little House Books: A Personal Story." In *Touchstones: Reflections on the Best in Children's Literature*, edited by Perry Nodelman, Vol. 1: 291–300. West Lafayette: Children's Literature Association, 1985.

Woodside, Christine. *Libertarians on the Prairie: Laura Ingalls Wilder, Rose Wilder Lane, and the Making of the Little House*. New York: Arcade Publishing, 2016.

Worsley, Lucy. "An Intimate History of Your Home." *The Historian* Autumn (2011): 6–9.

Worster, Donald. *Rivers of Empire: Water, Aridity, and the Growth of the American West.* Reprint ed. New York: Oxford University Press, 1992.

Zantop, Suzanne. "Close Encounters: Deutsche and Indianer." In *Germans and Indians: Fantasies, Encounters, Projections,* edited by Colin Calloway, Gerd Gemunden, and Suzanne Zantop, 3–14. Lincoln: University of Nebraska Press, 2002.

———. *Colonial Fantasies. Conquest, Family and Nation in Precolonial Germany, 1770–1870.* Durham, NC: Duke University Press, 1997.

Zastrow, Peter, and Hans-Werner Baurycza. *Eine Stadt Spielt Indianer. Aus den Anfangsjahren der Karl-May-Festspiele in Bad Segeberg.* Duderstadt: EPV, 2011.

Zochert, Donald. *Laura: The Life of Laura Ingalls Wilder.* New York: Avon, 1976.

# INDEX

Mexican-American War, 19

Miller, Alfred, 24

Miller, Julie Frances, 122, 124, 135, 219n48

Ministry for State Security, East Germany
(Stasi), 73–74, 81–82, 213n35

Miyamoto, Melody, 119

Modoc War, 22–23, 145

Möllhausen, Balduin, 28–29

Moran, Thomas, 25

Morche, Harry, 55–56

Munich Cowboy and Indian Club,
1913: and May, 41, 54–58, 69; recent
changes in, 167; subgroups, 87; in West
Germany, 41, 54–58, 69, 85–87, 162,
207n36, 207n38

NAAoG. *See* Native American Association
of Germany (NAAoG)

Namingha, Lindbergh, 164–65

national biography, 18–24, 36–40, 128–31,
140–41

national identity: German, 21, 30, 184; and
memory work, 134–35; and New West,
141, 144, 175–76; white American, 12, 14,
134–35, 141, 144, 171, 173–76

National Socialists. *See* Nazi Germany

Native American Association of Germany
(NAAoG), 161–62, 164–65

Nazi Germany: Hitler in, 49, 63,
71–72, 208n50, 209n52; and Karl May
Museum, 13, 44, 48–49, 54, 61–65, 69,
71–72, 208n50, 209n52, 213n35; and
Western fandom, 10–11, 13, 34, 44,
48–49, 54, 61–66, 69, 71–72, 208n50,
209n52, 209n55, 213n35

New Western historiography: history
of, 37–38, 139–42, 173, 176; imagined,
142–44; Indigenous North Americans

in, 37–38, 138–44; *Little House* books
in, 145–57; and national identity, 141,
144, 175–76; reforms of, 14–15, 37–40; in
Western films, 143–44, 223n15

No Child Left Behind Act of 2002, 134, 153

novels. *See* genre fiction, Western; *Little
House* novels (Wilder, L.)

Nscho-tschi (fictional character), 46–48,
62

Oakley, Annie, 25–26, 33

Old Manitou Club: in East Germany, 33,
54–56, 59–60, 66, 69, 73–75, 77, 80, 160,
167, 207n34, 207n36, 207n38, 228n79;
and May, 55–56, 59–60, 66; recent
changes in, 167

Old Shatterhand (fictional character):
German virtues of, 50–51; and May, 43,
45–48, 50–51, 58, 62, 71, 95, 168, 206n26

Old Texas Town, 41

*On the Banks of Plum Creek* (Wilder, L.),
103, 105, 115

one-room schoolhouse, 103–5, 131

open-air museums, 103, 120, 178–81, 187,
229n13, 232n39

open-air theatrical performances, 42, 45, 51,
65, 89–91, 96, 160, 169, 186

Osage Tribal Community, 125, 147–49,
224n27

participatory fandom, 4–5

Peers, Laura, 106–7

Penny, Glenn, 8, 32, 161, 163, 194n13, 195n16

Pepin homesite: and Indigenous cultures,
153; "Laura Days" festival at, 105, 121–22,
124, 153, 181; tourism, 99, 103, 105, 115,
121–22, 124, 130, 153, 181

Pierson, David, 143

and Indigenous North Americans, 2,
10–18, 21–40, 101, 108–9, 130, 133, 135,
137, 145–58, 166, 172–76, 223nn19–20,
224nn26–27; introduction to, 2, 10–12;
and Laura Ingalls Wilder, 14, 19, 23, 27,
101–3, 108–9, 112, 119, 130–33, 135, 145–57,
172–73, 186, 224n26; marketplaces
of remembrance of, 24, 101, 148; and
ownership of West, 17–34, 37–40, 144,
171; and property rights, 22, 34, 224n26
Wild West Girls and Boys Club, 41, 98,
203n2
*Wild West Show*, Buffalo Bill's, 25–28, 33–35,
50, 53, 98, 145, 172
Wilder, Almanzo, 103–6, 108–9, 112–13
Wilder, Laura Ingalls: award named for,
29, 114, 154–56; and Buffalo Bill, 145;
daughter of, 108, 110–14, 122, 124, 127,
176, 217n13; and evangelical Christians,
132–33, 174–76, 220n64, 222n13; father
of, 20, 103–6, 108–9, 111–12, 115, 124,
147–48, 172–73; and frontier thesis,
20, 27, 111–12; and gender identity, 14,
102–3, 112, 119, 130–31, 216n6; husband
of, 103–6, 108–9, 112–13; LauraPalooza
conferences on, 125–26, 187; "Laura
Days" festival, 105, 121–22, 124, 153, 181;
LIWLRA, 125–26, 156, 174; Memorial
Society, 114–15; mother of, 109–10,
131, 146–48; sisters of, 109, 122, 129;
and white settlement, 14, 19, 23, 27,
101–3, 108–9, 112, 119, 130–33, 135, 145–57,
172–73, 186, 224n26. *See also* homesites,
Laura Ingalls Wilder; *Little House*
fandom; *Little House* novels
Winnetou (fictional character): and
May, 45–48, 50–51, 58, 61–62, 64–65,
71, 90–91, 95, 167–68, 186, 206n26; as
Mescalero Apache, 45–46, 71; in slash
pairings, 196n20
*Winnetou, the Myth Lives On*, 167–68, 186
Wister, Owen, 22, 25, 27
World War II, 62, 64–66

# FANDOM & CULTURE